LOVERS OF DISCORD

Lovers of Discord

TWENTIETH-CENTURY THEOLOGICAL CONTROVERSIES IN ENGLAND

Keith W. Clements

SPCK

First published in Great Britain 1988
SPCK
Holy Trinity Church
Marylebone Road
London NW1 4DU

British Library Cataloguing in Publication Data

Clements, K. W.
Lovers of discord: twentieth century theological controversies in England.
1. Christianity—Great Britain—20th century 2. Theology—20th century
I. Title
230'.0941 BT30.G7

ISBN 0-281-04329-9

Photoset by Deltatype Ltd, Ellesmere Port, Cheshire
Printed in Great Britain by the Anchor Press, Tiptree

For Alec Vidler

Contents

Acknowledgements

The extract from *Hensley Henson: A Study in Friction between Church and State* by Owen Chadwick is reproduced by permission of Oxford University Press.

The extracts from the *Rise of Christianity* by E. W. Barnes are reproduced by permission of Sir John Barnes.

The extracts from *Soundings: Essays Concerning Christian Understanding*, edited by A. R. Vidler, are reproduced by permission of Cambridge University Press.

The extracts from *Objections to Christian Belief*, edited by A. R. Vidler, are reproduced by permission of Constable.

The extracts from *Honest to God* by J. A. T. Robinson and *The Myth of God Incarnate*, edited by John Hick, are reproduced by permission of SCM Press.

The extract from Karl Barth, *Letters 1961–1968*, trans. and ed. by G. W. Bromiley, is reproduced by permission of T & T Clark.

Preface

This book is intended to help the student of modern Christian thought, and the more general reader whose interest has been aroused by recent contentious episodes, to gain a longer perspective over the story of controversies in English theology this century. The justification for taking this topic is expounded in the first chapter, and so need not be elaborated on here. Suffice it to say that, just as one sign of advancing years is said to be a good memory of one's childhood and an inability to recall what happened last week, so one of the features of modern Christianity seems to be a scanty knowledge of events only just out of living memory for most of us, and indeed some events within living memory for many. During recent disputes, for example those surrounding Dr David Jenkins, Bishop of Durham, some reference has been made to earlier parallels, most notably of course Bishop Hensley Henson and the 'Durham affair' of seventy years ago. But such references in newspaper editorials, correspondence columns, and polemical booklets, inevitably tend to reflect the selective bias of the partisan. In trying to give a fuller picture of some of the major controversies and controversialists this century, I would not claim to have achieved total neutrality in each instance, and in any case such complete detachment would make for an excessively dull narrative. In fact, writing these accounts has sometimes resembled what I imagine it would be like to be both referee and commentator at a football match, with every now and again a lapse of discipline as I permit myself a cheer for one side or another. But my biases will probably be far more apparent to the reader than to myself.

Much of the material originated in lectures given in courses on twentieth-century religious life and thought, in the Department of Theology and Religious Studies at Bristol University. The germ probably lies a lot further back than that, however, in my own student days at Cambridge twenty-five years ago. That was when the 'Cambridge theology' of *Soundings*, the *Objections* lectures and the like, closely followed by Bishop John Robinson's *Honest to God*, were the excitement of the day. Whatever judgements are to be made of those days in retrospect, my testimony is that it was just such controversies which first aroused my interest in theology, and began to persuade me that theology and theologians were indeed wrestling with mighty and profoundly significant issues. Theological controversy, as far as at least one person was concerned, was therefore highly educative, even evangelistic.

At the centre of the Cambridge debates stood Dr Alec Vidler, Dean of King's College. Soon I was to have the privilege of being one of his students, and to him more than anyone else I owe the kindling of an interest in the history of modern Christian life and thought. As a small personal tribute, and as a recognition, with which I imagine many others will wish to be identified, of his integrity in both the making and the chronicling of controversy in modern English theology, this book is dedicated to him.

Keith W. Clements
June 1987

1 A Regular Troubling of the Waters

There are clear moral dangers in reading a book on theological controversies, and even greater perils in writing one. From early times the baser human instincts have been readily exploited and indulged by one form or another of spectator sport in which much blood is shed, from the gladiatorial combats in the amphitheatre to cock-fighting in sleazy cellars. An account of some theological disputes may, according to a not too cynical view, simply provide a refined and sublimated kind of indulgence to that deep-seated desire to watch, from a point of comparative safety, the merciless fight to the death, with or without money being laid out. Even more lurid possibilities are conjured up by the suggestion that the telling of these stories might be a way of compensating for the disappearance of public execution. The faintest scent of burning heretic (for which read 'martyr' as appropriate) can draw crowds from miles around. Those risks apart, however, there are equally valid reasons in favour of examining some of the theological disputes of the modern age.

One reason is purely educational. Many people are aware of very recent theological and doctrinal disputes, for example concerning the views of the present Bishop of Durham, Dr David Jenkins, on the virgin birth and resurrection of Christ, and, not quite so recently, the views of the authors of *The Myth of God Incarnate* which appeared in 1977. But beyond that the recollection is hazy. The year 1988 sees the twenty-fifth anniversary of the publication of the late Bishop John Robinson's *Honest to God*, but that event is well beyond the living memory of most of today's students and many in today's congregations. Theological controversy, especially when it involves figures of high position in the Churches, is often explosively disturbing, not least because of its newsworthy value in the secular media. The usual implication is that never before has such upheaval occurred, or such radically novel views been expressed in challenge to received orthodoxy. Not only so, but whereas controversy in a field such as politics may be expected by the very nature of the case, religion, it is commonly assumed, is contradicting its own nature by such clashes. After all, according to one of the most famous collects of the Book of Common Prayer, God is 'the author of peace and lover of concord'. The whole emphasis of so much Christian language, liturgy, architecture and music, is on the reconciliation of discord and disunity. It is therefore singularly disturbing when those concerned with the communication of Christian belief should be at odds with each other.

Whenever it occurs, it is often assumed to be unprecedented, the first time that the ark of God, cruising sedately down the river of history, has encountered rocks and rapids. The past, even the comparatively recent past, is quickly mythicized into tranquillity. The rocks and rapids of yesterday shrink to view with the distance, and the fearsome disturbance they caused is hard to appreciate. Only today, it is imagined, have theologians been so questioning of orthodoxy, or some bishops been so apparently heretical. Referring to the debate stirred up by Bishop David Jenkins, the Religious Affairs Correspondent of the British Broadcasting Corporation, Rosemary Hartill, writes:

> The recent theological controversy burst the dam between the theologians and the public. Perhaps it is not surprising this has caused an enormous wave; the pressure had been building up for years, and the previous lack of contact between theologians and the general public was bound to create some confusion once the barriers broke.[1]

The metaphor of the dam is useful, but slightly misapplied, betraying some lack of awareness of just what has been happening for several generations in this country. It would be better to speak of a continual stream of new theological thought running for well over a century, and regularly every few years flooding over the sandbags of intellectual complacency within the Churches. In the final chapter we shall remark on the significance of ministers as theological mediators, and, even more crucially, the importance of their own education into their roles as educators and communicators. In the intervening chapters we shall have cause to note repeatedly how, when the normal ecclesiastical channels of communication are bypassed in the secular media, the 'lay' public both inside and outside the Churches is often more interested in theological matters than official and clerical church opinion has reckoned.

It is, then, first a matter of becoming acquainted with the recent but unfamiliar story of modern theology and religious thought in its more dramatic episodes, of seeing that Maurice Wiles, David Jenkins and Don Cupitt, for all their reputation as questioners of tradition, in fact belong to a certain tradition of their own – as do some of their vociferous opponents. 'There is no doubt that we are passing through a period of unsettlement in religious beliefs,' said a prominent Anglican bishop, Charles Gore – in 1907. When A. R. Vidler in his popular history of the modern Church[2] headed his chapter dealing with the 1960s 'The Decade of Fermentation', he was using a title equally applicable to at least one earlier phase of the modern story, certainly to the decade 1910–20. As always, to understand involves setting the present scene in some kind of historical perspective. Only then can one really begin to assess the significance, or newness, of current debates; the extent to which they represent breakthroughs, or breakdowns, in religious thought; the extent to which they are revolutionary, or simply variants on already well-worn themes. This understanding does, however, presuppose something more than the acquisition of factual information about past episodes, namely, a *sense* of history. I am not too sanguine about the acceptability of such an attitude either in the Churches or in English society at large at the present time.[3] Memories are short, horizons are limited within the present, and, instead of engagement with carrying forward to a new chapter the best themes of the age-long story, there is more evident a desire to gratify either the flesh or the spirit with what today may bring. Least of all can a merely nostalgic harking back to what are imagined to have been the unquestioned orthodoxies of former Christian generations, or the Victorian values in society, be equated with such a historical sense. Such appeals to the past are so often merely thin disguises for power struggles by ideology or party.

There is a further, and more robust, reason for the study of theological controversy. In theology as in other disciplines it is often not merely in their development, but in their conflict, that ideas become most sharply defined and, indeed, most interesting. For instance, one might say truly, but rather blandly, that both the transcendence (or 'otherness') of God and his immanence (or 'withinness') play important roles in the Christian doctrine of God. But it is when someone claims, as R. J. Campbell did, that God must be conceived of in wholly immanentist terms, that we are forced to see most clearly just what is at stake in such notions. Or, while few would dispute that the Judaeo-Christian religious tradition is a highly ethical one, it is when Don Cupitt asserts that 'God' is purely a unifying symbol for our ethical ideals, that the whole question of the relation between theism and ethics is focused as nowhere else. To look at controversies, then, is to look at some of the more spectacular landmarks (and, on the human level, at some of the more colourful characters in the story). This of course carries with it some danger that the intervening, less dramatic terrain will be unjustly reduced in significance. It would be a morbid attitude to any sphere of life, theology included, which dealt only with conflict, and the least intention of this study is to give the impression that the story of modern theology is *purely* one of controversy. Much creative work, imaginative as well as solid, has been carried on by relatively uncontroversial figures.

At this point some definition and delineation is called for to indicate the scope of this study. By a *controversy* is here meant a dispute or debate which has developed into being more than a disagreement between one scholar or thinker and another, and, taking on a public significance, is recognized by the wider community in the Church or Churches – and often in society generally as well – to have serious implications for the way in which Christian beliefs are to be understood and accepted. By a *theological* controversy is meant one in which the dispute concerns one or more basic Christian doctrines such as the doctrine of God, or the person and work of Christ, or the nature of biblical authority. This is to be distinguished, not only from an erudite scholarly controversy confined to specialists (for example, over the precise dating of St John's Gospel, which may conceivably raise temperatures at gatherings of the Society for New Testament Studies, but nowhere else), but also from what are properly *ecclesiastical* controversies where issues of church order and authority take precedence. In practice the distinction is not absolutely watertight. A theological or doctrinal controversy may well arise as a result of conclusions drawn from scholarly research, and it is certainly the case that, particularly in the Church of England, a theological controversy can quickly become embroiled in ecclesiastical issues such as the extent to which bishops should disturb the peace of the Church, or the degree of theological latitude to be allowed to any member of the priesthood. At the present time, the issue of the ordination of women, and the doctrinal issues raised by feminist theology about the doctrine of God and gender, are intimately related in the minds of many. But the distinction should be preserved. Episodes, therefore, like that over the revision of the Anglican Prayer Book in the 1920s, in which theological issues were involved but were not as such the central subjects of debate, fall outside the scope of this book. At the same time, it has to be recognized that only rarely is any 'theological' controversy *purely* 'theological'. We shall be looking at some human, sometimes all too human, stories in which personal, social, cultural and political factors play varying parts. This account will therefore be about both theological ideas and the theologians who wielded them, and in turn the theologians will have to be described in the context of their times and the influences upon them. We are dealing with aspects of the history of ideas. But ideas never come disembodied, and it is their bodiliness or corporateness – psychological, religious and social – that will concern us as appropriate. At the end of the account, as we approach some of the disputes nearer our immediate context, and in some cases still taking place among us, it is to be hoped we may be in a position to reflect on the nature and significance of theological controversy in modern Christianity, and on whether or not we can – or should – expect its resolution.

One last point of circumscription needs explanation, namely the geographical. We are restricting ourselves to Britain, and within Britain almost exclusively to England. The intention is not one of wilful parochialism, but of being specific to the point of some detail. Nor is it the least intention to imply any lack of significance on the British scene outside England. Quite the opposite. For example, there are special factors on the Scottish scene which would require and deserve an extended treatment on their own, and which have played a part in the way in which, to name but one, the Barth *versus* Bultmann controversy was played out north of the border to a degree unique in the United Kingdom. It might well also be thought that Roman Catholic Modernism, which was represented on the British scene by Father George Tyrrell in particular, is deserving of special mention beyond the sketch we afford it as part of the background to the Anglican Modernists. But much has already been written upon the Roman Catholic Modernists elsewhere, and the main weight of that particular episode lay between France and Rome.

Why controversy?

Twentieth-century theological controversies, as we shall see shortly, are in some respects the continuation of a nineteenth-century tradition. That tradition of 'theology in turmoil'[4] is itself a product of the immense changes which began to affect Western thought and culture early in the seventeenth century, and which by the end of the eighteenth had, albeit in stages, effectively revolutionized the intellectual scene. These changes are so profound and far-reaching as to ensure that eventually virtually everyone who espouses religious belief does so in a 'modern' way, even if they consider their beliefs to be 'traditional'. There is nothing so modern, for example, as the phenomenon of biblical fundamentalism, and we shall in subsequent chapters find several examples where the defence of 'orthodoxy' had to resort to arguments which the original framers of those orthodox beliefs would have thought strange, if not actually heterodox. The passage to modernity has passed four main landmarks: the acceptance of the use of reason in free inquiry, instead of unquestioning acceptance of authority in religion; the rise of *critical historical* attitudes towards the past, including the Bible and creeds; the collapse of the metaphysical view of reality, that is, the view which claims to comprehend all that is natural, and all that is supernatural, in a general system of reality and being; and the primacy of 'subjectivity', that is, the feeling, knowing human self, in all discussion of the nature of truth and of how it can be known.

Many suggestions have been made as to the moment, or the person, in which this movement to modernity received its decisive impulse. Few would doubt that the French Catholic mathematician and philosopher René Descartes (1596–1650) played a decisive role. Descartes, as a young philosopher, determined on a means of acquiring certainty of knowledge that would be independent of the various systems of thought, still largely inherited from the medieval period, which relied heavily on the appeal to tradition and authority. Certitude, he argued, could be attained only by relentlessly pursuing a 'negative way' of doubt. How much 'knowledge' can be put beyond all shadow of doubt? Very, very little, concluded Descartes. My knowledge of the world, of other persons, even of my own body, ultimately even of my own existence, might all be illusory, the result of a giant confidence trick by some Being. If, then, all this is dubitable, what, if anything, is indubitable? Only the fact that I am doubting! My own self-consciousness, which in the midst of the severest uncertainties is at least certain of thinking these uncertainties, is then the final, absolutely secure knowledge – the famous *cogito, ergo sum*, 'I think, therefore I am.' Small in extent this area of certainty may have been, but Descartes considered it to be solid enough to serve as a foundation on which a new rational argument could be erected for the existence of God and the world.

Much has been written on the significance of Descartes for Western thought. In his location of certitude in the individual's mental self-awareness, many have seen the introduction of two fateful dichotomies: that between the knowing human 'subject' and the known 'object' of thought, and that between the intellectual or 'spiritual' realm of inwardness on the one hand and the outer, material physical world on the other. Certainly Descartes represented a crucial development in the post-medieval outlook: the possibility of a use of reason quite independent of received dogma and tradition, beginning from its own perceived *a priori* certainties instead of those dictated by external authority, and accountable for its conclusions only to the thinking subject himself. Descartes, far from being anti-religious, was wishing to find much firmer rational grounds for belief in God. But the method he adopted, of radically doubting until intrinsically certain propositions obtained, proved to be a highly versatile child with its own ambitions. The Age of Reason was in view, and with it, the slow but steady erosion of the unchallenged place of Christian orthodoxy in Western society and culture. Lord Herbert of Cherbury (1583–1648) stated succinctly a rational religious alternative to the claims of orthodoxy, comprising belief in a supreme Being exercising government over all things, whose worship consisted of the practice of virtue, and who would in the hereafter mete out just rewards and punishments. Such beliefs could be known by the exercise of the unaided reason innate in all human beings, and their universality constituted 'the only truly Catholic Church which does not err'.

Such beliefs were the essential basis of what was later popularly known as *deism*, the 'natural religion' of the 'Age of Reason', usually dated from the mid-seventeenth to the end of the eighteenth century. In part this alternative to external authority and dogma was the other side of that aversion to the wars of religion which had devastated Europe in the earlier part of the seventeenth century. When appeal to 'revealed truth' and 'authority' had wreaked so much havoc, it was perhaps not surprising that people began to suspect that a safer, if humbler, guide to truth might lie nearer to hand in man's common intellectual and moral gifts, than in the exaggerated claims to knowledge of 'special revelations' from on high. The *Enlightenment*, that progressive philosophical and cultural movement occupying most of the eighteenth century, saw the full flowering of confidence in this alternative possibility to reliance on received tradition and claims to supernatural revelation. Two major developments had massive consequences for religious thought. These were the rise of a *historical* consciousness and method of critical study, and the collapse of an assumed metaphysical framework for belief.

The rise of historical study was itself, in part, religious in origin, especially in Germany where it was a legacy of the Reformation and its insistence upon the Scriptures as normative for the knowledge of revealed truth. The historical foundations of Christianity were themselves subjected to scrutiny, as was much else in the ancient world. But by the mid-eighteenth century the presuppositions of the historians studying the ancient texts could no longer necessarily be assumed to coincide with theirs whose main concerns lay in the defence of dogma and ecclesiastical order of one sort or another. H. S. Reimarus (1694–1768), for example, argued that the books of the Bible could and should be studied as purely human documents regardless of any veneration of them by the Church as sources of revealed truth, and that the New Testament was capable of a purely naturalistic, non-miraculous interpretation. It is hard for us today to conceive how long-lasted was the veneration for the authority of antiquity precisely *because* it was ancient. The change was as though a people living on a plain had for long assumed that the distant sacred mountain with its striking outline on the horizon was a single land-mass, and now, thanks to those who had ventured to explore it in close detail, learned that, far from being a single mountain range, it consisted of many ridges and valleys, of very different geological age. The supposed massive unity of the past disintegrated, and therewith, apparently, its authority also. Creeds and Scripture alike had a history, instead of being dictated directly from heaven.

The decline in the metaphysical outlook was a consequence of the age's preoccupation with the problem of knowledge, and the growing acceptance of the element of subjectivity in all human knowing. The Scottish philosopher David Hume (1711–76) honed the scepticism of the British empiricist tradition to an unprecedented point of refinement. Was even 'causation' any more than an inference which our minds impose on the sequence of events we observe in the world about us? But it was Immanuel Kant (1724–1804) who both summed up the Age of Reason and pointed beyond it. He brought the Enlightenment to its head by insisting on the *moral autonomy* of man. The truly moral element in man, according to Kant, demands that man be responsible to his own discernment of what is intrinsically true and good, and not be in tutelage to some external authority. On the other hand, Kant in one sense destroyed the 'commonsensical' view of the Enlightenment as to the scope and powers of reason. Human reason, in Kant's view, is capable of dealing only with the sensible, empirical world. Moreover it does so by applying to the 'phenomena' perceived by the senses the innate or *a priori* categories with which the mind is endowed – such as the categories of 'space' and 'time'. These categories are not entities seen in the world, but irreducible mental principles by which the mind shapes what it observes in the world. In other words, a large part of what we call 'knowledge' is ineluctably 'subjective', that is, originating within our own thinking and feeling selves rather than received 'objectively' from outside us. There is no totally 'objective' knowledge of 'things in themselves', that is, completely independent of the knowing mind.

Kant's argument had quite revolutionary consequences for all concepts of human knowledge, and not least for the traditional understanding of the knowledge of God. The traditional proofs for

God's existence had presupposed that the human mind could comprehend realities beyond the spatio-temporal world. For example, the famous 'ontological' proof of St Anselm relies on a definition of the nature of God, namely, that he is the reality than which no greater can be conceived. Or, the 'Five Ways' of St Thomas Aquinas rely on the assumption that by probing the nature of the finite world we are led to deduce the existence of an infinite, self-existent reality on which this finite realm depends. The fact of God's 'aseity' was assumed to be meaningful, at least, to human reason. But on the Kantian view, reason was confined in its scope to the finite world – and even then was conditioned by our own subjectivity. The metaphysical assumption that the essence of what was beyond this world could, at least in outline, be known to human minds, went by the board. Not that Kant wished to abolish belief in God. Like Descartes before him, he wished to establish room for faith on a firmer footing – having removed 'knowledge'. This he did by a *moral* argument for God's existence. The inner voice of moral obligation is, when we obey it, significant of our acknowledgement of a moral *law-giver*. God is thus an inference from the moral sense (the 'practical reason'), not a conclusion to an abstract argument of 'pure reason'. So it is an element of human subjectivity which becomes the basis for belief in God, otherwise hidden and unknowable in himself.

It would be simplistic to say that Kant himself actually caused the revolution in Western thought, just as it is equally naive to pretend we can behave as if the Enlightenment can be totally reversed.[5] But he marks the point at which, ineluctably, human awareness, human feeling, all that makes for 'subjectivity', becomes central. Of course there is ambiguity in Kant, and he has very diverse interpreters. Was he, for example, effectively an atheist in saying that God is beyond human knowing, for is not that in effect to dispense with any kind of divine reality in an objective sense? Or does that 'epistemological transcendence' leave open the possibility that the hidden God *is* real, though unknown to human reason, and *can make himself known* by his own initiative and by his own means in 'revelation'? Either way the transcendent has become problematical in an unprecedented manner. It cannot be mediated simply by the weight of authority, or the aura of tradition, still less by the sheer power of a Church. Once autonomy has been granted to the human knowing and feeling subject, the doctrine of God has been destabilized. An attempt to restore stability may take several forms.

One attempt would be to speak of God as, frankly (to use Don Cupitt's phrase), 'only human'. Stability in religion will be recovered, on this view, only by admitting that there is not, nor can there be in any meaningful way, anything 'beyond' our own subjectivity and rationality. God is a term we use for that which is essentially of our own make-up, or at any rate, we and God are essentially at one. Philosophical idealism early in the nineteenth century took this latter line, most magnificently expressed in the grand and subtle system of G. W. F. Hegel (1770–1831). Hegel accepted what Kant said about the limitations of the scope of reason, but drew the conclusion that, if we cannot know what lies beyond the confines of our rationality, we may as well say that rationality is all. The basis of reality is therefore rationality, or the knowing mind, of which God, or Absolute Spirit, is the infinite pole, and of which human mind is the finite, self-conscious pole. This too contained a profound ambiguity, however, as the later idealist Ludwig Feuerbach (1804–72) realized. Whereas Hegel could be interpreted as a quasi-pantheist, seeing human mind as a kind of dialectical projection of the Absolute Spirit in finite form, Feuerbach thought that a better explanation of religion lay in entirely human terms. It is not that man is a finite projection of the Infinite Spirit. Rather, the infinite God is man's own projection of himself to form an infinite image of his own higher qualities, which are then worshipped as if they were the attributes of a separate celestial being. Man must reclaim his attributes of creativity, power and goodness, of which he has, as it were, robbed himself and sacrificed to the 'God' he has himself created.

The modern situation, in summary, is that man finds it virtually impossible to leave himself out of the reckoning when it comes to speaking of God. Even if one does not go all the way with Feuerbach, or with Cupitt, in arguing that in speaking of God we are simply describing one or more aspects of humanity writ large and hallowed, nevertheless the human, subjective element in all religious and theological discourse seems irreducible. And it is precisely in those claims to sheer 'objectivity', 'submission to revealed truth', and so forth, within which the most intense subjectivity is suspected of lying concealed. On the other hand, a historical religion such as Christianity, includes, as part of its essential structure, certain statements which are held to be determinative and normative as sources of the content of belief. They are part of the *given* of belief, which is simply *there* as the tradition – literally, that which is handed down. The tradition, in part, means something in itself. But that meaning can only be apprehended subjectively, as meaning is brought to it by the contemporary generation. Here is one of the main ingredients of controversy. On the one hand there will be those who, legitimately, call for the preservation of the tradition as that from which Christianity draws its truth and by which it maintains its identity. On the other hand there will be those who, with equal justification, see the need for *interpretation* of the tradition, for its meaning is never entirely self-evident. Controversy is therefore likely to occur whenever the traditional biblical and credal texts and formulae are examined with a view to their contemporary interpretation.

Nineteenth-century cases

The spread of ideas is usually a much less tidy affair than historical summaries may suggest. In philosophy and historical studies Germany led the field in the latter eighteenth century. Due partly to the Napoleonic Wars, England suffered an intellectual isolation at the turn of the nineteenth century, and it was not until the mid-century that the full impact of those studies began to make itself felt on theology. Significantly, for example, it was the novelist George Eliot who translated D. F. Strauss's *Life of Jesus* into English in 1846. As it was, the first major theological stirrings were provided by reactions to home-grown developments in the natural sciences.[6]

Evidences of Christianity by William Paley (1743–1805) was the standard manual of natural theology for much of the century. The orderliness of the world was regarded as clear evidence of the providential care of a beneficent Creator. Genesis was regarded as reliable cosmological history, the world being little more than 6000 years old. In 1830, Sir Charles Lyell's *Principles of Geology* appeared, arguing that the earth's crust and fossil remains pointed to immeasurably greater tracts of time than had hitherto been assumed, for the formation of the present-day landscape. Lyell was attacked as irreligious by some, and the quaint arguments began to be advanced to account for the existence of strange fossil remains: that these were the species which Noah had been unable to accommodate in the ark, or that God had placed them there in order to tempt the faith of many. Then in 1844 great excitement was aroused by the anonymous *Vestiges of the Natural History of Creation*, which eventually proved to be the work of Robert Chambers and was the first cogent and publicly stated British argument for the evolution of species from earlier forms of life. Finally, in 1859, Charles Darwin (1809–82) published his *Origin of Species*, which not only presented an unprecedented range and quantity of evidence for evolution, but moreover advanced the theory of natural selection as a *mechanism* for the process, by the purely natural effect of the survival of the fittest specimens of any species.

The impact was immediate, enormous and convulsive, not least on theology, where many felt that the opening of Genesis, and hence by implication the whole authority of Scripture, was being contradicted: a conflict epitomized by the notorious encounter between Bishop Samuel Wilberforce and Darwin's advocate Thomas Huxley, at Oxford in 1860.

The 'conflict' between religion and science at this point should not be exaggerated, however. In large measure the controversy begun by Darwin was between scientist and scientist, rather than between scientist and theologian, or theologian and theologian. And while it did stir up the debate on the interpretation of Scripture, from the beginning there were always those theologians like Charles Kingsley, F. D. Maurice, F. J. A. Hort and Henry Drummond, who had little difficulty shifting to a non-literalist understanding of the biblical narratives. In fact several years earlier, in 1853, Maurice had been expelled from his chair at King's College, London, for querying the traditional doctrine of 'everlasting punishment' in his *Theological Essays*.

The fact is that the debate around Darwinism was as nothing compared with the furore which erupted in 1860 over the volume *Essays and Reviews* by seven Oxford scholars (or scholars with Oxford connections): Frederick Temple (Head Master of Rugby School), Benjamin Jowett (Master of Balliol), H. B. Wilson, Rowland Williams, Baden Powell, C. W. Goodwin and Mark Pattison. These represented the first concerted attempt in England to take critical and historical questions seriously in relation to the Bible, and arose out of a sense of frustration on the part of the authors that basic intellectual questions were being ignored in the Church, which would have to be faced in the light of contemporary historical and scientific knowledge. Pattison protested that the defect of the eighteenth century was not in having too much good sense, but in having nothing besides, whereas in the current Church of England 'nothing is allowed but the formulae of past thinkings, which have long lost sense of any kind'. Much of the book will strike today's reader as commonplace – the concept, for example, of a progressive revelation, or the different fields of interest covered by science and religion. Much of the controversy centred upon Jowett's essay, 'The Interpretation of Scripture'. Change and development had occurred within both the Scriptures and the later doctrinal tradition. The meanings of the biblical writers, Jowett argued, had to be distinguished from the later doctrinal orthodoxy which tended to be read back into them in anachronistic fashion. But the moral and rational truth of Christianity had nothing to fear from critical study of the Bible: 'Interpret the Scripture like any other book. There are many respects in which Scripture is unlike any other book; these will appear in the results of such an interpretation.'

The book caused a profound shock to many devout church people. Here, apparently, was an onslaught on the edifice of revealed truth *from within the Church itself*. Even some outside the ranks of believers, such as F. W. Harrison, considered that the authors had no business to remain in the Church if such were their views. Conservative bishops like Samuel Wilberforce made wild attacks. Over 8,000 clergy signed a protest petition to the Archbishop of Canterbury. Williams and Wilson were arraigned before the Court of Arches (the Consistory Court of the Province of Canterbury) and found guilty of promulgating views incompatible with the doctrines of the Church of England. They appealed to the Judicial Committee of the Privy Council (which included the two Archbishops and the Bishop of London) which reversed the judgement of the Dean of Arches, on the grounds that the Church of England had no definitive ruling on the precise interpretation of such matters as 'everlasting punishment', on which the two had been charged. A certain liberty of opinion was to be allowed. While the two Archbishops dissented from this judgement, the Bishop of London, Tait, supported it. Once more alarm seized the Church, uniting High and Low Church opinion. Eleven thousand clergy signed another petition, while 137,000 lay people signed a letter congratulating the stand taken by the Archbishops. Meanwhile others were keeping cooler heads, notably A. P. Stanley, from 1864 Dean of Westminster, who, while not agreeing on every point with the essayists, defended them in print and asserted that the faith had more to fear from intolerance than from free inquiry. The consequences of the controversy were to persist for some years. In 1869, Temple was nominated to the bishopric of Exeter. There were heated but unsuccessful protests at his appointment.

Then there was the case of Bishop J. W. Colenso (1814–83), who in 1853 was appointed to be the first bishop of the new Anglican see of Natal in southern Africa. Unusual and unorthodox in more ways than one, it was largely when some of his African converts started asking him straightforward questions about the truth of the Bible, especially the Old Testament stories, that he began his own review of the problems of biblical history. Already he had some acquaintance with the work of German scholars. His commentary on the Epistle to the Romans appeared in 1861, in which he criticized the traditional view of eternal punishment, and much traditional sacramental theology also. Most alarm of all was caused back in England when during the

1860s and 1870s his pentateuchal studies appeared, challenging many of the conventional views of biblical authorship and historical veracity. Even Dean Stanley was alarmed. Colenso was, strictly speaking, outside the jurisdiction of the Church of England. Robert Gray, Archbishop of Cape Town, however, declared Colenso deposed from his bishopric. Colenso disputed the Archbishop's right so to act, and a long legal wrangle ensued. Colenso refused to move, even though Gray consecrated another bishop with jurisdiction over Natal.

Essays and Reviews, as often with pioneer works, was indeed in places brash and simplistic. But in the last three decades of the century, English biblical criticism was to develop a tradition of scholarship, as meticulous as it was creative, in the work of the Cambridge trio Westcott, Lightfoot and Hort. Meanwhile on the doctrinal level it was among Oxford High Churchmen of a younger generation that theology was to be opened up still further, with the publication of the collection of essays *Lux Mundi* in 1889. It was edited by Charles Gore (1853–1932), then Warden of Pusey House, and the essays aimed to carry forward the ideals of Catholic orthodoxy, as set out by the original Tractarians of the Oxford Movement, but taking into consideration the recent advances in historical and scientific scholarship. In particular, the essayists shared an acceptance of the presence in the Old Testament of much that was not necessarily literally and historically factual, though conveying religious truth. Gore, in particular, took seriously the idea of progressive revelation, with its underlying premise that God's self-disclosure to man at any point in history takes account of the limitations of human knowledge typical of that time and place. But Gore's real originality came when he dared, in a way quite venturesome for the time, to state the implications of this notion for the understanding of the incarnation. The incarnate Son of God, suggested Gore, would himself have shared in the limitations and particularities of human knowledge operating in first-century Palestine. Gore was later to develop this notion in his 'kenotic' Christology.

The older Anglo-Catholics, especially H. P. Liddon, who regarded Gore as his protégé, were much disturbed by such novelties which seemed to betray the classic Catholic tradition. G. A. Denison, Archdeacon of Taunton, who had been one of the leading thunderers against *Essays and Reviews*, condemned 'this negation issued from what was the Pusey House'. A. R. Vidler summarizes his views: 'Its rationalism was another symptom of the decadence of England under Mr Gladstone, to be classed with universal suffrage, Welsh disestablishment, secular education, and schemes for a Channel tunnel.'[7]

Nor were the Free Churches exempt from controversy. John Foster (1770–1843), a Baptist minister and essayist of some note, caused a posthumous stir when his correspondence was published in 1848, and it was revealed that he too expressed disagreement with the traditional doctrine of everlasting punishment – in his case on moral grounds. A more sustained and damaging dispute broke out in Congregationalism during the 1850s, the so-called 'Rivulet Controversy'. It centred around a hymnbook which Thomas Toke Lynch (1818–71) published in 1855, *The Rivulet: Hymns for Heart and Voice*. Lynch's hymns were a mixture of the sentimental and edifying, and, in a way which contrasted sharply with the largely biblical style of Isaac Watts, often waxed eloquent on the beauties of nature. This to some Congregationalists smacked either of deism or nature-worship rather than evangelical religion, and for some time the Congregational Union was sharply divided. In effect, some of the new theological breezes were blowing through the Free Churches sooner than through Anglicanism, though it has to be said that in this Congregational episode the issues were inflamed by personal factors which set Lynch at odds with John Campbell, editor of a number of Congregational journals.

The most serious Free Church dispute involving theological issues occurred among the Baptists in the Down Grade controversy of 1887–8. During the 1870s and 1880s, Baptists no less than other denominations were becoming increasingly open to ideas of biblical criticism and to the need to reconcile biblical faith with scientific knowledge. A significant number of ministers were seeking what they held to be a necessary reinterpretation of the evangelical faith of their fathers for the contemporary age. Notable among these was John Clifford (1836–1923), Minister of Westbourne Park Chapel in London, and destined to be the 'uncrowned king of militant Nonconformity' by the end of the century, who in 1886 published a volume of sermons, *The Dawn of Manhood*. Clifford, within his own chapel and well beyond, had a large following among younger people of inquiring mind – the new beneficiaries of the spread of education. On the other hand, Charles Haddon Spurgeon (1834–92), who from the Metropolitan Tabernacle reigned supreme over the evangelical Victorian pulpit, was disquieted over the liberal trend among Baptists, and over Clifford's publication in particular. Early in 1887, two articles (not by Spurgeon himself) in his monthly magazine *Sword and the Trowel* referred to the 'Down Grade' taking place in evangelical theology, a disastrous capitulation to rationalism.

Spurgeon followed these up with three articles of his own. At the autumn Assembly of the Baptist Union that year, several speakers were somewhat dismissive of Spurgeon's remarks. Spurgeon, deeply hurt, withdraw from the Union.

Spurgeon had a considerable following among Baptists and beyond, and throughout the English-speaking world. Many feared that the Baptist Union would split over the issue, although only very few ministers actually followed Spurgeon out of the Union. Spurgeon himself felt betrayed and treated flippantly. For their part, the Baptist Union leadership felt that Spurgeon, for all his sincerity, was gravely in error in refusing to be specific about precisely whom he was accusing of heresy in his charges, and in his remarks about the Union looking like a 'confederacy in evil'. In fact in 1888 the Baptist Union Assembly passed a resolution reasserting Baptist belief in the authority of Scripture as the word of God, while acknowledging that there were differences of interpretation over such matters as the last judgement (that perennial Victorian preoccupation). The Down Grade dispute was partially, if uneasily, resolved. Spurgeon remained outside the Union for the rest of his days, and as we shall see in a later chapter, echoes of the controversy were to be heard over forty years later.

The twentieth-century style

Theological controversy, then, was no stranger to the English scene by the end of the nineteenth century. The controversies we shall be examining in the rest of this study can be seen as the continuation of this series, with roots deriving from the deep-seated issues of encounter between traditional belief and modern culture. But while there is undoubtedly continuity, the twentieth-century controversies do tend to a distinctive colouring of their own. This is so in three main respects.

First, where controversy has arisen over biblical study and interpretation, whereas in the last century it was primarily the historicity and authorship of the Old Testament which were under debate, in this century the New Testament has been no less thrown open to critical inquiry. Charles Gore, we have seen, was prepared to allow a great deal of room to 'progressive revelation', myth, saga, poetry and so forth in the Old Testament. But he remained relatively conservative as regards the New, and as we shall see refused to countenance the views of younger scholars like B. H. Streeter who by the First World War were querying the miraculous elements in the

Gospels. The twentieth century has left no biblical stone, however sacrosanct, untouched.

Second, whereas in the nineteenth century certain doctrines and their customary interpretation were disputed, such as everlasting punishment, or the meaning of creation, in the twentieth century the whole doctrinal edifice has been questioned, including the incarnation, right down to the foundational doctrine of God, such that the very *meaning* of 'God' has been under review. The post-Enlightenment possibility, that God is a name for an aspect of being human, has made its fullest impact.

Third, the *context* in which controversy has occurred this century has intensified many of the debates. This century has seen not just the advance, but the *consciousness*, of the social process known as secularization, that is, the process whereby religion loses its public, social significance and increasingly becomes a private option for belief. Religious institutions and sanctions are left with a modicum of importance for believing individuals, but with very little role for society as a whole – beyond, perhaps, that of providing some ritual for state occasions. It is a process originating centuries ago with the break-up of medieval Christendom. But large-scale awareness of it really dates from about the turn of this century, as church leaders gradually began to wake up to the fact that no longer could an assumed Christian framework be taken for granted for the whole of society, that the industrial masses had been very little touched by religion, that increasing numbers of the educated middle classes were just not interested in it, and that the public influence of the Churches – on political life for example – was shrinking. Many of the nineteenth-century debates still assumed a religious ethos pervading the body politic, especially in Oxford, which until about 1870 was virtually the academic close of the Church of England. By the years just prior to the First World War we find churchmen anxiously talking about the 'modern age' as something not only quite distinct from the realm of organized religion but threatening it – and seeing it implicitly as *the norm* for the population. The new currents of social, cultural and political life were increasingly bypassing the Churches, which from now on manifested increasing signs of insecurity *vis à vis* society.

This continuing development has seasoned theological controversy. On the one hand, those who have felt led to question traditional forms of belief have often argued the necessity as lying in the unintelligibility of the old formulae and imagery to people of the modern age. The truth has to be expressed in a new way, the tradition has to be reinterpreted. On the other hand, the defenders of the old formulae have argued that it is the very distinctiveness – even their seeming archaism – which is their strength, that nothing will be gained and everything will be lost by any accommodation to contemporary fashions of thought. The former group want a faith with secular currency. The latter group want a faith which will impress the secular ethos precisely by its apparent strangeness. Both, in different ways, are responding to the phenomenon of secularization. Their conflicting concerns, not always clearly articulated, are quickly fed into the programmes of theological dispute, lending heat, if not always light, to the debates.

Notes

1 R. Hartill, 'My Message to the Churchmen', *Baptist Times*, 4 December 1986.

2 A. R. Vidler, *The Church in an Age of Revolution* (Pelican History of the Church, vol. 5), Harmondsworth: Penguin Books 1971.

3 See K. W. Clements, *A Patriotism for Today. Love of Country in Dialogue with the Witness of Dietrich Bonhoeffer*, London: Collins 1986, chapter 5 'Accepting a Heritage'.

4 For a review of controversial issues between 'conservative' and 'liberal' theologies since the early nineteenth century, see A. P. F. Sell, *Theology in Turmoil: The Roots, Course and Significance of the Conservative–Liberal Debate in Modern Theology*, Grand Rapids, Michigan: Baker Book House 1986. A comparison of Dr Sell's thesis with the last chapter of this study will indicate that I am not quite as sanguine as he concerning the possibilities for resolving such controversies.

5 This seems to be the implication of some of the welcoming responses, though not necessarily the views of the author himself, to Bishop Lesslie Newbigin's *The Other Side of 1984. Questions to the Churches*, Geneva: World Council of Churches 1984.

6 On nineteenth-century disputes, see A. O. J. Cockshut (ed.), *Religious Controversies of the Nineteenth Century: Selected Documents*, London: Methuen 1966.

7 Vidler, op. cit., p. 193.

2 An Indefinable Something: R. J. Campbell and the 'New Theology'

The classic formula for raising theological tempers is that a radical attempt to 're-state' Christian belief should be made by a leading church dignitary, and be given sensational publicity in the national press. The formula worked well for John Robinson and *Honest to God* in 1963, and it was no less important in the episode with which our journey into modern theological controversy begins. The debate began shortly before 1907 and arose around a theological viewpoint called by both its protagonists and critics the 'New Theology'[1] (not the last time that a brand of religious thought has confidently claimed this distinction). Its leading advocate was R. J. Campbell (1867–1956), minister from 1903 until 1915 of the City Temple of London – at that time the most prestigious Congregational pulpit in the land and, one might say, the Free Church equivalent of Westminster Abbey in symbolic significance. The debate caused most uproar within the Congregational Union but also excited the other Free Churches and drew considerable comment from the Church of England. Moreover, thanks to the popular press which then, as now, was quick to exploit the newsworthy potential of heretical clerics, for a while it became a talking-point in the country at large.

The controversy was relatively short-lived, emerging in late 1906, reaching its height in 1907 and subsiding to virtual extinction well before the outbreak of the First World War in 1914. But it was significant in that it brought to a head certain tendencies in liberal theology which had been at work through much of the nineteenth century. Some elements in it can also be seen as foreshadowing later debates on the doctrine of God. When *Honest to God* broke upon the scene in 1963, several octogenarian heads nodded knowingly with the comment that they had been there before, with R. J. Campbell.[2] They may have meant that Campbell was a prophet before his time, or merely that Robinson was an old-fashioned liberal born far too late. Either way, the fact that the English Churches could have produced a Campbell and a Robinson troubling the waters at more than half a century from each other, is witness to the recurrence of some of the questions facing an understanding of God in the modern age. Particular controversies may be relatively ephemeral, but the underlying questions which give rise to them are not, least of all the question of how to explicate the relationship of an infinite God to a finite world.

Basically, the New Theology emphasized to an unprecedented degree (as far as British theology was concered) the *immanence* of God, that is, his active presence inside nature and human history, his indwelling within the world, as distinct from his *transcendence*, that is, his difference from the world, his surpassing of the cosmos in his uniquely divine greatness. The New Theology so stressed God's immanence, pressing him into such close intimacy with the universe, that the distinction between 'God' and 'world' was virtually lost. In fact critics accused the New Theology of 'pantheism' (i.e. God is everything) although the New Theologians themselves preferred to speak of 'monism', that is, an understanding of all reality as essentially one, with God and man being but parts of the same spiritual whole.

Background: the immanent tendency

The New Theology controversy has to be understood against the background of the immanent tendency in theology which had been growing in strength throughout the nineteenth century. In Britain the tendency was fed from a variety of sources. Samuel Taylor Coleridge (1772–1834), the philosopher-poet who had a seminal if diffuse influence on English religious thought for at least a generation after his death, gave it a powerful impetus with his emphasis on Christian truth as a matter of inward, intuitive spiritual apprehension. Coleridge was reacting to what, after the Enlightenment, looked an increasingly shaky defence of Christianity: the reliance on 'external' evidences and proofs of God which looked upon the deity either as an arbitrary law-giver, or as one who interfered in the course of nature and human affairs by dubious miraculous means. Instead, Coleridge asserted, the truth of God must be found within, in the voice of that innate 'reason' which is both a faculty of the human spirit and the self-expression of the one God who is eternal truth and reason. Thus:

> There neither is nor can be but one reason, one and the same: even the light that lighteth every man's individual understanding (*Discursus*) and thus maketh it a reasonable understanding, *discourse of reason – one only, yet manifold: it goeth through all understanding, and remaining in itself regenerateth all other powers.*[3]

The scepticism of the Age of Reason had called for a halt to attempts at furnishing proofs of religion and the existence of God by the human mind, for man could not know what lay outside the reach of his mind.

The Coleridgean view answered the challenge by claiming that religious truth did not involve a vain grasping after what lay beyond man, but the realization of what was present within him. When man apprehends the inescapable verities of what his spiritual faculties are saying, he is being true not just to himself, but to the eternal truth or divine *Logos* in which his 'reason' shares.

If a search for God within human awareness and experience was demanded by the collapse of the old metaphysical systems, then the pursuit of a divinity within *nature* was felt to be required by the progress of science. The increasing acceptance of an evolutionary understanding of biology, especially after the impact of Darwinism, meant a total shift in the perception of 'creation' – if that concept was retained at all. The picture of a development of complex forms of life from simpler forms, and of a continuity between the animate, the organic and the inorganic levels of physical existence, put a severe question mark against all traditional notions of special or sudden life-creating acts by some celestial agent external to the natural world. In the wake of Darwin, many theologians who did not cling to a literalist interpretation of Genesis sought to rehabilitate the idea of a 'Creator God' by conceiving him to be continually active within the evolutionary process, rather than exclusively active at a particular originating point. Thus it became more congenial to look for God 'within' nature and history rather than 'coming down' on the world from outside. Preaching in 1875 at the funeral of the pioneer geologist Sir Charles Lyell, the Dean of Westminster Abbey, A. P. Stanley, took as his text Genesis 1.2: 'And the earth was without form, and void; and darkness was upon the face of the deep. And the Spirit of God moved upon the face of the waters.' Some of his opening remarks illustrate just how much the new science had caused a shift in gears as far as biblical exegesis was concerned: 'The language, however poetic, childlike, parabolical, and unscientific, yet impresses upon us the principle in the moral and material world, that the law of the Divine operation is the gradual, peaceful, progressive redaction and development of discord into harmony, of confusion into order, of darkness into light.'[4] God's creativity could therefore now be seen as the hidden, spiritual force within natural processes, and within human history too, the source and inspiration of man's continually onward and upward striving towards the higher and nobler life. It was a concept which linked human history to the evolutionary process in one grand cosmic vision of emergent life: from the primeval slime to Beethoven's Fifth Symphony, it could be said. It also keyed into the bourgeois cultural attitudes of the Western world at that time, expressed as the belief in progress harnessed to democracy, science, Christianity and the spread of European influence around the globe.

Literary influences were no less important. Romantic poetry cast a pervasive spell over the nineteenth century. Wordsworth had written of

> A presence that disturbs me with the joy
> Of elevated thoughts; a sense sublime
> Of something far more deeply interfused,
> Whose dwelling is the light of setting suns,
> And the round ocean and the living air,
> And the blue sky, and in the mind of man:
> A motion and a spirit, that impels
> All thinking things, all objects of all thought,
> And rolls through all things.[5]

The fragrance of the rose, the splendour of the sunset, now tended to have a religious significance not because they pointed beyond themselves to a Creator, but rather because their intrinsic beauty gave outward glimpses of indefinable mysteries and wonders within. The high-mindedness of Wordsworthian poetry was important especially to those who felt that the new industrial and urban scene was threatening established moral values. Man's essential life could be seen as lying not within the dark satanic mills, but in a beauty reflected in lake and upland. Conversely, the grandeur of mountain and torrent had an affinity with the nobility of human aspiration which trod the heights of endeavour on behalf of history's advance towards liberty. Social 'advance' in history could therefore be celebrated as an expression of 'the spirit of progress', especially in episodes at a safe distance away, whether in time (Magna Carta and suchlike) or in space (witness the admiration for Garibaldi for instance). Not surprisingly such attitudes spilt over from poetry into the hymnody of the time, which bears ample witness to the immanent tendencies of popular piety. Samuel Johnson, an American Free Churchman, could pen verses which found a ready echo among like-minded religious liberals in Britain:

> Life of ages, richly poured,
> Love of God, unspent and free,
> Flowing in the prophet's word,
> And the people's liberty!
>
> Never was to chosen race
> That unstinted tide confined:
> Thine are every time and place,
> Fountain sweet of heart and mind.

Breathing in the thinker's creed,
Pulsing in the hero's blood,
Nerving noblest thought and deed,
Freshening time with truth and good.

It was a simple matter to transpose 'spirit' into 'Spirit', and if the heavenward-pointing finger now seemed a little unreal as a pulpit gesture, the preacher could instead clasp his bosom and make fervent reference to 'the indwelling Spirit'.

Then, in the last third of the century, the immanent tendency received powerful intellectual backing from the philosophy of idealism. Coleridge and Thomas Carlyle had been well acquainted with the thought of G. W. F. Hegel (1770–1831), the founding figure of German idealist philosophy. But it was not until Hegel's influence was well past its zenith on the continent that his thought was really discovered and exploited in Britain. Oxford, one might say, acquired a system second-hand from Berlin, where it was no longer in demand. According to Hegel, reality is rational, and one. The universe is the unfolding of a single spiritual principle or mind (hence 'idealism'), in and through the processes of nature and the course of history. This process allows differentiations to emerge between distinct entities and levels of existence – but always within a more comprehensive unity enfolding these distinctions. The parts can only be understood in relation to each other and to the whole, whether in a local community, or the state, or the cosmos as a whole. History moves on through a 'dialectical' process whereby each new development (thesis) provokes a counter-development (antithesis), and the two are eventually comprehended in a higher unity (synthesis). Within such an all-embracing system there could be no ultimate dichotomies, not even between 'God' and 'man'. Divinity is simply a name for Spirit in its absolute and infinite primordiality. The human mind is Spirit in differentiated, finite and self-conscious mode – the infinite Spirit becoming aware of itself in space and time. But the infinite and finite are poles of the same universal Spirit.

In Britain, as in Germany previously, philosophers of 'idealism' varied greatly in their precise attachment to and use of Hegel. But broadly speaking, in the dominant philosophy of the last two decades of the century, especially at Oxford, there was a Hegelian emphasis on mind, consciousness or rationality as being more fundamental than the material aspect of the world, and on the unity of reality at all levels. Objects exist for the knowing mind, and the unity of all things must be comprehended by a single Absolute Mind. Edward Caird (1835–1908), Master of Balliol College from 1893, particularly emphasized the evolutionary dimension. F. H. Bradley (1846–1924), also of Oxford, asserted the nature of ultimate reality as the Absolute which lies beyond all changes, all relationships and all individuated selves – and yet contains all these within itself. The compatibility of this philosophical idealism with traditional theism was obviously a matter of some debate. Bradley, for instance, held that the 'personal God' of religion is but a crude representation of the ultimate truth of the Absolute which lies beyond all notions of personality. But not a few theologians felt that idealism was an ally to Christian doctrine. In face of scientific materialism, philosophical idealism at least argued for the primacy of the 'spiritual' as against the merely physical, and for that the theologians were grateful.[6]

These ingredients in the immanent tendency created an atmosphere in which *continuities* in thought and experience were given greater prominence than the discontinuities: the continuity between nature and history, between one historical period and another, between religion and philosophy, between human spirit and (divine) Spirit. Hard outlines and distinctions were softened and blurred, as in the landscapes of the most distinctive English painter of the century, Turner, where the solidity of ships, trains and bridges dissolves into the mist and melts in the sunlight. Religiously, the age required a haze to accommodate the divine. Nor was this propensity peculiar to the theologians themselves. Victorian and Edwardian drawing-room conversation was entertained with the writings of Sir Oliver Lodge (1851–1940), noted physicist and first Principal of Birmingham University, whose researches extended beyond electromagnetic theory into psychic phenomena. Lodge claimed to be able to offer a new religion for the age, reconciling scientific knowledge with spiritual values in what seemed to be an esoteric blend of Spiritualism and evolutionary pantheism.

Christianity, however, in its traditional expressions asserts some powerful *dis*continuities: eternity and time, infinite God and finite world, Creator God and creature, holiness and sin, heaven and hell, this age and the age to come. Much Victorian religion and theology, of course, still conveyed these formulae – they were not lost to view, however dominant a motif 'God within' may have been. But could the immanent tendency and these traditional disjunctions really be squared with each other? Remarkably, around the turn of the century both approaches could be found not only at the same time or in the same Church, but even within the same individual. For example F. B. Meyer, a leading Baptist Evangelical, a favourite speaker at the annual Keswick Convention and a fervent believer in the literal and imminent personal return of Christ, could strike the immanentist note within history as forcibly as any on occasion:

> [Christ] is moving towards an end which He has had in view from all eternity, and is bearing with Him the destinies of men and nations . . . But since the world discerns Him not, it is for the Church to read His handwriting on the wall, to bear witness to Christian ideals, to aid Him in the work of reconstruction, and to secure . . . freedom instead of slavery, peace instead of battalions and warships, self-sacrifice instead of self-interest, for of such is the Kingdom of Heaven.[7]

It was perhaps inevitable that eventually questions would have to be asked as to the compatibility of the immanent tendency with orthodox theology – or at least, since few would deny that the Bible itself witnesses to the 'nearness' of God as well as his transcendence, whether there were to be limits to the degree of immanentism acceptable within Christian belief. That is what happened in the New Theology controversy, and to its central figure we now turn.

R. J. Campbell

Reginald John Campbell was born in 1867, in London, the son of a Free Methodist minister of Scottish descent. But, apparently for reasons of health, his childhood was spent in the care of relatives in Ulster and his earliest religious impressions were those of a devout if austere Presbyterianism. He returned to England in his late teens, became attracted to the Church of England, and was confirmed. After a period as an assistant teacher he went up to Christ Church, Oxford, in 1891 with a view to eventual ordination. He was by then comparatively mature for an undergraduate (twenty-four) and already married. He read, not theology, but history and political science. He evidently had intellectual gifts, but ill-health and a nervous collapse prevented anything more than an average performance in examinations.

High Church Anglicanism was still the dominant religious force at Oxford, and from it Campbell received what he later called his 'first great spiritual impulse'. It was personified in two characters who left an indelible mark on him – the saintly Francis Paget, then Dean of Christ Church, and Charles Gore, Warden of Pusey House. When Campbell arrived in Oxford the talking-point there was still *Lux Mundi*, the volume of essays edited by Gore that had appeared two years previously and which marked a new era in Anglo-Catholic thought. The essayists were younger High Churchmen, led by Gore, who were seeking to establish a new and sounder footing for Anglo-

Catholic theology in relation to contemporary scientific and historical knowledge. Since the first generation of the Oxford Movement in the 1830s, there had come evolutionary science and historical criticism, and the High Church emphasis, which laid so much store by tradition, was in danger of degenerating into a religious antiquarianism by ignoring the new currents of thought. Gore and company wished to be no less true to the deep-seated roots of Catholic tradition than Pusey and Newman had been. Those pioneers had by no means been theological obscurantists. Newman's *Essay on the Development of Christian Doctrine* (1845) was a highly sophisticated attempt to cope with the historicity of thought – 'here below to live is to change, and to be perfect is to have changed often'. But the young generation of Anglo-Catholics knew that in the eyes of their educated peers dogma was equated with either an ignorance or a denial of the intelligent use of scientific and historical knowledge. Gore, for instance, argued for a view of progressive revelation, recognizing that the Old Testament contained saga and myth which need not be taken as literal, historical fact, and also for a view of the incarnation which allowed that Jesus, as an element in his genuine humanity, would have assumed the world-view normal to a Jew of his time and place. This rejuvenated Anglo-Catholicism combined a continuing sense of tradition with a contemporary intellectual alertness and (in Gore's case at least) a strong social concern. Above all, it fostered a deeply sacramental spirituality. It was an exciting mixture from which Campbell, as others, drank deeply at Oxford.

He did not, however, quite drink it to the lees. A reading of English church history, and a residual loyalty to his Protestant nurture, led him to question the Anglo-Catholic claims that the boundaries of the true Church excluded Nonconformity. He was, moreover, discovered to have a natural gift of eloquence and was already delivering sermons, mostly among Free Church congregations in and around Oxford, to the disquiet of his Anglican mentors. Taking advice from A. M. Fairbairn, the Principal of Mansfield (Congregational) College, shortly after graduation he accepted a call to the pastorate of Union Street Church, Brighton, in 1895.

What followed was a re-enactment of the classic saga of the Victorian Nonconformist pulpit star: a modest beginning in a somewhat down-at-heel provincial chapel attended by the faithful few; a rapid rise in attendance as news of a new prince of the pulpit spread abroad; the church filling to capacity; plans adopted for demolition and building of larger premises; fame spreading . . . especially to the metropolis. Campbell did not thunder hell-fire and damnation, and eschewed all histrionics. Indeed it was precisely his gentleness of speech and demeanour, aided by an angelic appearance, thanks to prematurely whitening locks, which seemed to fascinate. His was an eclectic congregation, comprising many Anglicans and people who wanted what he had to give: evangelical and spiritual religion in terms consonant with what thinking people knew about the world of the time.

Meanwhile at the City Temple, London, one of the greatest Victorian preaching ministries was drawing to its close as Dr Joseph Parker, full of years, faded in health. At this citadel of Nonconformity congregations of 3,500 were a normal occurrence every Sunday morning and evening. There was also a sermon delivered every Thursday morning, and when it became clear that Parker could not maintain this additional weekday burden, it was Campbell who was asked to serve instead. This established beyond doubt his reputation, and few were surprised when, on Parker's death, Campbell was called to the full charge of the City Temple in 1903, at the age of thirty-six. Soon he was a national and indeed international figure (he had toured South Africa and the United States), and his sermons were published throughout the English-speaking world. Many admitted that it was the preacher as much as his message which appealed. An eyewitness commented:

> He is a striking personality in the pulpit. He wears a Geneva gown, which hides the slimness of his figure. But this detail does not arrest you. It is the face! pallid, beardless, slightly oval, ending in a protuberant chin. And the eyes! Large and clear, they seem to possess a luminous attractive power, inspiring confidence and friendship. The wavy grey hair forms almost an aureole, and is a reminder of old age – a suggestion which is, however, dispelled by the winsomeness of youth in the face and figure. As we look at this young preacher and pastor, we know that personality tells. There is an indefinable something in his appearance in the pulpit which impels attention.[8]

The 'indefinable something', however, was not simply in the preacher's personality, nor in his manner, but in the actual content of his preaching. People might compare his impact on London with that of C. H. Spurgeon a generation earlier, but Campbell's message was hardly Spurgeon's. It combined to an unusual degree a deep personal reverence for Christ, with an almost mystical vision of the cosmic scope of belief. Thus:

> I believe not only in my own mind, but I believe in a Mind which is the source of mine; I believe not only in my own soul, I believe in the Oversoul. Moreover, I believe in an essential relationship between my soul and that Soul; the Father of my spirit is ever speaking unto me.[9]

Jesus is the soul of the Universe. He is the Self of our selves, and the Life of our lives.[10]

The Cross of Calvary is the key to creation.[11]

Here was the immanent tendency in full stride. Certainly Campbell's preaching from the start seemed more speculative than evangelical. 'The incarnation,' he said in an early City Temple sermon, 'is the process whereby humanity is being taken to its home in God; or, better still, the incarnation is the discovery that humanity is in God'.[12] On the other hand, he could present in a strikingly simple and fresh way the meaning of the atonement:

Your sin can be taken from you as though it had never been. The Gospel that we have to preach is the declaration of Christ's power of so dealing with your sin that it is his, and not yours . . . It is as though you were to say, 'I am not guilty; the Sinless One is . . . My redemption has meant the passion of Deity; my Redeemer has the assets of my character. My broken life is his, and the way of opportunity has opened before me because of the holiness of Christ, as well as his passion.'[13]

Those who from the beginning had suspicions about Campbell's orthodoxy – and such there were – could for the time being be quieted by this strand in his preaching. It was the evident absence of this element a few years later which provoked controversy.

There was a direct relationship, not always to be assumed in preachers, between Campbell's well-stocked bookshelves and his sermons. During his Brighton years he had sought to compensate for the lack of formal theological education by a voracious reading in theology and philosophy, which was to be maintained throughout his life (a standing joke was that in order to find out what German theological works had arrived in England in the past week, one had only to slip along to the City Temple of a Thursday morning). It was, above all, the neo-Hegelian idealism of Caird and Bradley, of which he had heard so much at Oxford yet never read first-hand, which engaged him, together with the continental Liberal Protestants (the French representatives like Sabatier rather than the Germans such as Harnack), and the writings of the mystics. Mysticism was in fact enjoying a revival of interest in England at the turn of the century, thanks particularly to W. R. Inge, Dean of St Paul's Cathedral, of whom Campbell was a professed admirer. He was also well versed in the most recent advances in biblical criticism. Out of all this, and his own spiritual instincts, he forged his peculiar brand of liberal theology.

During 1903–6 his standing increased unimpeded. He was hailed as a sign that the age of preaching was by no means over. Free Church pulpits and platforms throughout the land vied for the honour of his presence, and many an Anglican sat in the pew at the City Temple. One prominent Low Church layman solemnly declared, after sampling a service there, that he could verify that the Holy Ghost had also attended. Public wonder increased as it became known that Campbell did not laboriously toil over sermon preparation, but rather relied upon extempore inspiration. On one occasion at a Baptist Assembly in Edinburgh, he suddenly realized during the hymn preceding his address that he could not remember the chapter and verse of his chosen text. After hurried whispers among the platform party a concordance was frantically consulted in the vestry below, the verse located, and all was well (just) in time. Such improvisation was greeted as a sign of genius – while his popularity lasted.

Two further features of Campbell's City Temple ministry deserve mention. The first is his remarkable ministry of pastoral counselling. After every service his vestry was besieged by a queue of inquirers beset by moral and spiritual dilemmas, and who in some cases had even come from overseas to seek him out. He did not remain several feet above contradiction, and knew that as a pastor it was as important to listen to the questions people were actually asking, as to declaim upon what the answers to life's problems might be. The second was his political conversion to socialism. Campbell had ventured some opinions in print on the subject of working-class attitudes to Sunday observance. This had caused offence among some trade union leaders, who challenged him to a public debate. Campbell accepted the invitation, and the result was a new awareness on his part of working-class life, so much so that he threw himself into the socialist movement as a speaker and writer. It was very much a platform socialism, but in those days the platform mattered a great deal in politics, and the Labour movement was grateful to have secured Campbell's voice, so much so that in 1907 he was invited, at Keir Hardie's personal request, to contest the Cardiff seat for the Independent Labour Party at the next election.[14] It was an unusual degree of involvement for a Free Church minister of the time, for most Nonconformists were still strongly identified with the Liberal cause in politics and were viewing the rising Labour movement with unease. It was in turn a revelation to Campbell to discover just how far the masses were alienated from organized religion, and how irrelevant the Churches seemed to the political left.

'O woeful blunder!'

In September 1906, Campbell addressed a private meeting of London

Congregational ministers on 'The Changing Sanctions of Popular Theology'. Hints of what he said leaked into the religious press, and as a result another meeting of ministers was called for discussion of the issues he had raised. This meeting was held behind strictly closed doors, but the scent of an interesting story was picked up in the offices of the *Daily Mail*, at that time the most widely read and popular national newspaper. So one day in January 1907, Campbell found himself face to face with a reporter in his study, and the sight of pencil poised above notepad ignited his eloquence as readily as did the serried ranks on Sundays at the City Temple. The resulting feature article appeared on 11 January. Campbell was quoted at length:

> I do not like the term 'New Theology' . . . but it is in common use, and so it must be allowed to stand. It is a term of convenience employed to describe a certain tendency towards liberalism in modern religious thought. It denotes an attitude and a spirit, rather than a creed. We object to the formal statements of belief which have distinguished the theology of the past. We object to ecclesiastical labels. Everyone knows that for the past twenty years there has been considerable uneasiness in the Churches, due largely to the development of scientific knowledge, the progress of archaeology, and the study of comparative religion. This uneasiness has affected every Church, even Rome. From the side of science, the New Theology is typified in the work of men like Sir Oliver Lodge.
>
> Unitarianism made a great gulf and put man on one side and God on the other. We believe man to be the revelation of God, and the universe we mean to be the revelation of God . . . Believing this, we believe that there is thus no real distinction between humanity and deity. Our being is the same as God's, although our consciousness of it is limited. We see the revelation of God in everything around us.
>
> From all this it will surely be clear that the New Theology brushes aside many of the most familiar dogmas still taught from the pulpit . . . We reject wholly the common interpretation of the Atonement – that another is beaten for our fault. We believe not in a final judgment, but in a judgment that is ever preceding . . .
>
> We believe that Jesus is and was divine, but so are we. His mission was to make us realise our divinity and our oneness with God. And we are called to live the life which he lived.

Next day, a Saturday, the paper was already acknowledging that this broadside on traditional belief was shocking many readers, and the subject was dealt with in a somewhat defensive editorial. Mr Campbell, it was claimed, was merely trying to engage with an exaggerated conception of the place of evil in the universe. As for his views: 'If we cannot endorse them, we can at least discuss them in the light of modern thought, and point to their significance.'[15]

At any rate, all this meant that next day the congregations at the

City Temple were at least as large and certainly more excited than usual. Two days later Campbell left for Newcastle-upon-Tyne, where he had been booked to speak. Tickets had already been sold out and crowds were turned away at the doors. Meanwhile, the initial public response was already reverberating in the *Daily Mail*. On Monday 14 January, Campbell himself claimed in a letter that there were some distortions in the report of his interview, and that he had not denied the atonement. 'On the contrary, I have little else to preach about. The New Theology is an attempt to restate the Atonement in terms of the ethical ideal.' Two other correspondents demanded to know what Campbell was really meaning, if not proclaiming the old Sabellian heresy and pantheism.

Next day, 15 January, the paper published a selection from the enormous volume of mail received. Most were hostile to the New Theology: 'It can be concisely expressed in one word – Buddhism'; 'Surely the New Theology should be called "The New Theoliver-lodgey".' One correspondent found it had all been said by Tolstoy but with a better rationale, another that it was simply reiterating what was already being propounded in Germany and America and by 'a northern Dean' (presumably Hastings Rashdall of Carlisle). One reader congratulated Campbell on having at last seen the light in Spiritualism, and yet another saw it as the plainest Unitarianism. Only one published letter offered Campbell support, to the extent of complaining of tendencies towards a heresy hunt. The same edition carried another article on Campbell and his career, adorned with a large photograph. The paper carried the controversy for several more days, reporting reactions from far and wide. Sir Oliver Lodge opined that there was actually little new in the New Theology except the sudden public interest.[16]

Having erupted on to the public scene via the secular press (and note again the parallel with *Honest to God*), the controversy was inevitably pursued for far longer and with greater seriousness within the Churches themselves and their own periodicals. Much Free Church opinion was astonished and perplexed, especially in the Congregational Union, and the counter-attack was led by the *British Weekly*, the main interdenominational organ of Nonconformity. The editor, Robertson Nicol, was nerved by a sense of betrayal, having claimed some of the credit for 'discovering' Campbell in Brighton, and having also opened the columns of his paper to Campbell in the form of articles answering readers' questions. The first issue of the *British Weekly* to appear after Campbell's *Daily Mail* interview carried large sections of the offending article, together with a cutting comment from P. T. Forsyth, Principal of Hackney Theological College: 'His is not the New Theology – it may be an amateur one.' Next week Robertson Nicol himself launched the attack with a front-page article on 'City Temple Theology'. He began with a display of pained reluctance to indulge in anything so unpleasant as a prosecution for heresy, especially where Campbell was concerned:

> He seemed to us a precious gift to the Free Churches of England. We were among the first to hail his accession; we have refrained from criticising him, even when in mute opposition. We have done all that ever we could to keep him in the ranks. We hoped great things from him. Nor have we abandoned our hopes.[17]

Nicol then rounded on those aspects of Campbell which had previously evoked a mischievous admiration: his entry into the ministry without any seminary experience or formal theological education, and his avowedly improvised approach to preaching. He was out of his depth in theological and philosophical technicalities:

> Not having the language of those problems, and having no time to choose it, he sinks as it seems to us, and especially of late, into complete intellectual chaos. The preacher is at sea on all points. He can spin his fabric by the square mile of whatever texture it may be . . . but many of us may think that the texture is gossamer, twaddle and no more.[18]

Deprived of the preacher's winsomeness, alleged Nicol, the City Temple preaching was a mere nothing.

The *British Weekly* offensive was maintained every week through the spring and into the summer. On 31 January Nicol was able to parade some weighty evidence for the prosecution in the form of a particularly infelicitous pulpit utterance heard at the City Temple the previous Sunday:

> . . . However startling it may seem, sin itself is a quest for God – a blundering quest, but a quest for all that. The man who got dead drunk last night did so because of the impulse within him to break through the barriers of his limitations, to express himself, and to realize more abundant life. His self-indulgence just came to that: he wanted, if only for a brief hour, to live the larger life, to expand the soul, to enter untrodden regions, and to gather to himself new experience. That drunken debauch was a quest for life, a quest for God.

This of course hardly appealed to Nonconformists who had for years been campaigning against the drink trade as a work of the devil, and who were now seemingly being told that the public house was but a somewhat more circuitous route to heaven than the chapel. Campbell tried to amplify his thinking the following Sunday. He admitted that to speak of sin as a quest for God, albeit a misdirected one, was startling. What he was arguing for, he explained, was a view of all life and all history as an exhibition of two competing tendencies: the deathward, sinful tendency of self-seeking, and the lifeward tendency of love and sacrifice, the Christ-tendency. But, he insisted, *both are seeking God*, correctly or otherwise. Thus: 'Your *roué* in Piccadilly, who went out to destroy innocence, was seeking life while spreading death. It seems almost blasphemy to say it, but he was seeking God, and thinking – O woeful blunder! – that he would find Him by destroying something that God has made beautiful and fair.'[19] At this point, it was not only puritanical Nonconformists who were moved to object. G. K. Chesterton, still at that time a High Anglican, thought it sounded too much like an apology for sin – 'The "New Theology" denies the only part of Christian theology that can really be proved from experience: positive sin' – and wryly commented that whereas atheism might use the sordid fact of Piccadilly as an argument against the existence of God, the New Theology 'offers us a modern and rational settlement by denying the existence of Piccadilly Circus'.[20] Then, still more pointedly: 'The policeman who tortures women in some central European dungeon will quite agree that there is no such thing as positive evil; he will smilingly assent as you tell him that he is only a shadow where there might be light.'[21]

From being the most brilliant star in the Free Church sky, Campbell suddenly found himself eclipsed by the controversy and the welter of caricature and innuendo which such disputes generate. Engagements to preach and speak were in some cases withdrawn overnight. Questions were asked by some Congregationalists as to whether Campbell could legally preach this theology under the terms of the trust deeds of the City Temple – though the congregation and officers of that church did themselves remain steadfastly loyal to him throughout the crisis. Free Church leaders were acutely embarrassed by the whole affair. John Clifford, the most famous campaigning Baptist and champion of individual liberties, displayed as much integrity as any when he deputized for Campbell one Sunday at the City Temple pulpit, stating his disagreement with Campbell while affirming the right of a preacher to be true to his own conscience in his own pulpit (to loud applause from the gallery). F. B. Meyer safeguarded both his piety and his reputation for courtesy by saying that even if the New Theology was true, it would not make the traditional interpretation of the New Testament untrue.[22] Fortunately for himself he was not required to enlarge on such a vacuous remark. Others were far less polite. John Oman, writing in the *British Weekly*, commented:

> Most people labour under the illusion that for any exposition to be popularly effective, it must be concrete. But no German could be more abstract . . .
>
> . . . In all seriousness, this air of a pundit over things so crude, this tone of an oracle over a poor pantheism on which no one could for any time carry out effectively the business of life, is no step towards any theology.[23]

Perhaps in all this there was an element of sour grapes, an outburst of jealousy at the upstart from Brighton who had achieved renown before his time. But there was, too, a genuine concern for theological coherence. The question then to be asked is whether Campbell's views had really changed, or whether it was merely that the fuller implications of what he had always preached were now being comprehended. Certainly there are sermons from both before and during the actual controversy which are equally matched for their immanentist and quasi-mystical tone. But the view of sin as 'a blundering quest for God' does mark a definite shift of position, for in 1903 Campbell had quoted approvingly Joseph Parker's famous description of sin as 'a raised hand, a clenched fist, and a blow in the face of God'.[24] From sin as a blow in the face of God, to sin as a hand falteringly groping out for God – this was the crucial change in understanding which precipitated the New Theology controversy. Campbell, in his critics' eyes, was so redefining the human condition as to obviate the need for redemption. On the other hand, Campbell felt that this understanding of man was of a piece with the theology and philosophy which he had been absorbing and propounding for years. In the midst of the uproar he gave himself the opportunity of a considered reply to his critics by taking himself off to Cornwall and writing *The New Theology*, which appeared in March 1907.[25]

The New Theology

The New Theology, Campbell's major apologia for his views, was written hurriedly, even angrily in parts. His point of departure was what he alleged to be a sharp dichotomy between Christian beliefs as traditionally taught and preached, and the actual experience of people in the present-day world. There was the danger of a wholesale departure of modern civilization from the Christianity in which it had grown. The vital world, particularly in the socialist movement, was dismissing Christian belief not only on intellectual but also on moral grounds. The world had no use for it – certainly not for those theologians who were 'rehabilitating truth in the grave-clothes of long-buried formulas'.[26]

The New Theology, declared Campbell, would rectify this by placing God's immanence decisively at the centre of its thought, so countering the key failure of traditional theology, which was, in effect, a dualism: thinking of God 'as above and apart from the world instead of expressing himself through the world'. This meant a quite new understanding of God's relationship with the world and with man:

> When I say God, I mean the mysterious Power which is finding expression in the universe, and which is present in every tiniest atom of the wondrous whole. I find that this Power is the one reality I cannot get away from, for, whatever else it may be, it is myself.[27]

Campbell was quite explicit that the basis of this monistic view lay in idealist philosophy: 'I can only think of existence in terms of consciousness: nothing exists except in and for mind. The mind that thinks the universe must be immeasurably greater than my own, but in so far as I too am able to think the universe, mine is one with it.'[28] One might say, Campbell stated, that the universe is God's thought about himself, and we are tiny parts of that great consciousness. So it becomes clear why Campbell could describe sin as a search for God – there could not be any ultimate dichotomy between human consciousness and divine consciousness, however wayward the former might be. Likewise all evil, all pain, must by definition be ultimately harmonious with the purpose of the whole. According to Campbell the traditional doctrine of the 'Fall' was misleading, and indeed a survey of history supplied grounds for optimism, not despair, about man. 'Slowly, very slowly, with every now and then a depressing setback, the race is climbing the steep ascent towards the ideal of universal brotherhood.'[29]

The nerve of any Christian theology is its understanding of the person and work of Christ. Campbell, like other liberal theologians, had a deep personal reverence for the figure of Jesus. But, given that on his view humanity and divinity were but parts of the same great consciousness, the traditional understanding of Christ as a unique union of divine and human natures had to be drastically revised. 'Humanity is Divinity viewed from below, Divinity is humanity viewed from above.'[30] We call Jesus divine, says Campbell, because in his human life he displays perfect love, and such love is the innermost essence of what divinity is. Anticipating the protests of those who would say that this made Jesus 'only a man', Campbell retorted: 'I make Him the only Man . . . We have only seen perfect manhood once, and that was the manhood of Jesus. The rest of us have got to get there.'[31] What, then, of Jesus as uniquely divine? Campbell unflinchingly exposed the full implications of the monistic stance: 'Jesus was God, but so are we. He was God because His life was the expression of Divine love; we, too, are one with God in so far as our lives express the same thing . . . Fundamentally we are all one in this eternal Christ.'[32] Clearly 'incarnation' no longer meant a once-for-all occurrence in a particular historical person, but the expression of the divine through the whole human story. Jesus is the sign of what is happening all the time, the struggle of the divine to manifest itself through the human. 'To think of all human life as a manifestation of the eternal Son renders it sacred. Our very struggles and sufferings become full of meaning. Sin is but the failure to realize it; it is being false to ourselves and our Divine origin.'[33]

Not only the incarnation, but also the Trinity and atonement, were rehabilitated by Campbell into his monistic metaphysical system. Historical doctrines became symbolic of universal truths. Gone, too, was the idea of the Church as a unique community of the saved. Its work was to serve the Kingdom of God for the salvation of the world, making the world a happier and safer place. The Church has no exclusive part in God's purpose, for God is equally at work in all movements for human betterment, most notably the socialist movement. In fact also in 1907 Campbell's *Christianity and the Social Order*[34] appeared, and central to its argument is an attack on 'other-worldliness' as a distortion of the primitive Christian preaching:

> This has led to a view of the function of the Church entirely different from that which Christianity began . . . The whole emphasis is different, for primitive Christianity confined its interest to the establishment of the kingdom of God in this world, whereas modern Christianity has weakened its efforts in this direction by its other-worldism. This will have to be given up . . .[35]

Not that Campbell rejected immortality or miracle as such (though historical criticism led him to question severely the historicity and theological significance of the virgin birth). The 'bodily' resurrection of Jesus was less problematical to him than to some liberals, since one of the implications of his monism was that the 'physical' and 'spiritual' could not be rigidly separated, being but different ways of describing the same reality or stuff of the universe.

Those who had known the gentle Campbell of the seraphic countenance were taken aback by the waspish tone of much in *The New Theology*, not least the sweeping, scornful dismissals of 'pulpit theology' and 'theological college Christianity'. Such language could hardly make friends when friends were sorely needed, and while the book was intended as a defence, it quickly proved to offer a still larger target to his opponents. But before attending to the second wave of criticism which descended upon Campbell, some notice should be taken of his allies.

Campbell's allies

Campbell was not entirely on his own. For one thing, as has been said, his City Temple congregation stood loyally by him. For another, there were Free Churchmen like Clifford who were as concerned for liberty of conviction as they were in disagreement with Campbell's theological excesses. Moreover, Campbell's theology could not be rejected *in toto* without raising embarrassing questions regarding the strongly immanentist strain in much theology and preaching of the time, which had close affinities with the New Theology while still distinguishable from it. What is more, there were other Congregationalists who were as radically immanentist as Campbell. The New Theology was by no means confined to the City Temple. Nor was Campbell himself even the first to venture into print under the 'New Theology' banner.

As early as 1905 T. Rhondda Williams of Bradford published *The Evangel of the New Theology*.[36] Claiming to be a piece of anti-Unitarian apologetic, it was trinitarian only in a drastically modified sense. Like Campbell, Williams was an avowed monist:

> If God had one kind of spiritual nature, and man a different kind, man could never receive any revelation. We are bound . . . to believe in the essential oneness of man with God. The question, therefore, as to whether Jesus was divine or human is meaningless; from the point of view of the New Theology the old controversy between Trinitarian and Unitarian drops out.[37]

Another New Theologian, J. Warschauer of London, had in fact migrated from Unitarianism to Congregationalism. His book *The New Evangel. Studies in the 'New Theology'* (1907)[38] called for the completing of the Protestant Reformation by allowing the formation of a truly spiritual religion, freed from all external authorities and the 'yoke of the letter'. Compared with Williams and Campbell, Warschauer comes across as strongly immanentist rather than explicitly monist: 'We could not behold the presence of God in Christ but for the fact, however dimly apprehended, of the presence of God within ourselves; and Christ, in turn, wakens and strengthens the consciousness of that presence in us, until it becomes a clear and governing conviction.'[39] Nevertheless, Warschauer too was reluctant to concede to Jesus a wholly unique 'incarnation'. Probably the most radical of all the New Theologians was K. C. Anderson of Dundee, who was moving towards the 'Christ-myth' position, that is, seeing the human, historical Jesus (if he existed at all) as incidental to the 'eternal Christ' who is for ever expressing himself through history.

Not only was Campbell not alone, therefore. He was not even the originator or the most radical of the 'New Theologians'. But by virtue of his reputation and position he was certainly the most prominent, and the others were glad to adopt him as their standard-bearer. Despite their differences of emphasis they all shared the radically immanentist approach and the determination to break with traditional theology. Further, they all wished to unite radical religion with socialism. Some attempt at giving the movement coherence resulted in the formation of 'The New Theology League', succeeded by 'The Progressive League'. A summer school was held in 1907 at Llandudno in North Wales, bringing together members of the movement with socialists. Reports were heard at this gathering of some younger ministers who had been forced out of their Churches thanks to their espousal of the New Theology, and proposals were made for their financial relief.[40]

The critical reaction 1: Congregationalists

The fact that there was indeed a 'movement' of extremely liberal theology, though of uncertain extent, among Congregational ministers was unnerving to the leadership of the denomination. Scarcely had *The New Theology* appeared in print in March 1907, than its unacceptability was made plain, first in the *British Weekly* and then in a collection of essays, *The Old Faith and the New Theology*, edited by C. H. Vine of Ilford, in which thirteen eminent Congregationalists pronounced their anathemas.[41] A restatement of Christian truth in terms of the modern mind may be desirable, stated Vine in his introduction, 'but to destroy that truth in order to substitute a strange variety of metaphysical dogmas is quite another matter'. That view of the situation summed up the tenor of the essays as a whole, uneven though they were, as such collections usually are. Indeed the unanimity of the authors was striking, representing as they did a wide spectrum of Congregational outlook, from the staunchly evangelical to some who had hitherto been considered 'liberal' or 'modern'. Charles Silvester Horne, one of the most popular preachers of the day, who combined an evangelical message with a strong social conscience (and, for a time, a seat in the House of Commons), typified the view that the New Theology seemed to lack Christian common sense:

> The fact of Christ, the fact of sin, the fact of salvation, do not seem to be sharply defined. We seem to be transported into a region of rosy haze, very pleasant and genial, where the stern, hard, jagged facts of life lose all their ugly realism, 'the wizard twilight Coleridge knew'.[42]

In terms of academic theology, the most significant contributor, and Campbell's severest critic, was P. T. Forsyth (1848–1921), then Principal of Hackney Theological College and rapidly approaching his status as the most significant Free Church theologian of the age. He was himself no stranger to liberalism, having as a student sat at the feet of none other than Albrecht Ritschl, the founding father of German Liberal Protestantism, and as a young minister he had enjoyed startling his congregations with progressive religious ideas. However, he had come to be severely disillusioned with the superficiality and sentimentality of late Victorian religion as compared with the biblical faith of the reformed tradition proper, and turned from extolling the joys of 'love' to the awesome nature of *grace*. God's love was *holy*, a matter of fearful mercy, demanding a recognition of God's holiness and of man's profound moral plight. Forsyth proceeded to work out a renewed understanding of the cross as the event in which divine judgement and reconciling love met in an act of costliest atonement. With his emphasis on the discontinuity between God and man, which could be bridged only from God's side, Forsyth was already sounding the note which Karl Barth was to strike on the continent a generation later.

Not surprisingly, therefore, the whole style and content of the New Theology was anathema to Forsyth, and the exchanges between himself and Campbell comprised the bitterest personal aspect of the whole controversy. As we have seen, Forsyth dismissed Campbell as an 'amateur', and it was undoubtedly Forsyth who was the target of Campbell's cutting remarks about 'theological college Christianity'. As with Nicol, Forsyth probably felt a sense of betrayal. On leaving Emmanuel Congregational Church, Cambridge, for Hackney College in 1901, he nursed a hope that Campbell might succeed him as minister there, on the grounds that a person of Campbell's background might find more acceptance within university circles. But far more important to Forsyth was the feeling that the New Theology represented the culmination of an insidious tendency in modern Christianity, a tendency to evacuate its objective, historic core and to lose sight of – to use the title of one of his books – 'the cruciality of the cross'. Before launching a full-blooded thrust at Campbell, however, Forsyth carefully guarded his rear with a *British Weekly* article explaining that his own youthful involvement in a measure of controversy some thirty years before was of a quite different kind to the present disorder.[43] Then, the 'Leicester Conference' on doctrine – wrongly accused in some quarters of infiltrating Unitarianism into the Congregational churches – had been seeking deliverance from a dead, sterile orthodoxy. Freedom for the truth had been the issue. What had now arisen was a campaign for freedom *from* the truth.

Forsyth's essay in *The Old Faith and the New Theology* was entitled 'Immanence and Incarnation', and it was precisely a confusion between the two terms which Forsyth held to be the cardinal error of the New Theology. In fact immanence, he argued, was a very dubiously Christian concept. It was from just such pagan Hellenistic ideas that primitive Christianity had striven to distinguish itself.

> We owe something to a theory of the divine immanence which, more than a century ago, rescued us from a distant deism, confirmed our faith in the rationality of the world, and went on to deepen our cosmic emotion to be almost an order of religion. It is a theory which has thus had its effect on some moods and expressions of religion. But with evangelical faith it has little to do. It preoccupies us with the physical notion of monistic progress, instead of the moral notion of personality and freedom of action and crisis, sin and sanctity. It does not go to the depths. It speculates about a Christ made flesh, but it never gauges the true seat of Incarnation – a Christ made sin. It is not a theology of Incarnation.[44]

Christ, said Forsyth, did not come to teach or convey 'God's presence', but to redeem and transform the moral personality by moral means. By contrast, the New Theology 'loses redemption in evolution'.

Forsyth's thought dealt in antitheses and his style was always epigrammatic, sometimes to excess ('fireworks in a fog', Silvester Horne once quipped). His rhetoric certainly provided an outlet for his feelings in this essay, and focused as few others could have done the points of inadequacy in the New Theology from an intelligent orthodox standpoint. But the essay did little more, especially as Forsyth indulged in that favourite ploy of the theological polemicist – to identify the position of one's opponent with the direst of heresies from the Christian past and so give oneself licence to pillory it for all it is worth. To Forsyth, the New Theology was all too reminiscent of Gnosticism, that strange blend of cosmology and religious syncretism which attempted to seduce Christianity in the post-apostolic age. 'The present conflict in the Church is more critical for Christianity than any that has arisen since the second century. The issue in the Reformation was small beside this. What is at stake is the whole historical character of Christianity.'[45]

So leading Congregational opinion had its say. How much impact was made by the actual content of the essays is uncertain. For most Congregationalists it was probably enough to know *that* eminent and respected thinkers and preachers had rejected the New Theology, without troubling to read much further. (Nearly sixty years later, on examining the copy of *The Old Faith and The New Theology* in the University Library at Cambridge, A. R. Vidler found the pages still uncut.[46]) Campbell himself never mentions the volume in his autobiography. There is simply the hint of a gulf of bitter contempt between himself and Forsyth. But it was clear that 'pulpit theology' and 'theological college theology' were not going to give way to the 'indefinable something' of the New Theology.

The critical reaction 2: Charles Gore

Now, a touch of melodrama. Just as the hero seems to be sinking ever deeper into tragedy, a father-figure from his long-forgotten past appears on stage, with momentous consequences. Charles Gore, Campbell's Anglo-Catholic mentor of Oxford days, was now Bishop of Birmingham and had followed Campbell's post-Anglican career with interest as well as regret. The New Theology had caused considerable comment in the Church of England and, erupting as it did early in the year, provided a convenient topic for Lenten lectures and sermons in not a few cathedrals during 1907. That, in fact, was the origin of Gore's *The New Theology and the Old Religion*[47] (note the severe shortage of original titles in this controversy) which appeared in 1907. The book was the most creative piece of theology to emerge from the debate, and quite apart from its intrinsic theological value, it is a model of how to conduct an argument as distinct from simply venting one's spleen. The Congregational essayists had bombarded the New Theology from afar, with varying accuracy. Gore was far more subtle. Donning for a while the enemy uniform as a disguise, he slipped inside the perimeter defences and carefully laid charges against the key points from within. Gore, in other words, engaged much more closely with what Campbell was actually saying and took his questions far more seriously. In the end, he took him prisoner.

Gore begins on a note of gratitude to Campbell for articulating certain questions which have been gathering over the years, and he welcomes the theological ferment, for it is, he suggests, in such periods of mental upheaval that so much creative thought has emerged in the past. 'A living theology must always in a sense be a new theology.'[48] In a masterly way Gore sets the whole contemporary debate in a long-term historical perspective, and not in a one-sidedly 'anti-heretical' way as Forsyth had done. He concedes (as Forsyth did not), for example, that there *is* an immanentist strand in Christian thought, which early Christian theology took over from Stoicism. But it was only *adopted*; it was kept in its place and was not allowed to determine the primary perspective of theology, which was that of revealed truth. Yes, Christianity is about moral and social striving (Gore had been a leading Christian Socialist long before Campbell's sudden conversion to the Labour cause). But it is precisely in Christianity's assertion of God's transcendence, his eternal righteousness, that there lies a source of moral uplift which inspires hope and confidence. Monism, or pantheism, cuts the moral nerve by making sin relative and denying grace:

> For the Christian, God is in the world in all its parts and at every moment, revealing himself in varying degrees in all its force, and order, and beauty, and truth, and goodness. But the universe does not exhaust him or limit him. Beyond the universe and independent of it, he is himself, limited by nothing outside himself, in the eternal fellowship of his own being.[49]

According to Gore, in rebelling against what it called 'dualism' the New Theology had not been attacking the truly orthodox notion of God but a distorted form of it, the deism of the eighteenth and early nineteenth centuries. This had so separated God from the world as to make him a kind of remote mechanic and the world a physical machine. So Gore could go on to argue deftly that the New Theologians' real enemy was the *Protestant* 'orthodoxy' which had fostered such Deism. Gore thus turned his critique of the New Theology into a powerful apologia for orthodoxy, not just in a general, but in a specifically Anglo-Catholic, sense. He had begun by taking Campbell's questions seriously. By the end of his reading of the book, Campbell was beginning to take Gore's answers seriously.

Reconsideration and recantation

Strictly speaking, Campbell did not lose many friends in the New Theology controversy, for he had made very few during twelve years of Free Church ministry. If he had attended a theological college after leaving Oxford he might, or might not, have taken a different theological direction, but he would at least in all probability have had more personal acquaintances in Congregationalism. He ruefully remarked that Nonconformity seemed to operate a kind of trade union among its ministers, and to a degree he always felt an outsider. His position after 1907 was increasingly isolated. As late as 1910, there were unsuccessful attempts to remove him from the Congregational ministerial list. There were, in addition, aspects of Anglicanism which he made no secret of missing inwardly since Oxford, in particular the sacramental ethos and the interest in mystical theology and spirituality. Perhaps, after all, what Campbell really represented was a spirituality in search of a theology, a sense of the world suffused by the divine. If a monistic universe was to prove a false trail, where could the answer be found? Hardly in Nonconformity, specializing as it did in moralistic verbal jousts from the pulpit. As for the New Theology movement itself, Campbell was growingly uneasy over some of its tendencies after 1907, especially the speculations of K. C. Anderson, and the movement lost whatever coherence it might once have had. What, then, of the Church of England?

Campbell was impressed by what Gore had written, and the way he had written it. As time went on, he felt that his own understanding of sin had indeed been inadequate, as was his Christology; or rather, what he had been feeling after in Christology could perhaps be better expressed in classical terms than he had realized, and as Gore had suggested. It was the Liberal Protestant Jesus, not the Christ of Catholic belief, which was defective. Study of Gore and others in the years up to 1911 led him ever further away from the brash assertions of 1907. Heresy had been a blundering quest for truth. By mid-1914 he was inwardly clear as to where his future lay: in the Church of England he had left twenty years earlier. By now there were even some disagreements with the officers of the City Temple, though less over theology than on policies of pastoral oversight of the church. In 1915 he made the first decisive break, by withdrawing *The New Theology* from circulation and buying up the publishing rights. No repudiation could be clearer. In the autumn of that year he resigned from the City Temple, and was received back into communion with the Church of England by Charles Gore. Early in 1916 he was ordained to its ministry.

Campbell's new career began at Birmingham Cathedral, and continued at Christchurch, Westminster, where it was hoped he might re-establish himself as a London preacher. But in the pulpit he was never again the force that he had been as a Free Churchman. *The Times* obituary said of him: 'He would not stoop to the sensational methods that attract crowds of a certain type, while to thoughtful people many of his sermons seemed little but a succession of commonplaces though charmingly delivered.'[50] After six years at Brighton, the remainder of his long life was spent quietly at Chichester, as a cathedral canon and theological teacher. He died in 1956.

Retrospect: a blundering quest for truth?

Enough was said about the shortcomings of the New Theology at the time to obviate the need for any further comment, it may be felt. The final word, in that case, was Campbell's own in his retractation. The whole episode could then be regarded as a mere historical quirk of theology, or perhaps significant as marking the high-water mark of liberalism. And high-water marks, one observes, are typically littered with all kinds of rubbish brought in on the tide. Or, it may be felt, Campbell is as much a psychological as a theological curiosity, the lonely child dispatched by his parents to distant Ulster and thus ever after in search of home. After a vain search for a monistic universe (that is, an environment where all is friendly and nothing is really evil), home was found in a sacramental Church, where immanence was at least recognized in a real Presence.

Before making a final judgement, however, we should pause and ask whether the significance of a theological controversy is confined to the more lurid or sensational ideas it generates. What actually prompted Campbell to make his bold if misguided and ill-fated venture? Amid the heat and dust of the controversy his own stated motives were ignored in the successive waves of condemnation which poured down upon the New Theology. Even Gore, who was sympathetic to the need for a renewal of theology, did not light upon the actual reason which Campbell gave for urgent reappraisal of Christian teaching.

That reason is in fact to be found set out in the first chapter of *The New Theology* – and it has an impressively contemporary flavour:

> There is a curious want of harmony between our ordinary views of life and our conventional religious beliefs. We live our lives upon one set of assumptions during six days of the week, and a quite different set on Sunday and in church. The average man feels this without, perhaps, quite realizing what is the matter. All he knows is that the propositions he had been taught to regard as a full and perfect statement of Christianity have little or nothing to do with his everyday experience; they seem to belong to a different world.[51]
>
> The masses of the people on the one hand, and the cultured classes on the other, are becoming increasingly alienated from the religion of the Churches.[52]

If these are thought to be commonplaces, it should be recalled that they were uttered at a time when the Free Churches were at the zenith of their numerical strength and social influence. Confident claims were heard that ere long the established Church would be outstripped numerically as well as politically by Nonconformity (the 1906 Liberal landslide victory owed much to Nonconformist votes). And these were the words of a minister who was himself, to all appearances, the epitome of success as a public communicator of belief. He was not, as happens sometimes with 'radicals', trying to rationalize his obvious failures or find a scapegoat for them. There were no such failures on view at the City Temple, for there were no empty pews. But, as the above statements show, Campbell was already percipient of a deeper kind of failure which, as the twentieth century proceeded, would increasingly haunt the churches like a spectre. Perhaps it was through his vestry ministry of counselling, perhaps it was through his involvement in the labour movement, but whatever the cause, Campbell was detecting – earlier than most – the currents flowing beneath the surface which had the most serious implications for organized religion and the theology which was employed by that religion. He spells out to theologians the dark warning of 'a whole civilization breaking away from the faith out of which it grew'. This was not to be interpreted as an apostasy from the faith, but rather as a signal that the vital movements of the contemporary world were finding traditional expressions of religion irrelevant: 'The world is not listening to theologians today. They have no message for it. They are on the periphery, not at the centre of things. The great rolling river of thought and action is passing them by.'[53] The traditional dogmas, says Campbell, neither square with experience nor do they interpret life:

> The consequence is, that religion has come to be thought of as something apart from ordinary everyday life – a matter of Churches, creeds and Bible-readings, instead of what it really is, the co-ordinating principle of all our activities. To put the matter in a nutshell – popular Christianity (or rather pulpit and theological college Christianity) does *not* interpret life. Consequently the great world of thought and action is ceasing to trouble about it.[54]

Campbell, one could say, was beginning to be aware of what later sociologists and theologians would call *secularization* – the displacement of religious beliefs from the centre of social significance. He must be given credit for this, especially as most of his contemporaries saw the problem (if they saw it at all) simply in terms of the need for increased effort at saying and doing what the churches were already saying and doing. Campbell at least saw that the whole question of the *meaning* of Christianity was being raised by the emergence of a form of daily life which was increasingly autonomous. In face of this, was religion to become a special, circumscribed area of life with its own language, rules and activities? Or was it indeed 'the co-ordinating principle of all our activities' and the interpretative key to the whole of life? If the latter, then theology cannot be an academic extra to life, but the means by which all human – or as was said half a century later, 'secular' – experience is examined in depth and totality.

The subsequent history of theology this century has shown that these issues are in themselves more than enough for a substantial agenda of inquiry and debate. Campbell must be acknowledged as one of the first to raise the issue of theology and belief in these terms. His tragedy was that he rushed into a package of answers before even the questions were fully articulated or their importance was recognized by others. The answers were shouted down and ultimately repudiated by himself, and in the din the original questions were forgotten. Beginning with the problem of a pathological dichotomy between religious life and daily life, he identified the fault in what he saw as a false dichotomy between God and the world, and so rode roughshod over any significant meaning to 'transcendence'. That may have been naive, but the original question as to how *faith* can be immanent throughout all human experience and activity, was not. It is, moreover, a question which has insisted on being heard again and again, in different forms and in various contexts, during this century. In retrospect, it can only be seen as a serious loss that a dialogue between Forsyth and Campbell did not spring up around this issue, instead of the diatribes which enveloped the speculations of the New Theology.

Finally, it has to be remarked that the major fault of the New Theology, in the view of its critics, was that it substituted a certain philosophy, that of monistic idealism, for the Christian revelation. Even as late as 1907, it could not have been foreseen how quickly and drastically the philosophical climate would change in Britain, that not only idealism, but all grand, comprehensive system-building would crumble in face of an analytical and linguistic approach to knowledge, and a rejuvenated empiricism. In that new situation, Christian theology, far from being in danger of seduction by philosophy, would have to make some desperate attemps to qualify even for recognition as a meaningful enterprise in the eyes of philosophy. On the other hand, the very nature of the change in philosophy after the First World War meant that it became rather unreal to talk about 'the philosophy of the time' for there was no longer any single agreed metaphysical world-view to typify the age – unless it was in the purely negative sense of questioning whether such a perspective was possible any longer. Christian theology was thus handed an ambiguous freedom, the freedom to develop its own distinct identity, which might or might not carry significance in a time of collapsing systems. Some forms of Anglican 'modernist' theology, as we shall see in a later chapter, operated within an idealist framework into the early 1920s, but the controversies which they raised had less to do overtly with that philosophical basis as such, than with their apparent variance with the credal formulae of the Church. The New Theology controversy, centred as it was in the less credal environment of the Free Churches, forced open much more radically the age-old question of the relation between the Bible and philosophy, Jerusalem and Athens. The beginnings of a more biblically-based orthodoxy in English Protestantism certainly seem to be traceable from these years just before the First World War.

Notes

1 General accounts of the New Theology controversy may be found in R. Tudur Jones, *Congregationalism in England 1662–1962*, London: Independent Press Ltd 1962; J. W. Grant, *Free Churchmanship in England 1870–1940*, London: Independent Press Ltd 1955; A. R. Vidler, *Twentieth Century Defenders of the Faith*, London: SCM Press 1965. R. J. Campbell's own account is to be found in his autobiographical *A Spiritual Pilgrimage*, London: Williams and Norgate 1916.
2 See W. R. Matthews, *Memories and Meanings*, London: Hodder and Stoughton 1969, p. 56.
3 From *Aids to Reflection* (1825), cited in B. M. G. Reardon, *Religious Thought in the Nineteenth Century*, Cambridge: Cambridge University Press 1966, p. 243.
4 From 'Sermons on Special Occasions', cited in A. O. J. Cockshut, *Religious Controversies of the Nineteenth Century: Selected Documents*, London: Methuen 1966, p. 242.
5 'Lines Composed a Few Miles Above Tintern Abbey'.
6 For Hegel and the British idealists, see citations in Reardon, op. cit.
7 Presidential Address to Baptist Union Spring Assembly 1906, cited in *Baptist Times*, 27 April 1906.
8 C. T. Bateman, *R. J. Campbell: Pastor of the City Temple, London*, London: S. W. Partridge 1903, p. 94.
9 R. J. Campbell, *City Temple Sermons*, London: Hodder and Stoughton 1903, p. 3.
10 ibid., p. 6.
11 ibid., p. 12.
12 ibid., p. 224.
13 ibid., p. 71.
14 *The Times*, 26 July 1907.
15 *Daily Mail*, 12 January 1907.
16 ibid., 15 January 1907.

17 *British Weekly*, 17 January 1907.
18 ibid.
19 R. J. Campbell, *The New Theology*, London: Chapman and Hall 1907, p. 161.
20 Quoted by C. S. Horne in C. H. Vine (ed.), *The Old Faith and The New Theology* (see note 41 below), p. 156f.
21 ibid., p. 157f.
22 *Daily Mail*, 17 January 1907.
23 *British Weekly*, 7 February 1907.
24 Campbell, *City Temple Sermons*, p. 67.
25 See note 19 above.
26 ibid., p. 10.
27 ibid., p. 18.
28 ibid., p. 26.
29 ibid., p. 63.
30 ibid., p. 75.
31 ibid., p. 77.
32 ibid., p. 94f.
33 ibid., p. 109.
34 London: Chapman and Hall 1907.
35 ibid., p. 146f.
36 London: W. Daniel 1903.
37 ibid., p. 22.
38 London: James Clarke 1907.
39 ibid., p. 103.
40 *The Times*, 10 August 1907.
41 C. H. Vine (ed.), *The Old Faith and The New Theology*, London: Sampson Low, Marston and Co. 1907. The contributors were, in addition to Vine: A. Goodrich, D. W. Simon, P. T. Forsyth, G. S. Barrett, W. F. Adeney, A. Rowland, J. D. Jones, C. S. Horne, R. Vaughan Pryce, R. F. Horton, W. H. S. Aubrey, and H. E. Lewis.
42 ibid., p. 154f.
43 *British Weekly*, 7 March 1907.
44 Forsyth, in Vine (ed.) op. cit., p. 48.
45 ibid., p. 57.
46 Vidler, op. cit., p. 30.
47 London: John Murray 1907.
48 ibid., p. 19.
49 ibid., p. 57.
50 *The Times*, 2 March 1956.
51 Campbell, *The New Theology*, p. 3.
52 ibid., p. 5.
53 ibid., p. 8.
54 ibid., p. 9.

3 Oxford versus Zanzibar: The *Foundations* Debates

The saga of R. J. Campbell might have been read by sober Anglicans as an object lesson in the folly of deserting the vessel of *ecclesia anglicana* for the rudderless raft of Nonconformity. Whatever criticisms might be levelled at the national Church, its broad credal tradition could be seen as supplying the necessary ballast which individualist and subjectivist dissent lacked. Anglicanism, however, was in no position to cast aspersions on the theological stability of the Free Churches. By the time he received Campbell back on board the Anglican ship, Charles Gore was fighting what many saw as nothing less than theological mutiny in the Church of England – a mutiny based on what had traditionally been the Church's most secure and loyal deck: Oxford. The plain fact is that during the decade 1912–22 the Church of England was riven by doctrinal controversy as never before or since, to the extent that many despaired of the future of the Church and warned darkly of its disintegration. If ever there was a book with a *déjà vu* title, it is surely the recent *The Church of England: Where is it going?*[1]

In broad terms, it should not be surprising that the Church of England should have been disturbed during these years. A body claiming to be a *national* Church can hardly fail to reflect in some measure the social, intellectual and cultural trends of the age, and Edwardian England was an increasingly argumentative society. Seen in retrospect through the smoke of 1914–18, the age casts a spell of escapist enjoyment and innocence over succeeding generations, of music hall jollity, sunny picnics and extravagant garden-parties. The contrary evidence is plentiful enough: of increasingly bitter industrial strife, of women campaigners battling with police in Trafalgar Square, and of Ulster on the brink of civil war in 1914. New political cross-currents were at work. Conservatives and Liberals still shared the parliamentary stage, and the Liberals won their celebrated landslide victory in 1906. Yet not only were there divisive feuds within the two main parties – especially within the Conservative ranks, following Joseph Chamberlain's campaign for protection of British imperial trade – but both parties watched with unease the rise of socialism as a political force. Keir Hardie could at first be tolerated as a lone oddity in the House of Commons, but the 1906 election brought the Independent Labour Party victory in twenty-six seats. Behind this socialist presence lay a growingly assertive trade union movement, provoked in part by the infamous Taff Vale judgement of 1901, which threatened the bargaining rights of unions. As well as trade unionists, so also feminists, Ulstermen, nonconformist Liberals, Manchester free traders and Birmingham protectionists were all demanding their stake in the future. Shibboleths were being passionately challenged and vehemently defended. Asa Briggs comments:

> Edwardian society was picturesquely but perilously divided, and the greatest of the many contrasts of the age was not with that which had gone before but that between the divergent outlooks and fortunes of different groups within the same community. The implications of the clash of outlooks, fortunes, and tactics could seldom be completely evaded, and . . . more particularly during the four years after the king's death in 1910, there was open and violent internal conflict. Will transcended both law and conviction. The greater international violence of 1914 was a culmination as well as an historical divide.[2]

The crisis of modernity was engulfing all the industrialized, urbanized societies of Western Europe, and in Britain no less than elsewhere.[3] A given, accepted system of values and beliefs as the necessary framework for a stable order was being steadily eroded. The very idea of a single, authoritative, unifying system appeared increasingly suspect to the intellectuals of the day. In philosophy, Moore and Russell were boring into the idealism which had held sway since the last quarter of the nineteenth century, and demolishing the coherence theory of truth. Fragmentation, dissonance, relativity, seemed to be sweeping through social experience, and equally through intellectual and artistic activity.

Within the Church of England, there was plenty of party-spirit to match that in society at large. There was rising bitterness between Anglo-Catholics and others over ritual and ceremonial. On a more fundamental level there was the growing tension between those who wished Christian belief to accept, in some measure at least, the presuppositions of modernity if the faith was to maintain any credibility, and those who by contrast insisted on maintaining inviolate the classical formulations of the faith once delivered to the saints, regardless of the climate of the age. And the nineteenth-century religious tendency to organize the like-minded into a party, found entry into theology. In 1898 there was formed the 'Churchmen's Union for the Advancement of Religious Thought', of which we shall hear more in the next chapter. One of its leading members,

Hastings Rashdall, of New College, Oxford, taught an idealistically based, immanentist Christology not dissimilar to that of R. J. Campbell. 'We cannot,' he wrote in his *Philosophy and Religion* (1909), 'say intelligently that God dwells in Christ, unless we have already recognised that in a sense God dwells in and reveals himself in Humanity at large, and in each particular human soul.'[4]

A measure of Anglican anxieties at the direction of some liberal versions of belief was registered in 1905, when the Convocation of Canterbury felt it necessary to pass a resolution reaffirming the Catholic faith in the Holy Trinity and the incarnation, as contained in the Apostles' and Nicene Creeds and in the so-called Athanasian Creed (the *Quicunque vult*) as statements of fact, and as the necessary basis of the teaching of the Church. Then in 1908, the bishops of the Anglican world communion meeting at the Lambeth Conference resolved that: 'This Conference, in view of tendencies widely shown in the writings of the present day, hereby places on record its conviction that the historic facts stated in the Creed are an essential part of the Faith of the Church.' If such solemn strictures were symptomatic of unease over current tendencies, they were hardly effective in curbing those wayward impulses. Sterner measures were required – and applied. When he was Bishop of Worcester, Charles Gore insisted on obtaining the resignation from his benefice of one C. H. Beeby, for denying the miracles in the Creed. More celebrated still was the case of J. M. Thompson, Fellow of Magdalen College, Oxford, who in 1911 published his *Miracles in the New Testament*. A stir was created by his detailed examination of the New Testament documents and his radically negative conclusions. Bishop Talbot of Winchester, the College Visitor, applied his episcopal jurisdiction and withdrew Thompson's licence to preach. Thompson had vocal supporters, but to no avail. God might not work miracles, but bishops could still enforce discipline.

Presiding over the factious Anglican scene of the Edwardian era was Archbishop Randall Davidson, enthroned at Canterbury in 1903. Far from being factious himself, Davidson was the epitome of ecclesiastical diplomacy. A cautious Scot, he made no pretensions at theological or any other kind of intellectual prowess (his critics were not above pointing out the incongruity of an Oxford third in occupancy of Lambeth Palace), choosing rather to defer to 'earnest and reverent' scholars, and to rely for his part on a simple, though not naive, piety. To calm, to cool, to defuse, was his attitude to disputes in matters theological, ecclesiastical and political. If he had not been so well served by his biographer George Bell – Davidson's chaplain, and later himself to be one of he most outspoken prelates of the century – he might have been dismissed as the archetypal time-serving cleric. In fact it was precisely his cautious detachment, for example, which saved the Church of England from being engulfed in mindless chauvinism during the First World War, and it was his ability to take the long, broad view of affairs, which helped to prepare Anglicanism for the ecumenical era. He gave an important address at the Edinburgh Missionary Conference in 1910, usually regarded as the birth of the modern Ecumenical Movement.

Some of the ablest theologians of the time were much exercised in discussion of the humanity of Christ. Davidson might have found his mind uncomfortably stretched by abstract speculations about 'humanity', but he had a sure perception of that humanity liable to be forgotten by the theologians – their own. To no one did this apply more than Charles Gore, by the early 1900s the patriarch of Anglo-Catholicism, with a justly earned reputation as the most able interpreter of orthodoxy for the modern age. His abilities, as was seen in the previous chapter, were amply displayed in the debate with R. J. Campbell. He was, however, as liable to irritate by his assumed eminence as he was likely to impress by his erudition. In December 1912 Archbishop Davidson received a complaining letter from Bishop Jayne of Chester, asking: 'Are Bishops' meetings to become largely gatherings at which the Bishop of Oxford delivers constant, copious and highly impassioned, if not minatory, allocutions to his brethren? This may be a hygienic safety-valve for him, but he has, I think, done something to change the atmosphere of the meetings.'[5] Following the Thompson episode, Gore had wanted a full debate in the Convocation of Canterbury and had gone so far as to draft a strong resolution against publications by ordained clergy which 'brought into doubt or, positively denied' the virgin birth and the resurrection. He had to be content with a private discussion among the bishops. But by 1912 a far bigger target had appeared in his sights, heralding the most violent controversy of his whole career.

Foundations *and its editor*

It seems to be a peculiarly Anglican way of producing theology, for a collection of essays to emerge from a circle of 'minds' which have been meeting for some time, perhaps over several years, to discuss questions of common interest and concern. To some it may betoken a desire to seek safety in numbers, or a means of getting into print the second-rate article which on its own would not have merited the light of day. But the 'essay' has a distinct quality of its own, as conveyed by its root meaning of 'attempt'. It need not claim finality, though it should certainly have clarity and direction. It may raise questions and should infect the reader with interest in them, even if its own answers are to be regarded as provisional. A volume consisting of several such essays by different authors is liable to have an effect quite other than a monograph of equal length or that produced by the essays published individually. If the essays are in the least questioning of established ideas, taken together they will suggest conspiracy. *Essays and Reviews* shocked many on the English religious scene in 1860. *Lux Mundi* healthily disturbed the Anglo-Catholic world in 1889. *Foundations: A Statement of Christian Belief in Terms of Modern Thought: By Seven Oxford Men*,[6] which appeared in 1912, could therefore almost claim to be in a tradition, however untraditional certain of its contents appeared to be in the eyes of many readers.

The seven were B. H. Streeter, who edited the volume, N. S. Talbot, R. Brook, William Temple, A. E. J. Rawlinson, W. H. Moberly and R. G. Parsons. All were relatively young (Streeter was twenty-seven) and were, or had been, fellows of Oxford colleges. They had been meeting informally in their 'Holy Lunch' club for some years.[7] Partly because of his central role in the project and partly because of views expressed in his own essay, much of the controversy was to centre around the editor. Burnett Hillman Streeter (1874–1937) was Dean of Queen's College, already establishing himself as one of the most authoritative teachers in New Testament historical and literary criticism, and carrying forward the work of his own notable Oxford teacher W. B. Sanday. But Streeter was no narrow specialist. He was trained in philosophy no less than in theology, and he was stirred by the intellectual challenges facing religion in the modern age, particularly as they were felt by students. Prayer, relations between science and religion, mysticism, other religions, the afterlife – all came within reach of his mind and his pen.

As well as being young and Oxford, several of the group had something else in common, incidental in itself, but accorded sinister significance by their severest critics. The examining chaplain to a bishop has the responsibility – directly or indirectly – of ensuring the theological competence and orthodoxy of candidates presented for ordination in that diocese. Brook was in this relation to the Bishop of Wakefield, Parsons to the Bishop of Winchester and – until the publication of *Foundations* – Streeter to the Bishop of St Albans. Temple was a chaplain to the Archbishop of Canterbury. His own passage through ordination, as is now well known, had not been untrammelled by doubts as to the historicity of the virgin birth, though these had evidently been resolved.

Streeter and his colleagues were united not by any defined theological position, but by a shared attitude to the current intellectual climate and to the situation of traditional belief within it. Streeter stated in his Introduction:

> The modern world is asking questions. Christianity and its traditional theology have come down to us from an age very different from our own, an age when the sun and the stars moved round the earth, when the meaning of natural law and evolution was only dimly apprehended, when the psychology of religion, the historical method and the critical study of ancient documents were yet unborn. These things touch the foundations of the old beliefs, and it is about the foundations that the world is enquiring.[8]

Behind such a statement lies an assumed distinction between 'religion' and 'theology'. The Oxford seven did not doubt that their contemporary world needed and wanted a 'religion', but felt that the obstacle to acceptance of religion consisted in its theology, its intellectualized expression, and its lack of conformity with modern science, philosophy and scholarship. The foundations of beliefs as traditionally stated therefore required re-examination in the light of modern knowledge, right down to the fundamental question of the existence of God. But, and here Streeter is recognizably 'modern' in his approach, he insists that such questions cannot be tackled before one has first examined the nature and contents of the primary sources, in the Scriptures and other documents of the early Church. There is a clear recognition that doctrine has a *history*, and the historical nature of the sources of Christian belief must be laid open to all the known techniques of historical inquiry.

The liberal consciousness of the *Foundations* team is expressed very clearly in N. S. Talbot's opening essay, 'The Modern Situation'. He begins:

> This generation in Great Britain is modern in the sense that it is not Victorian. Its members were born while Queen Victoria was still alive, but they never knew – they were not themselves moulded by – the times before the 'sixties'. They were not born, as their parents were, into the atmosphere of pre-'critical' and pre-Darwinian religion. Their education did not begin with the statement 'Creation of the World, 4004', nor are their minds governed by the assumptions it implies.
>
> In fact, the change from genuinely Victorian times to today is a change from the reliance upon, to the criticism of, assumptions.[9]

The essays all exhibited this welcome to questions, and the authors did not pretend to have reached any agreed or final position, still less a system. Brook's essay, 'The Bible', argued for the worth and authority of the Scriptures in terms of the spiritual experience which they record: 'We go to the Bible in order to deepen and correct our religious lives by the aid of the Biblical writers: we read the Bible in order that we may find God in the way in which religious men at all times have found him.'[10] Rawlinson dealt with the variety of christological ideas in the New Testament, and in another essay, 'The Principle of Authority', he argued against both the Roman Catholic doctrine of papal infallibility, and Protestantism's reliance upon biblical infallibility. Instead of either, he posited a comprehensive Anglican type of catholicism, where authority lies in the corporate witness of Christians to the validity of the spiritual experience on which their lives are based. He based his argument not solely on history, but, in quite a novel way, on a kind of religious psychology, an understanding of how persons develop spiritually through relationships with others in the corporate life of a religious institution. Temple wrote two essays, on 'The Divinity of Christ' and 'The Church'. In his Christology he sought to move away from reliance upon the concept of Christ's 'natures', human or divine, towards a more dynamic understanding based upon the category of 'will'. His doctrine of the Church was a sacramental one, that is, seeing the totality of the Church's life on earth as a sacrament of the risen life of Christ present in the world. Moberly wrote on the atonement, seeking a view of Christ's work based on his moral influence upon believers. He also wrote the final, and most philosophical, essay in the collection, on 'God and the Absolute'. As its title suggests, this attempted to state a philosophically acceptable concept of God in terms of ultimate reality as Mind or Spirit.

Streeter's own essay was on 'The Historic Christ'. It was the longest, it was by the editor, it was that which stamped the collection with a particular identity in the public mind, and therefore should be examined in greater detail. Over seventy years later, much of it now reads as fairly commonplace historical criticism of the New Testament. In relation to its own time, what is interesting is that it begins with a fairly full, and sympathetic, exposition of the 'eschatological' interpretations of the Gospels which had recently been put forward on the Continent by scholars such as Johannes Weiss and Albert Schweitzer.[11] Streeter was enthusiastic for this rediscovery of the apocalyptic note in Jesus' preaching, where Jesus appears as prophet of the end-time, proclaiming the imminent collapse of the present human and cosmic order and the advent of the supernatural Kingdom of God. This was in mighty contrast to the well-meaning nineteenth-century attempts to reconstruct a 'life of Jesus'. These, as Schweitzer had shown, all too often produced a portrait of Jesus which simply reflected the late nineteenth-century interests and values of the theologian himself. But Streeter added a cautionary note: '.. . if we agree with Schweitzer here, yet it is not without a feeling that he himself cannot quite escape the charge of modernizing, and that his own boldly-outlined portrait is a little like the Superman of Nietzsche dressed in Galilean robes'.[12]

For Streeter, the chief merit of this approach was that it restored to Jesus his own individuality, in his own time, and made his sayings much more meaningful in their context, and thus less embarrassing to the modern sensibility. Ever since the Enlightenment, theology had been on the retreat, effectively accepting the rationalistic presuppositions of the age and tailoring the outline of Jesus and his teaching to accord with those presuppositions. 'A Christ whom apologists have first to "save" is little likely to save mankind,' said Streeter. Schweitzer's Christ at least stood out in his own right, surrendering himself to the absolute and inexorable demands of the new age breaking in upon the world, and bidding others surrender themselves with him. There follows a lucid presentation of the history of the Gospels as reconstructed by recent scholarship: the historical priority of Mark, the Q material, and so forth, and the peculiar nature of the fourth Gospel. Streeter argues for the historical accuracy of the synoptic material (pointing out the oriental propensity for accurate oral transmission), though also showing how the material was shaped, used and rearranged chronologically according to the particular purpose of each Gospel writer in turn.

So far so good. The essay might well have ended there, and would have constituted an effective and useful introduction to modern New Testament scholarship. But Streeter went on to a lengthy concluding discussion of the resurrection of Jesus. The presupposition for his whole argument was the necessity for a belief in life after death – for ourselves and for Jesus. 'No-one who really believes in a Heavenly Father such as our Lord spoke of, can believe that the life of Jesus ended upon the Cross.' What is at stake in belief in the resurrection is belief in the power and goodness of God, which are otherwise left questionable by the facts of suffering and death, the suffering and death in the world at large, but above all that of Jesus himself. Something happened after the cross, which was clearly a sign to the first disciples that Jesus did indeed survive death, and that God does rule. But what was it that happened? Streeter's chief difficulty lies with the concept of 'physical' resurrection:

> . . . the theory that the actual physical body laid in the tomb was raised up seems to involve . . . that it was subsequently taken up, 'flesh and bones', into heaven – a very difficult conception if we no longer regard the earth as flat and the centre of the solar system, and heaven as a definite region locally fixed above the solid bowl of the skies. In the mediaeval universities the question was seriously debated, whether the body of our Lord was taken up into heaven clothed or naked. To us the very idea of such a debate seems irreverent and absurd, and I know of no living theologian who would maintain a physical *Ascension* in this crude form, yet so long as emphasis is laid on the physical character of the *Resurrection* it is not obvious how any refinement of the conception of 'physical' really removes the difficulty.[13]

The fact of the empty tomb, says Streeter, does not decide the issue, for it is always possible to produce naturalistic explanations to account for it, however unlikely. The real issue for Streeter is the nature of the resurrection life itself, which, according to the teaching of Jesus (in answer to the Sadducees), and to that of St Paul, is of a totally new and spiritual kind, transcending the physical, and that must surely be true of the risen life of Christ as of ours. Streeter therefore speculates that Jesus survived the death on the cross in some kind of spiritual state, from which he was able to communicate to his disciples through visions that he was indeed so alive. 'On such a view, the appearances to the disciples can only be styled "visions", if we mean by vision something directly caused by the Lord himself veritably alive and personally in communion with them.'[14]

This naturally leads to a discussion of 'miracle' in general. Streeter anticipates the objection that, while rejecting miracle of a physical type, he has opted for another form of miracle with the same difficulties as the traditional miracle, namely an occurrence of an unprecedented kind. Streeter argues that the 'unprecedented' type of event he now has in mind does not violate the continuities of natural occurrences. Evolution, for instance, produces what is unprecedented, yet the unprecedented is also organically related to and continuous with what has gone before. Religious faith sees God working with the normal forces of nature, not suspending them. The resurrection appearances would be a divine 'intervention' of this kind, that is, a new form of human communication with the divine, but not a physical occurrence which interrupts the ordinary course of physical nature. He concludes:

> There are some, I know, to whom such an interpretation . . . seems

> lacking in reality and substance, but for myself I feel I am on firmer ground than if I were to rest all on a view of miracle which the lapse of time and the growth of knowledge seems ever to be making less secure, and which in the last resort appears to mean that God did things in Palestine nineteen hundred years ago which he will not or cannot do for us today, and that Christ was raised from the dead in a way that we shall not be.[15]

It was clear even before the book went to press that such views, especially in the wake of the Thompson episode and the like, would provoke controversy. The book carried a disclaimer stating that, on the matter of the resurrection, Streeter's chapter expressed only his own views and not those of the group as a whole.

An Oxford reply: Ronald Knox

Foundations caused a good deal of comment, and some murmuring, in England during 1912–13. Ronald Knox, Chaplain of Trinity College, Oxford, an Anglo-Catholic and close friend of several of the essayists, composed a satirical Drydenesque poem, *Absolute and Abitofhell*, for the *Oxford Magazine* almost as soon as the book appeared. He was persuaded by like-minded friends to attempt something more serious, and so there appeared in 1913 the no less wittily entitled *Some Loose Stones*,[16] a volume which was in fact to be the most substantial criticism offered to *Foundations*. The book defended an avowedly conservative standpoint – and Knox was in due course to make a famous entry into the Roman Catholic Church – but it made its points with delicious humour:

> 'The Christian religion,' so Mr Talbot assures us . . . 'could never have brought salvation had there not been a situation for men to be saved from.' It may seem captious to observe, that in ordinary old-fashioned Christian theology our religion is said to save us, not from a situation, but from sin. 'Being then made free from the Situation.' . . . 'You, being dead in your Situation.' . . . 'Where remission of these is, there is no more offering for the Situation.' . . . It hardly rings familiar.[17]

But Knox was also displaying an insight, at that time relatively unusual, into the social and cultural conditioning of theology. In fact he describes his book as a piece of psychology rather than of theology, and his first chapter bore the title 'How Much Will Jones Swallow?' He alleged that in querying traditional understandings of God's providential action, or Fatherhood, or kingly rule, liberal theologians were submitting to 'quasi-political modifications of our outlook on the Divine government of the world', in an age demanding greater political rights, women's suffrage and humanitarianism. Hence, he argued, a distinct change has come about in the *motivation* of modern theological debate:

> In modern doubt it is not so much our own beliefs we worry about, as those of the man next door.
>
> That is why modern theology is all at heart apologetic; that is why it shows, at times, such a cynical indifference to abstract truth. For we are not concerned, now, to find how we can represent truth most adequately, but how we can represent it most palatably. We ask of a doctrine, not, 'Is it sound?', but, 'Couldn't we possibly manage to do without it?'; not, 'Is it true?', but, 'Can I induce Jones to see it in that light?'[18]

Knox's 'Jones question' has nagged liberal thinkers ever since. At least one of the *Foundations* team, Temple, had a high and grateful regard for it as constructive criticism. But such intra-Oxford banterings were presently to be deafened by a barrage released from a seemingly unlikely quarter: Zanzibar, on the far distant east African coast, the diocese of Bishop Frank Weston. The range was long, but for a time it seemed as though the Church of England might go up in flames.

The conservative counter-blast: Frank Weston

Frank Weston (1871–1924)[19] has an assured place among the most colourful ecclesiastical figures of the twentieth century – provided it is realized that 'colourful' is often a euphemism for 'contentious'. What may not be gainsaid is that he epitomizes the great Anglo-Catholic missionary tradition which, out of love for Africa, has spent itself, heart, mind and body, for that continent. Though he came from a family with evangelical sympathies, he already considered himself a High Churchman when he went up to Oxford in 1890 to read theology, and he was amply confirmed in this loyalty by the influence of Gore and the worship at Pusey House. Thereafter the Anglican Church meant for him the *Catholic* Church. In theology he was fortunate in having as one of his tutors W. B. Sanday, making a name as one of the foremost New Testament scholars of the day. He took a first, but, together with the firing of his Anglo-Catholicism, the most decisive impulse he received at Oxford was the missionary call of Africa, via the Universities Mission to Central Africa. His health being somewhat suspect, he first gained experience of parish ministry in London until the doctors were satisfied that he could face the rigours of the tropics. He left for Zanzibar in 1898. There, punctuated by fairly frequent home visits to England, the rest of his intense life was spent.

Weston was that kind of individual of strong, some would say rigid, convictions combined with great personal sensitivity; of tight-lipped, barely suppressed emotional energy; who is as often as much a trial to himself as to those who have to live with him. Within months of his arrival in Zanzibar the fresh young missionary priest penned an Open Letter to the Bishop of the Diocese, highly critical of the Church's missionary policies and methods, and calling for much greater participation by African priests and laity. He may have been right, but such angry presumption by so recent a newcomer dismayed his seniors. In fact the need for the Church to be thoroughly 'Africanized' was to be a major and increasing preoccupation of Weston, along with his Anglo-Catholicism. Perhaps he should have been called a Zanzibaro-Catholic. When he became a bishop himself, he despaired at times of the Church of England and speculated on the possibility of removing his diocese from communion with Canterbury, to let it simply be an African diocese. The Church of England, he claimed, was riddled with a racial and caste mentality. Since his Oxford days, and again thanks to Gore, he had been a committed Christian Socialist, and much of his time during his later years in Zanzibar was spent in combating the forced labour of Africans under colonial rule. Conservatism in theology is not invariably yoked with reactionary social and political attitudes.

Despite his early record as an angry young missionary, Weston's devotion and patent spirituality, his labours as priest, schoolmaster, seminary teacher and Cathedral Chancellor made an impressive record, and he was consecrated Bishop of Zanzibar in 1908, at the age of thirty-seven. Back in England, he had a large and enthusiastic following among High Church people, and he was in great demand as a preacher and platform speaker on his frequent furloughs. Nowhere was he more popular than at Oxford and Cambridge, where he captivated generations of students with his impassioned pleas on behalf of the missionary needs of Africa. Many regarded as the peak of his oratory the address he gave in the Senate House at Cambridge, during the jubilee celebration of Livingstone's appeal, in 1907–8. Nor did his mind lie fallow amid all the pastoral and administrative toil of a tropical diocese. His continuing theological interest was expressed in his christological study *The One Christ*, in which he took a far more cautious position than Gore, by refusing to admit that the fullness of Christ's humanity necessarily implied a limitation or fallibility in his knowledge.

In the fetid climate of the East African coast, where Christianity of any sort comprised a minority enclave beset by fervent Islam on the one hand and by traditional witchcraft on the other, the theological speculations of the Oxford lecture room seemed remote and ineffectual. Weston was growingly impatient of academic theorists who, he felt, were unwittingly supplying Muslim propagandists with ammunition to be used against Christianity. Preaching in London in 1911, he exclaimed: 'Save our converts in Africa from reading in books by Christians at home all those things which are calculated to make them doubt whether there be a God at all, and such a thing as a Catholic Revelation.'[20]

In 1913, a copy of *Foundations* reached Weston in Zanzibar, accompanied by Hensley Henson's *The Creed in the Pulpit*.[21] Weston could not contain his shock, and affected bewilderment that, while he was in the front line of the missionary struggle against Islam, the Church at home should be undermining the central convictions which motivated that mission. Muslim writers would not be slow to point out that European Christian scholars were doubting the veracity of the New Testament. Weston's shock was doubtless genuine, but it is not clear how far he would have been spurred into action had not two other issues arisen which, he felt, similarly called in question the integrity of the Church of England.

One was the Kikuyu Conference. In 1913 there was proposed a form of federation of non-Roman missionary bodies and Churches in East Africa, to the extent of allowing intercommunion. Weston was incensed at the least suggestion of any Anglican participation with 'Protestants' in such a scheme. It would betray the *Catholic* nature of the Anglican fellowship. The other matter was comparatively minor, but no less significant in Weston's eyes. In England, a High Church clergyman in the diocese of St Albans had been disciplined by his bishop for the practice of invoking the saints in prayer. Why, queried Weston, was the Church so eager to suppress such a benign form of Catholic piety, while apparently tolerating the far more wanton theological licence of the seven Oxford men? The coincidence of *Foundations*, the Kikuyu Conference and the St Albans case struck Weston with the force of a divine summons. His response was to pen another Open Letter, the most famous piece of writing – though brief – of his career. Formally the pamphlet was addressed to the Bishop of St Albans, whose examining chaplain Streeter had been until publication of *Foundations*. That Streeter had been in such a post, and others of the essayists in similar positions, made what might otherwise have been a dubious exercise in theological speculation into a fundamental issue for the Church. What, Weston asked, was to be the standing of such men who were advocating opinions quite contrary to the declared credal basis of the Church? What, indeed, was the standing of the Church itself, if it acquiesced in such heterodoxy? What doctrinal norms were now to be permitted in those commissioned to preach, teach and administer the sacraments in that Church?

So the diatribe was called *Ecclesia Anglicana – For What Does She Stand?*[22] Its message was clear: the Church of England was 'entirely unfit to send missionaries to heathen or Muhammedan lands'. As a missionary diocese dependent upon and in communion with Canterbury, Zanzibar needed assurance of the home Church's self-expression – otherwise the missionary enterprise was a lost cause. 'The Church at home . . . is in a state of mental chaos: it is more than ever talkative but what it expresses is anything rather than its true self.'[23]

In one glorious paragraph, mixing truth and caricature, as always happens in the liveliest polemics, Weston arraigned *Foundations*:

> The book, briefly speaking, *permits* priests to believe and teach, among other things equally heretical,
> (a) that the Old Testament is the record of the religious experiences of holy men who lived roughly from 800 B.C. onwards; some of whom wrote the so-called historical books in order to show how, in their view, God acted in circumstances that quite possibly, and in many cases probably, never existed;
> (b) that the Christ's historic life opens with his baptism, at which he suddenly realised a vocation to be the last of the Jewish prophets;
> (c) that Christ did not come into the world to die for us; but having come, he died because of the circumstances of the case;
> (d) that Christ was mistaken in what he taught about his Second Advent, thinking that the world would not outlast St John;
> (e) that therefore he did not found a Church, nor ordain Sacraments;
> (f) that his body has gone to corruption;
> (g) that there is no Authority in the Church beyond the corporate witness of the Saints, many of whom are now unknown, to the spiritual and moral value of the Christian religion.
>
> Thus it is allowed by the Seven to any priest to deny the Trustworthiness of the Bible, the Authority of the Church, and the Infallibility of Christ.[24]

If episcopacy, sacraments, the Bible and Christ himself are on the 'official list of Open Questions', asked Weston, what was there left in the 'Deposit' to be handed on to Africans? A Church which had two views on such matters had lost all chance of winning the Muslim, whose dependence on *his* traditions would not be broken by a debating society but by 'the living, speaking Church of the Infallible Word Incarnate'. Nor could loose talk about the 'mediating' nature of the Church of England be permitted, for how could there be 'mediation' between two *contradictory* views – such as that Christ is virgin-born on the one hand, and that he is son of Joseph on the other; or that Christ is an infallible guide, and that Christ was seriously mistaken about the need of a Church and Ministry? *Foundations* claimed to be written by young men wishing to 'reconcile' faith with 'modern thought'. In fact, alleged Weston,

> Without faith, they sacrifice in the name of reason much that faith found in Creed and Book and Tradition: which done, finding their logic pointing them to complete unbelief, they exercise in the end the very faith they had mislaid, making pretence that it is reason which has led them to their goal. Which means that we may sacrifice what the modern mind dislikes, in the name of reason; and in the name of reason we may cling to what the modern mind tolerates: while in fact what is sacrificed is lost through lack of faith, and what is kept is kept because of faith. But this faith is nigh to perishing, because it is markedly individualistic: it is more and more removed from that corporately-exercised power of vision which marks the catholic Church, and makes for her saints.[25]

No less directly did Weston address the matters of the Kikuyu Conference ('Pan-Protestantism') and the 'Denial of Catholic Practices'. But the chief need was 'a united front against Modernism, our most deadly danger'.

Weston was a spiritual agonizer. Christ in Gethsemane was the model of devotion to which he always returned in his preaching and teaching. The Open Letter concludes with a call for a 'Gethsemane of Mind' for the sake of Truth (note how Weston heightened the absolutist tone of his declamations by capitalizing initials whenever possible) – 'we must be content to endure distress and even agony of mind, until the matter be finished'.[26] *Ecclesia Anglicana* must tell her flock for what she came into the world:

> If she have need of us to catholicize the heathen world for Christ, I am at her service now as always. But if to Protestantize the world, and modernize the faith, be the works that she officially undertakes, I for my part have no longer place or lot within her borders. Let the *Ecclesia Anglicana* declare herself, that we may know her fate.[27]

The Open Letter was published in England in November 1913. The *Church Times*, main organ of High Church opinion, at first pursed its lips at this indecorous outburst from a foreign field. 'We must say', stated the editorial of 5 December, 'of the Bishop of Zanzibar, as we have said of others, that he does injustice to Mr Streeter, who deserves some censure, but not such censure as he seems to demand.' Such tepidity completely misjudged the mood among Anglo-Catholics in the country, however. Next week brought a page full of letters deploring the faint praise by which Weston seemed to have been damned. A correspondent asked:

> To how many points of Catholic doctrine contained in the Creeds she [the Church of England] presumably holds, and enshrined in the Prayer Book she puts forth does the living voice of the Church of England bear unflinching witness? Most of them are on all sides flouted, watered down, or explained away; and the mind of the Catholic priest and layman, whether he be living and working in the loneliness of the country, or in the turmoil of the town, is distressed and perplexed and bewildered thereby. Numbers of people who have become so reconciled to our doctrinal confusion as to regard it almost as the normal will doubtless disapprove of the Bishop's letter as unwise . . .[28]

Weston was voicing what many Anglo-Catholics were longing to hear. Within weeks pamphlets, sermons and open letters were being exchanged in all directions. A group of London clergy approached their bishop with a Memorial to be presented to Convocation, asking for the repudiation of

> the claim of some clergy to reject the miracles of Our Lord's Birth of a Virgin and the actual resurrection of His body from the tomb, because we believe that these truths lie at the very centre of our faith, and that the statements of the Bible and the Creeds with regard to them are perfectly plain and unambiguous.[29]

For the Oxford seven and their supporters, the front to be defended was that of the freedom of academic inquiry; for their opponents, what was at stake was the authority of the Church as the guardian of the revelation given once and for all.

In the midst of these exchanges no one occupied a more painful position than Charles Gore, now (since 1911) Bishop of Oxford. Not only did his see have such obviously close connections with the university from which *Foundations* had emanated, but as the leading prelate and theologian of High Churchmanship he could not be expected to remain silent. The acuteness of the dilemma can readily be imagined, for Weston's broadside carried with it an implied rebuke not only to theological liberalism, but also to the English 'Catholics' who had failed to contain and counter it. Oxford was in danger of being upstaged by Zanzibar as the citadel of Anglo-Catholicism. On the other hand, Gore was not nearly so conservative as Weston in matters of biblical criticism and Christology. A whole-hearted *ecclesiastical* alliance with Weston was required, but could Gore's theology provide sufficient intellectual basis for that partnership?

Gore: The Basis of Anglican Fellowship

Gore's theological response took the form of his own Open Letter, addressed to the clergy of his diocese, *The Basis of Anglican Fellowship in Faith and Organization.*[30] It acknowledged that Weston had opened up a much-needed debate within Anglicanism, and sought to discuss the three major issues he had raised. On *Foundations*, Gore saw the chief question as that of miracle. He allowed that some of the ideas in the book were permissible as tentative possibilities, but urged that sooner or later a man must make up his mind if he is to accept a clerical office requiring repeated recitation and teaching of the Creed. Indeed, Gore went so far as to identify himself with the idea of progressive revelation in the Old Testament as set forth in *Foundations*, and to allow the place of poetry and legend therein. Here he was facing a criticism that had already been voiced in the press, that Gore was no fit person to champion the cause of orthodoxy since his own earlier writings had taken a relatively liberal attitude towards the Old Testament. Gore was able to meet this challenge by insisting that for him revelation came to its consummate fullness in Jesus Christ. Was he then insisting that all the items in the Creed which refer to Christ are to be taken as literal, historical fact? At this point Gore introduced a distinction between one type of item and another:

> Human language is practically limited by what has fallen within present human experience. With regard, therefore, to what lies outside present human experience, we can only be taught, or formulate our beliefs, in *symbolical* language – language which is in a measure diverted from its original purpose. This is what St Paul means when he says 'We see through a glass, darkly', that is a blurred reflection of truth, as in a metal mirror, or as conveyed in a symbolic story. So it is about the being of God, or about the beginnings or endings of things ('Genesis' and 'Apocalypse'), or about heaven and hell. When I say Christ ascended into heaven, I am first of all referring to a certain symbolical but actual and historical demonstration which our Lord gave to his disciples forty days after his resurrection. But when I say 'He descended into hell', and also when in a more general sense I say 'He ascended into heaven, and sitteth, etc' I confess to the use of metaphor in a historical statement, because the historical statement carries me outside the world of present possible experience, and symbolical language is the only language that I can use.'[31]

But, continued Gore, the symbolical did not apply to the incarnation itself, for there God does reveal himself within human historical experience, including the miraculous, for 'the glory of incarnation is the glory of literal fact'.

On the ecclesiastical front, since the Thompson episode of 1911 Gore had in fact been working behind the scenes for an unequivocal condemnation by Convocation of too liberal interpretations of the Creed. As if unsure that Thompson's de-licensing would in itself be enough to discourage others, Gore in that year pressed Randall Davidson to allow a strongly worded resolution to come before Convocation in July. Davidson, with his native caution, invoked the aid of the Bishop of Winchester (who had withdrawn Thompson's licence) and the Bishop of Ely to consider the matter. They managed to dissuade Gore from precipitate action. But the appearance of *Foundations* and Henson's *Creed in the Pulpit* stirred him to campaign again, with a request to Davidson to have the whole matter raised at a private meeting of the bishops in January 1913. When this took place Gore found himself unexpectedly isolated, and in private correspondence with Davidson he dropped gloomy hints of resigning. Davidson's emollient epistles persuaded him that such a course would be disastrous for the Church. Then, late in 1913, came Weston's Open Letter and the ensuing furore. As we have seen, the initiative to demand an authoritative pronouncement was taken by the Bishop of London and clergy of his diocese. Their Memorial was presented to Convocation in February 1914, and the Bishop announced that he would move a resolution on the subject at the next sessions.

Gore was increasingly drawn into the manoeuvring for such public moves, and readily helped the Bishop of London in drafting possible resolutions. Meanwhile, respectful if tense private exchanges took place both in conversation and correspondence between Gore and the Archbishop. Gore's first suggested draft resolution was seen by Davidson in March 1914. After reaffirming the Lambeth Conference statement of 1908 (see p. 51 above), it continued:

> And further, inasmuch as the claim has been widely made that those Creeds can legitimately be recited by Clergymen in their public ministry when they themselves deliberately ceased to believe that our Lord was in fact born of a Virgin or did (in the sense of the New Testament) rise again the third day from the dead, and inasmuch as the public opinion of the Church has been repeatedly challenged to allow this claim, we feel it to be our duty solemnly to affirm that we can give no countenance to what we cannot but regard as seriously contrary to that sincerity of profession which is especially necessary for the Christian ministry.[32]

Davidson was appalled by this draft, and told the Bishop of London that he could not possibly support any such statement which would effectively pronounce 'loyal churchmanship to be incompatible with a readiness to allow any "reserve" or "suspended judgment" as to the manner of receiving and holding certain credal clauses which the impugned men willingly, habitually and reverently use'.[33] Davidson, as Gore himself had done two years previously, brought in the ultimate deterrent of implying that his own position might become untenable if the issue were thus forced, and that he would have to resign the primacy. A troubled correspondence involving the Archbishop, Gore, and the Bishops of Ely and Winchester ensued. Davidson and Bishop Chase of Ely were desperately anxious to secure some space for those who wished to recite 'reverently' the creeds while suspending judgement on the precise interpretation of certain clauses. For his part, Gore was even more determined to repudiate what, in his view, was no such 'reserve' on the part of Streeter and company, but plain *denial* of the historical miracles.

In the middle of April 1914, only days before Convocation was due to meet, Davidson and Gore had a two-hour conversation in Bath. Perhaps the secular gentility of the resort provided a context of relaxed neutrality denied to both Lambeth and Oxford. Some such atmosphere was necessary as the opposing forces gathered to lay siege to Convocation. Petitions were on their way, including one signed by 45,000 Evangelicals who were no less worried than the Anglo-Catholics at what they saw as the impugning of biblical authority, and several from clergy and laity in various dioceses, and even one from Members of Parliament. From the liberal side petitions were to be presented by the Dean of St Paul's, W. R. Inge, by the Churchmen's Union, by the Bishop of Southwark and by a number of academics. Davidson and Gore finally agreed on a resolution which, after noting the anxiety and disquiet in the Church over doctrinal matters, called attention to the Convocation resolution of 1905 and the Lambeth Conference resolution of 1908. It continued:

> These Resolutions we desire solemnly to re-affirm, and in accordance therewith to express our deliberate judgment that the denial of any of the historical facts stated in the Creeds goes beyond the limits of legitimate interpretation, and gravely imperils that sincerity of profession which is plainly incumbent on the ministers of the Word and Sacraments. At the same time, recognising that our generation is called to face new problems raised by historical criticism, we are anxious not to lay unnecessary burdens upon consciences, nor unduly to limit freedom of thought and enquiry, whether among clergy or among laity. We desire, therefore, to lay stress on the need of considerateness in dealing with that which is tentative and provisional in the thought and work of earnest and reverent students.[34]

This resolution was presented to Convocation by the Bishop of London on 29 April. The petitions were also presented, the Anglo-Catholic and Evangelical hot air was released, while Inge's petition pleaded the case for liberty:

> While asserting without reserve our belief in the Incarnation and resurrection of our Lord Jesus Christ, we submit that a wide liberty of belief should be allowed with regard to the mode and attendant circumstances of both.
>
> We believe that real study, thought, and discussion will be discouraged if clergymen, who, in matters not affecting the essential truth of Christianity, arrive at conclusions which are opposed to traditional or momentarily dominant opinions, are to be removed from their offices or denounced as dishonest for retaining them. We venture to recall to your lordships the dictum of Archbishop Temple, 'If the conclusions are prescribed, the study is precluded.'[35]

Two days' debate followed. Bishop Percival of Hereford attempted to bury the whole issue by proposing an amendment sympathizing with the liberal petitioners concerned for their freedoms, and calling for no declaration to be issued at all. But most bishops were anxious to resolve the issue somehow. Gore spoke mildly, if sadly, for the main resolution which he and Davidson had agreed upon at Bath, and which said what had to be said, even if he could have wished for more. It was evident that the resolution contained just enough 'on the one hand . . . and on the other' to make people on either wing hesitate before refusing it. It left open where the main weight should be placed – whether on the earlier part affirming the historicity of the creeds and the need for clerical 'sincerity', or on the later sentences acknowledging the status of modern critical scholarship and the inquiries of 'earnest and reverent' scholars. Davidson summed up the debate in a long speech in which he certainly gave encouragement to the 'search for truth'. Even in the case of accredited clergy, who as public spokesmen for the Church had a particular responsibility in credal affirmation, he eschewed any 'inquisitorial' intention. 'We desire with earnestness beyond words to show to them throughout their investigations and enquiries a considerateness, a respect, a patience, a hopefulness, and an encouragement to the utmost of our power.'[36]

The resolution was carried *nem. con.* Gore was still not wholly at ease, in view of some remarks Davidson made at the close of his speech, comparing the wording of the resolution with that of the liberal petition presented by the Bishop of Southwark and a number of academic theologians. Davidson found 'nothing in the two that is radically or essentially inconsistent' in so far as both of them called for reasonable liberty. Gore privately sought reassurance that this did not readmit *denial* of the historic credal facts. Davidson assured him that he had been referring simply to the actual form of words in the Southwark petition, and not to what may have been the intention of some of those who had signed it. Yes, the Bath agreement stood, and we may imagine the weary sigh with which Davidson signed his reply.

Nor was Frank Weston to remain particularly sanguine about the outcome. Bishop Percival of Hereford, having been rebuffed by Convocation in his attempt to divert the house from what he feared would be a heresy hunt, sought compensation by installing Streeter as a canon in his cathedral. It caused little comment in England, but when the news reached distant Zanzibar a notice appeared on the door of the cathedral there. Couched in the heraldic language of ancient ecclesiastical courts, it solemnly declared that the Bishop and diocese of Zanzibar were no longer in communion with John, Bishop of Hereford, and those who adhered to him. It is an entertaining if improbable picture, to imagine the swains of deepest Herefordshire pulling thoughtfully on their ale, and shaking their heads over their excommunication from Zanzibar.

The continuing debate

Weston did not let the theological issue rest. During the First World War he wrote *The Christ and His Critics*, which earned him a reply from his old Oxford teacher W. B. Sanday, now Lady Margaret Professor of Divinity and, to Weston's dismay, numbered among the liberals. In 1912, at a meeting in Oxford, Sanday had confessed to being unable to accept that the birth of Christ took place through *unnatural* means, though the incarnation as such was certainly a 'supernatural' event. Now, in *The Position of Liberal Theology*,[37] Sanday set out for his former pupil what he saw as the unavoidable conditions recognized by modern scholarship in dealing with miracle and the historicity of events recorded in Scripture. Like Streeter, he was content to regard as 'miracle' an event which elicits wonder, but not with any implication that there occurs thereby 'a breach or suspension of the order of nature'. In modern research there is an assumed *continuity*: 'The secular historian, dealing with the events of the past, assumes that the surrounding external conditions were the same as those which we see about us today. Are we not to make that assumption for the particular century that comes first in the series of Christian centuries?'[38] This leads Sanday to a fine statement of the basic affirmation of liberalism:

> It stands fundamentally for what I have called elsewhere 'the unification of thought'. The liberal feels that he cannot at any point stop short of this. It is the same mind that has to think of things secular and sacred, and the processes of thinking for both are the same. What are called the laws of

> thought are applicable alike to both . . . Unification of thought means unification of life. It means that the universe is all of a piece; it means that life from the beginning has been in essence just what we see it around us today.[39]

'The unification of thought': one is reminded again of R. J. Campbell's ill-fated attempt to overcome the 'dichotomy' between religious belief and modern secular thought and experience. In his own way, Weston too was of course wanting a 'unification' of thought, but one determined by the acceptance of revealed truth in dogmatic form, around which secular knowledge would have to take its place. The real issue was therefore the question of where was the fixed point around which unification could take shape. For such as Streeter and Sanday, the modern consciousness of the continuum of nature and history was axiomatic. For Weston, the traditional formulae of revelation were absolutely normative, self-contained and self-explanatory. Along with these intellectual stances, and perhaps highly determinative of them, went different perceptions of identity and responsibility. Streeter and the other Oxford liberals saw themselves not just as a clergy of their time, but as university teachers, and the university in which they lived and worked had long outgrown being the preserve of the Church of England, or indeed of any form of organized Christianity, no matter how deeply embedded Anglicanism remained within it. A modern university is a place of dispassionate inquiry, and theology, pursued within that setting, and accountable to that community, could only remain with integrity if its conclusions were not prescribed in advance. Knox was to a degree correct, it *was* a matter of psychology to determine how belief could be made 'acceptable' to Jones. But, the liberals felt *themselves* to be Jones at one level of their consciousness. It was not simply the doubt of the 'man next door' which troubled them. It was the modern world-consciousness within themselves which they wished to unify with their adherence to the Christian tradition. But the likes of Weston can equally well be seen to display psychological and social motivations. They viewed the world from within the well-marked ramparts of the Church, and moreover the *Catholic* Church in its English form. Even Weston's own biographer and fervent admirer admits that Weston knew practically nothing of the Church of England beyond the confines of the Anglo-Catholic wing. One's identity lay not within the wider world of the time but within this corpus of tradition, defined, absolute, bequeathed from the past and to be safeguarded for the future. The controversy between liberal and conservative, then, was not simply an intellectual one. It stemmed from very different senses of where one belonged, which set of social relationships and obligations were the substance of one's existence.

Theologically, Charles Gore continued to occupy something like the middle ground in an uneasy attempt to maintain the traditional formulae of miracles in the creeds, at the cost of admitting a 'symbolic' element at certain points. A number of critics, both to left and to right, pointed out that his distinction between those elements in the creeds which pointed beyond human historical experience, and which therefore employed symbolism, and those which indicated realities within history and therefore were to be taken literally, was of dubious consistency. Indeed, it was a suspiciously *modern* distinction to make. Would a fourth-century Christian, given the assumed cosmology of the time, have necessarily assumed the ascension to be 'symbolic', in contrast to the virgin birth, which was to be taken as literal historic fact? It was becoming evident that options for particular theological positions, even conservative ones, were having to be taken ever more self-consciously and, indeed, with ever greater sophistication. Paradoxically, one could remain a traditionalist only by employing very non-traditional arguments, as did Gore in effect. Unless, that is, one just refused to argue, as did Weston, and declaimed instead.

Inconsistency, however, was no monopoly of the conservatives. Streeter's approach to the historical Jesus in *Foundations* was curiously uneven. His enthusiasm for the newly discovered apocalyptic Jesus meant, as he rightly saw, that Jesus could be given back to his first-century Palestinian context instead of being an artificial figure-head for modern European values. But, having placed Jesus back in the first century, Streeter failed to see the problem of just how a faith relationship to this Jesus can exist, across the divide from the twentieth century and its culture. In the conclusion to his essay, Streeter fell back on a rather conventional, even sentimental, argument that the morally beneficial influence of Jesus and his followers supports the claim that he who died on a cross was nevertheless vindicated. The questions of the relationship between the transcendent and the historical, and of the relation of faith to the cultural conditioning of human knowledge, were barely beginning to emerge on the English scene. But what had arrived, for good and all, was the historical method to be applied to the Bible from cover to cover, and not to the Old Testament only. That, at least, had been secured in the latter part of the 1914 Convocation resolution, and to that fact liberals and 'Modern Churchmen' were henceforth to anchor their claims to rightful churchmanship.

Theology at war

On 4 August 1914, Britain found itself at war with Germany. The great conflagration at once seemed to quell into insignificance the internal disputes that had been sundering English society. In face of the threat from without, there was certainly some closing of the ranks between Tory and Liberal, between suffragettes and their opponents, between business and trade unions. About the only quarrel which the war did not immediately end, was the doctrinal controversy in the Church of England. Indeed in some important respects the war added fuel to keep this particular home fire burning.

Streeter and other liberals had made clear their debt to German scholarship, and for some years there had been rumblings of disquiet in various quarters about the 'rationalizing' tendencies of professors on the Continent. The abstruse German academic had been a folk-target of British satire, all the way from Carlyle's Teufelsdröckh in *Sartor Resartus*, to Gilbert and Sullivan. Once war broke out, virtually everything German became poisonous, and much theological sentiment was sucked into the anti-German hysteria. Indeed, there were genuine grounds for suspecting German theologians and churchmen of serving Caesar at the expense of God, as their manifesto supporting the Kaiser's cause showed. British church leaders replied in kind. By many, German theology was held to be implicated in, perhaps even responsible for, German militarism and all that it was doing to Belgium. Those who had drunk at the wells of German learning had now to be made to see their folly. One of the most vehement attacks on the German influence was launched by Leighton Pullan, Fellow of St John's College, Oxford, in a pamphlet of 1915:

> Up to the very brink of the war the reverence which was paid in this country to a certain class of German professors went beyond all reasonable bounds. It encouraged in many among our clergy, and some of our laity, a temper which was unpatriotic and even anti-Christian. It was asphyxiating vocations to the ministry. Second-hand versions of second-rate German divinity flooded the country. In our universities Germany, and not the most religious part of Germany, was coming to be regarded as the Englishman's 'spiritual home' . . . We prudently overlook the fact that when the Bishop of Winchester and the Bishop of Oxford showed their resolve to maintain within the limits of their jurisdiction the teaching of the New Testament, writers of such different talents as Mrs Humphrey Ward and Dr Sanday appealed to the opinions of the Protestant universities of Germany. The German movement is still being actively organised and the Creed steadily assailed by clergymen and laymen who call themselves 'Modern Churchmen' or 'Liberal Churchmen' . . . It is enough for them to repeat the words of evangelists and saints, and then to suggest 'restatements' drawn from Harnack, Loofs and Schweitzer.[40]

To be liberal was now therefore to be unpatriotic. The issues were no longer seen in black and white, but in red, white and blue. It is probable that the immediate pre-1914 period marks the highest reach of German theological influence in Britain, and the Great War was one of the most dramatic non-theological factors to affect a theological dispute.

Streeter maintained his liberal perspectives and developed still further his critical approach to the New Testament, which bore fruit in his most influential book, published in 1924, *The Four Gospels: A Study of Origins*. His broader philosophical studies produced *Reality: A New Correlation of Science and Religion* (1926), and his Bampton Lectures of 1932, *The Buddha and the Christ*. He remained in Oxford, becoming Provost of Queen's College in 1933, and was always in demand as a speaker at conferences of the Student Christian Movement. Like others of his time and place he was an enthusiast for the Oxford Group Movement. He was killed in a flying accident in Switzerland, in 1937. Others of the *Foundations* team were to take honoured places in academic and church life. Brook, Parsons and Temple became bishops, and Temple of course proceeded to York and Canterbury. His Christology matured, or at any rate returned to more traditional categories. Right from the start there had been a certain distancing of themselves from Streeter by the rest of the essayists, at least as far as his views on the resurrection were concerned, and so association with *Foundations* proved no bar to preferment. In any case, much that was in the volume soon came to appear as the commonplace and accepted thought of educated Christians. Weston, spent with toil and finally overtaken by a poisonous fever, died, as he would have wished, in Zanzibar, in 1924.

Notes

1 D. Holloway, *The Church of England: Where is it going?*, Eastbourne: Kingsway 1985.

2 A. Briggs, 'The Political Scene', in S. Nowell-Smith (ed.), *Edwardian England 1901–1914*, Oxford: Oxford University Press 1964, p. 45f.

3 For an account of the disintegrative impact of 'modernity' on European thought, and its implications for theology, see R. P. Eriksen, *Theologians Under Hitler: Gerhard Kittel, Paul Althaus and Emanuel Hirsch*, New Haven, Conn.: Yale University Press 1985.

4 H. Rashdall, *Philosophy and Religion*, London: Duckworth 1909, p. 180.

5 G. K. A. Bell, *Randall Davidson, Archbishop of Canterbury*, Oxford: Oxford University Press 1935, p. 673. Much use is made of the biography in this chapter.

6 London: Macmillan 1912.
7 For an account of the early meetings of this group and the genesis of *Foundations*, see F. W. Iremonger, *William Temple: Archbishop of Canterbury*, Oxford: Oxford University Press 1948, pp. 155–66.
8 *Foundations*, p. vii.
9 ibid., p. 4.
10 ibid., p. 66.
11 A. Schweitzer, *The Quest of the Historical Jesus: A Critical Study of its Progress from Reimarus to Wrede*, London: A. & C. Black 1910.
12 *Foundations*, p. 77.
13 ibid., p. 131f.
14 ibid., p. 136.
15 ibid., p. 140.
16 R. A. Knox, *Some Loose Stones*, London: Longmans, Green and Co., 1913.
17 ibid., p. 1.
18 ibid., p. 8f.
19 see H. M. Smith, *Frank, Bishop of Zanzibar: Life of Frank Weston 1871–1924*, London: SPCK 1926.
20 ibid., p. 171.
21 See chapter 4.
22 *Ecclesia Anglicana – For What Does She Stand? An Open Letter to Edgar, Lord Bishop of St Albans*, London: Longmans 1913.
23 ibid., p. 8.
24 ibid., p. 10.
25 ibid., p. 13.
26 ibid., p. 29.
27 ibid.
28 *Church Times*, 12 December 1913.
29 Bell, op. cit., p. 674.
30 Charles Gore, Bishop of Oxford, *The Basis of Anglican Fellowship in Faith and Organization: An Open Letter to the Clergy of the Diocese of Oxford*, London: A. R. Mowbray, 1914.
31 ibid., p. 19f.
32 Bell, op. cit. p. 676.
33 ibid.
34 ibid., p. 683.
35 ibid., p. 683f.
36 ibid., p. 686.
37 W. B. Sanday, *The Position of Liberal Theology: A Friendly Examination of the Bishop of Zanzibar's Open Letter*, London: Faith Press 1920.
38 ibid., p. 17.
39 ibid., p. 31.
40 Leighton Pullan, *Missionary Principles and the Primate on Kikuyu*, Oxford 1915. p. iv.

4 From Miracles to Christology: Hensley Henson and the 'Modern Churchmen'

The controversy provoked by *Foundations* had centred on the miraculous items in the creeds. Had they really occurred, or had they not? Behind this question, however, there lurked another: Why was the historicity of these elements so important? The traditional answer had always been in terms of the bearing of these events on belief in the divinity of Christ, incarnate Son of God and second Person of the Trinity. This in turn invites a further question: Precisely what is the connection between miracle and divinity? Are the miraculous (or 'supernatural') and the divine synonymous? Does belief in the divinity of Christ require – or flow from – belief in the miraculous events asserted by tradition to have accompanied his birth and to have followed his death, not to mention many episodes of his intervening life and ministry? Put at its most general, does belief in God involve belief in miracle, and can God only reveal himself and prove himself to humankind by doing something out of the ordinary course of nature?

For long enough, ordinary believers and sophisticated theologians alike had answered in the affirmative. Proofs of the truths of Christian revelation had appealed not just to the authority of Scripture or the teaching role of the Church *per se*, but to the evident 'miracles', 'signs and wonders' recorded in the Bible, and associated particularly with Jesus himself. Jesus' divinity was both expressed in and attested by these happenings which could not be explained in terms of ordinary nature or human history, but only as of direct, divine intervention. Above all, it was belief in Jesus' birth of a virgin mother, and in his bodily resurrection on the third day, leaving a tomb physically empty of the crucified flesh, which was virtually synonymous with belief in his divine sonship.

The twentieth century has seen a dramatic, if partial, collapse of this assumed equation of the miraculous with the divine. At least, it is no longer self-evident that to believe in Jesus as both human and divine requires one to accept that any or all of the miraculous items are literal fact. It is a 'partial' collapse in that for many people the equation still holds, as is apparent in the reaction to Bishop David Jenkins' refusal to identify either the incarnation or the resurrection with particular miraculous events. But even among the devoutly orthodox there have been major concessions as to the status of the miraculous in belief – even Charles Gore, as was seen in the last chapter, probably gave away more than he intended with his distinction between the 'symbolical' and 'literal historical' elements in the Creed. In this chapter, we shall examine how, during that tumultuous decade 1912–22, crucial steps were taken in this modern process of shifting the area of debate from that of miracle as such, to the doctrine of the person of Christ. Christology proper – in traditional terms the question of how the divine and human natures are related to each other in the one person Jesus Christ – became identified as a matter distinct from that of miracle. By 1921–22, the christological debates centred less on whether or not *X* denied the virgin birth, than on whether *X*'s formulation of how divinity was expressed in Christ really did justice to the intentions of the classic incarnational doctrines. The route to this point led through several controversial episodes, culminating in the furore provoked by the Conference of Modern Churchmen at Cambridge in 1921.

The 'Modern Churchmen' were indeed highly important in promoting these christological debates, but they had no monopoly of theological irritant. To a casual observer, around the time of the First World War it must have seemed that 'liberals' or 'modernists' were generally running amok with orthodox doctrine in the Church. But already, important differences were emerging among the pioneers of the newer theology. Apart from Streeter, hardly any of the *Foundations* group were to be associated with the main controversies involving the 'Modern Churchmen' which we are to describe now. Moreover, the figure who in the second decade of the century most typified progressive theology to the public mind, Hensley Henson, and who caused one of the most acute crises for the Church of England during 1917–18, was to distance himself markedly from those to whom the title 'modernist' or 'Modern Churchmen' is to be more strictly applied. He did, however, play a highly significant role in helping to create a climate of receptivity for the more radical thinking which he was to criticize so sharply. In focusing upon his part in the story first of all, therefore, we bring into clearer view what was happening in – to use R. J. Campbell's phrase – the 'changing sanctions' of theology.

Hensley Henson (1863–1947)

In 1900 a collection of Anglican essays appeared with the none too euphoric title *Church Problems*. The opening essay, by the editor himself, began: 'The Church of England is the most perplexing of institutions. It provokes the most various sentiments, and lends itself easily to the most contradictory descriptions.'[1] The author had himself already exemplified much of the paradoxical nature of Anglicanism in his own career, and in succeeding years was to do so still more dramatically.[2] H. Hensley Henson had an upbringing in Low Church piety – his father, a businessman, in fact virtually forsook the Anglican Church for Nonconformity. Perhaps it was in reaction to this that Henson, who read History at Oxford and was elected to a Fellowship of All Souls, became a staunch, fiercely anti-Nonconformist Anglo-Catholic – only to reject this High Churchmanship on the death of his father. Instead, he embraced what he held to for the rest of his life, a broad, liberal churchmanship. A 'latitude man who had strayed from the seventeenth century into the twentieth' was his own best self-description. After serving as vicar of Barking, and chaplain of St Mary's Hospital, Ilford, in 1900 he was appointed rector of the fashionable St Margaret's, Westminster, in the shadow of the great Abbey, where he was also given a canonry. In both Westminster pulpits Henson made his name as a preacher, and much of his literary output was to be in the form of his published sermons. From the turn of the century Henson's churchmanship combined in a singular way – and almost uniquely so in its time – a staunch advocacy of the establishment of the Church of England with an unusually open and sympathetic attitude towards dissenting Nonconformity. The ideal English Christian constitution for England, in Henson's view, would be an establishment including Nonconformity, if that was not a contradiction in terms. In fact even while at Barking and Ilford, Henson proved to have the Midas touch in controversy. Almost everything he said, or did, became newsworthy in the local press. Once at St Margaret's, he determined to make the church a centre for preaching rather than musical appreciation. He dismissed the organist, who had other views. With the organist many of the congregation left also – but a new congregation soon arrived in their place.

Nor were his controversies always with other people. There were agonized debates within himself, many of which were transferred on to the pages of his private journal. On 8 May 1904 he recorded:

> This day is set for the celebration of the 1300th anniversary of the founding of the Bishopric of London . . . It is the first occasion on which I myself have preached in St Margaret's on this Sunday's appointed purpose, and now I do so heavily suspected of all kinds of fatal heresies, and, for some weeks past, the object of insult and denunciation, public and private. More and more I am persuaded that my life is governed by a Higher

Power, and that I move along pre-ordained lines towards pre-determined ends; and yet I am no fatalist because, along with this, I am more and more impressed with a haunting fear of personal failure to answer to the calls and plans of God. Yet I can in no way reconcile these conflicting convictions. To be a Man of Destiny, a straw on the stream of Divine Purpose, is one thing: to be a disobedient and self-willed servant is another. Yet I know myself to be both.[3]

There was a touch of Kierkegaard in Henson's inward agonizing. He was determined to be no one but himself, and placed spiritual candour and intellectual honesty above public esteem, to the point where it cost peace of mind and risked preferment. The incident which occasioned the above remarks was a brief controversy early in 1904 when in an article in the *Hibbert Journal*, and in his Easter sermon, Henson had drawn attention to the treatment of the resurrection of Christ in the New Testament. The fact of Christ's resurrection was central to the apostolic preaching and was affirmed throughout the New Testament.

But the New Testament no less clearly showed that, even in the Apostolic age, there was an impressive conflict of opinion as to the precise character of that crucial fact. Was the Christian Church really bound to believe the crudely material version of the truth which was set forth in the 4th Anglican Article? Had the liberty of opinion, which existed without challenge in the first century, become inadmissible in the twentieth? Might not *the method* of the Lord's resurrection be still left an open question?[4]

His sermon was reported in the press and something of a public hue and cry ensued.

Henson read widely in biblical criticism and recent theology. He was convinced that the intellectual challenge to belief could not be shirked, and should be faced publicly in the pulpit no less than in scholarly journals and erudite discussion groups. In common with many liberals, he distinguished sharply between the essential and non-essential elements in Christianity.

It is profoundly significant that the Apostles, even while they attest and exult in the amazing tokens of the Holy Ghost's presence within the Church, never by so much as a single word encourage their converts to think that such tokens are necessary, or even normal, evidences of sincere discipleship. Miracles in their view might be the deceiving devices of Demons, as well as the proofs of Divine Action: and, accordingly, they followed their Master in attaching no importance to them as factors in religion. Rather they were at great pains to make clear to their converts that the test of true discipleship lies always in the sphere of character and conduct.[5]

Not least, for him, among the cardinal virtues were intellectual honesty and integrity. In 1912 a collection of his sermons, *The Creed in the Pulpit*, was published. A copy accompanied *Foundations*, published that same year, to Zanzibar, where it too aroused the ire of Frank Weston. Certainly from that point on, if not before, Henson was numbered among the heretics by the orthodox. *The Creed in the Pulpit* reiterated the non-necessity of the miraculous for essential religious belief. The 'nature miracles' of the Gospels were, to historical science, incredible. Jesus possessed a 'severely normal' humanity, and St Paul's doctrine of the resurrection 'definitely disallows the theory on which alone the "empty tomb" can have any vital relation to the Christian faith'.

That same year, 1912, Henson was appointed Dean of Durham (he had earlier declined the offer of an Oxford chair). The Church of England has generally been highly tolerant of the deans of its cathedrals, and indeed such positions have provided admirable niches for highly gifted clergy, whose heterodoxy, or plain eccentricity, might otherwise have precluded them from episcopal office. Few begrudged Henson his translation to Durham, and indeed some probably sighed with relief that his views would no longer be aired weekly at the heart of the metropolis, but in the sparser setting of his new northern outpost. In fact Henson was highly successful as Dean of Durham, quickly establishing a warm relationship with both the clergy and people of the city. The onset of war in 1914 did not deflect Henson from his critical detachment. In fact it provided more opportunity for him to exercise it. In July 1915, on a return visit to Westminster Abbey, he preached a sermon in the course of which he dismissed the much-cherished myth of the first months of war, that angelic beings had clearly been seen in battle assisting the British troops at the retreat from Mons. Angry correspondents berated his unpatriotic scepticism. He was equally cool towards the National Mission of Repentance and Hope, which the leaders of the Church hoped would turn the crisis of war into a religious revival. 'Those who are running about the country, exhorting little companies of puzzled women, have no vision of any larger teaching than that which has passed on their lips for years, and is now admittedly powerless. A dervish-like fervour cannot be maintained, and is not really illuminating or morally helpful.'[6] Then came the stormy year of 1917.

It began with an episode which, from today's perspective, seems almost unreal. Henson received an invitation to preach at the City Temple in London, the Congregational pulpit till recently occupied by R. J. Campbell. Winnington Ingram, the Bishop of London, by all means tried to persuade and cajole Henson into refusing the invitation to occupy a Nonconformist pulpit, but to no avail. The year closed with the greatest crisis of Henson's life, and one in which, in the view of many, he held in his hands the destiny of the Church of England as well as his own.

In early December Henson received from the Prime Minister, David Lloyd George, an invitation for his name to be submitted for the vacant see of Hereford. Lloyd George's motives were, apparently, related to Hereford's proximity to Wales, where disestablishment of the Church had been set in train. A bishop firmly committed to establishment in England, while unusually open to Nonconformity, would be an asset. Henson, while he had initial and natural private doubts as to his capacities as a bishop, seems to have had little hesitation about accepting. However, by the middle of December news of the impending appointment had leaked out into the national press, and immediately the orthodox klaxons were sounding action stations. First to open fire were a group of clergy in the diocese of Oxford, who passed a resolution of protest and called upon the Dean and Chapter of Hereford to refuse election. A second round came from the High-Church English Church Union, urging clergy and others to write what they euphemistically called 'suitable letters' to the Prime Minister. The *Church Times* exploded with a leader under the title 'Unhappy Hereford'. But the more significant exchanges took place in the secular press, most notably *The Times*, where Lord Halifax, lay prince of Anglo-Catholicism, stated grandly:

> If the Prime Minister knew how deep and wide the feeling is against the nomination of the Dean of Durham to the Bishopric of Hereford he would have hesitated before taking a step which, if he had known anything about the mind and affairs of the Church of England, he would have seen has nothing to recommend it. Cleverness is not the only quality required in a Bishop. The scandal of such a nomination is great; the trouble and distress it causes widespread, and the consequences which may result from it such as a Minister, unless he desired to promote the separation of Church and State (which may be Mr Lloyd George's object), would be most anxious to avoid.[7]

Such assertions of course betray the polemical tendency, once the temperature rises above a certain point, to project on to the wider community one's own unease and sense of threat. The feeling in the Church of England was not nearly so uniform as Halifax had divined. J. N. Jarrow, of Durham, responded to the English Church Union by stating that, apart from members of that Union itself, in the north of England the only protest that would obtain 'would be one against the removal of a Dean who has proved himself a unifying influence amongst all classes, parties and sects in the industrial north, and who by his width of sympathy and independence of thought has won our respect, and whose departure we greatly regret'.[8] A correspondent writing under the pseudonym 'Laicus' hoped that the 'suitable letters' urged by the English Church Union upon the Prime Minister would somehow be preserved.

> If they could be assembled and printed in a handy volume they would, as a record of a certain current of Church Thought, be simply priceless; and there must be many who, like myself, would gladly give them a place on their bookshelves by the side of the earlier 'Epistolae Obscurorum Virorum'.[9]

Such a view was evidence that the calming sense of the relativizing effect of a longer historical perspective was gaining ground. Nor was it only a matter of distant history that had to be taken into consideration. E. G. Selwyn complained of the short memories of those claiming to be pained by Henson's preferment, and, with an unkind but apposite allusion to the effect of Gore's *Lux Mundi* in *its* own time, wrote: 'Do they not remember how an eminent living bishop by his theological concessions nearly broke the heart of Canon Liddon? Yet his ideas, too, have been absorbed.'[10] Selwyn too referred admiringly to Henson's effect of promoting *rapprochement* with Nonconformists at home, as the padres had also done at the front. This, in face of the High Church nature of the opposition to Henson, may have been slightly disingenuous as a defence, but it did expose one of the main motives behind the Anglo-Catholics' mistrust of him: the fear of a pan-Protestantism such as had reared its head with the Kikuyu Conference. Henson, it was felt, would by his consecration be appointed to an apostolical succession in which he himself did not believe and which he would betray.

Almost at the end of December, H. Wace, Dean of Canterbury, lent fellow-decanal support to Henson by stating in *The Times* that the opponents of Henson's appointment had not shown any real case for his disqualification.[11] This particular gauntlet prompted the next bout of exchanges early in the new year, when the debate moved away from the realm of party and personal issues towards theology proper. Darwell Stone, the Head of Pusey House, Oxford, took up Wace's challenge, and cited several passages from *The Creed in the Pulpit* which, he alleged, demonstrated clearly that Henson was fatally compromised in his stated beliefs, or unbeliefs, on the divinity of Christ, the bodily resurrection and empty tomb, and the great nature miracles of the New Testament gospel narratives.[12] This prompted W. B. Sanday to rush to the defence of Henson and liberal theology generally, in a long letter[13] which made up in fervour whatever it lacked in modesty:

> My own general position is so similar to Dr Henson's that I believe he will accept me as an advocate. And I also think that he will forgive me if, in defending him, I prefer to use language of my own. I have little doubt that he means to say very much what I have myself said. But it has perhaps happened to me more than him to lay stress on the affirmative rather than the negative side of the beliefs which we hold in common.
>
> Our own generation, and in particular the present decade of our generation, has to face a question of fundamental importance. It has to ask whether the fundamental truths of Christianity can be stated in terms that are acceptable to the modern mind. Dr Henson and I agree in thinking that they can, and if they can they assuredly must be so stated. The essence of the attempt at such restatement turns upon the distinction between ultimate belief and the expression of belief. The ultimate belief remains constant; but the expression of belief varies of necessity from age to age.

Sanday proceeded to cite extended quotations from his own writings, and then asserted:

> The Virgin Birth, the physical Resurrection, and physical Ascension, are all realistic expressions, adapted to the thought of the time, of ineffable truths which the thought of the time could not express in any other way. To conceive of them realistically was natural and right in the age in which they took shape.

Henson was grateful for Sanday's support, although Sanday was probably seeing something of his own reflection in Henson. Sanday was confident as to why and how the 'miraculous' needed restating in terms of modern understanding. Henson had not proceeded quite so far. He was simply *agnostic* as far as such elements were concerned, and could not see what vital relation, if any, they had with the living heart of belief in God through Christ. Privately, in his journal, Henson was less sanguine about Sanday's intervention than in his letter of thanks to the Oxford professor. 'It must needs have the effect of adding gravity to the controversy raised by the E.C.U.' he reflected.[14] It certainly made his position far more exposed, since he was now inevitably seen as representative of liberalism generally, and however extreme.

The gravity indeed increased. Among others, the Bishop of Chelmsford, Watts-Ditchfield, wrote to Henson, wanting assurances 'that what you have written does not imply that you have departed from the traditional and almost universal meaning which is attached to the words of the Creed, "Born of the *Virgin* Mary," "The third day he rose from the dead." '[15] More serious still, Charles Gore, spurred on by the protest resolution from his diocesan clergy in Oxford, published his own appeal, addressed to the two Archbishops and all the other bishops, pleading the case for Henson's disqualification on the ground that 'he falls outside the limits of tolerable conformity as recognized in our recent declaration in Convocation'. Davidson invited Henson to retract the views which had caused offence, but Henson refused. The Archbishop's position consequently became critical. He himself was convinced of Henson's deeply personal faith and piety, but if driven to the point where, on objective grounds, he would have to refuse to consecrate Henson, he might well have to tender his own resignation as Archbishop. For some days the Church of England, in the eyes of those who knew what was going on in the correspondence between Lambeth, Durham and Oxford, seemed to be on the verge of an unprecedented and disastrous collapse of the authority of its leadership, even to the point of schism on the part of many Anglo-Catholics. Finally, Davidson staged an opportunity for Henson to clear his reputation somewhat, by writing him a note, the form of which had previously been agreed between them, and which together with Henson's reply would be published. The Archbishop's note referred to the disquiet being caused to 'many earnest men of different schools' at Henson's supposed

> disbelief in the Apostles' Creed, and especially the clauses relating to our Lord's birth and Resurrection. I reply to them that they are misinformed, and that I am persuaded that when you repeat the words of the Creed you do so *ex animo* and without any desire to change them.

Henson replied by return to the effect that 'what you say is absolutely true. I am indeed astonished that any candid reader of my published books, or anyone acquainted with my public ministry of thirty years, could entertain a suggestion so dishonourable to me as a man and as a clergyman.'

Davidson's question and Henson's reply constituted a study in ambiguity, but it was now possible for Davidson to announce that he could consecrate Henson with a clear conscience and in assurance of his essential orthodoxy. But what did *ex animo* actually mean? Henson meant by it a deliberate and sincere acceptance of the religious intention of the Creed, a commitment to it, but not necessarily one which was 'nakedly and unintelligently literal'.[16] The two clauses in question were, in Henson's view, concerned to affirm the essential humanity and deity of Christ. If *those* were believed in, then there was *ex animo* acceptance of the Creed. Not all of course were convinced. Darwell Stone and the Anglo-Catholics remained highly suspicious. Many of the bishops were conspicuous by their absence from Henson's consecration, a fact which deeply wounded him (and must have sorely embarrassed Davidson too). Ever after for Henson, the anniversary of the consecration was a painful day in the year, so bitter was the memory of that ostracism. Nor were all the critics on the conservative side. Some of the Modern Churchmen like Dean Inge regarded Henson's admission to Davidson as a betrayal of the liberal cause, and Kirsopp Lake suggested that *ex animo* should be rendered *cum grano salis*. In fact, as we shall see, there was a *theological* divergence growing between Henson and the Modern Churchmen.

Henson's relations with Frank Weston took on the air of tragi-comedy. Hereford was already associated in Weston's mind with the execrable canonry conferred on Streeter. Henson, however, now became for him the *arch-heretic*. Not long after Henson's enthronement, Weston was conducting a clergy retreat at Malvern, in Worcestershire. Shortly before delivering one of his addresses, he was found staring long and fixedly out of the window, in a westerly direction over the rolling border countryside towards Hereford, and explained that he was mentally casting anathemas at '*that man*'. He again put pen to paper with a somewhat tortuous work *The Christ and His Critics*, dubbed by Henson the *Zanzibarian Fulmination*. However, at the 1920 Lambeth Conference Weston and Henson actually *met* – and took to – each other. The respectful friendship which ensued probably owed much to the ability of each to perceive something of himself in the other, advocacy of Protestant federalism and Anglo-Catholicism notwithstanding. Each was a man of profound convictions, of patent sincerity, determined to be slave to no one and nothing but his conscience before God. Both were supremely *pastoral* bishops. Certainly, if the trust, affection and respect of ordinary people and parish clergy were to supply the credentials of episcopal authority, Henson's brief time at Hereford was an unqualified vindication of his appointment. In 1920 he was translated to the see of his beloved Durham, where he remained as bishop until 1938 – controversial as ever but providing for the Church of England one of the most colourful stories of Christian leadership. Henson's career defies simple description. He offended the Durham miners (for whom he had the warmest personal sympathy and by no means naive understanding) by opposing the strike of 1926. His advocacy of liberty and inter-Christian communion continued unabated. In contrast to at least one other prelate, he knew from the start that there could be no Christian apologies for Nazi Germany and that Niemöller and the Confessing Church merited unqualified support.

Henson made no pretensions at being an original, or even particularly academic, theologian. He was a mediator to the public of the work of modern scholarship, which he believed had to be faced with integrity. By putting himself in the spotlight of honest belief, however, he played a highly important and educative role. Owen Chadwick sums it all up thus:

> Were men distressed and alarmed, as Bishop Watts-Ditchfield had said? Some of them, undoubtedly. The argument whether a good Christian man, and especially a good Christian teacher, might be agnostic about what happened in the two great miracles of the New Testament, continued to raise its head until the Second World War. And since, in the intellectual climate of that age, philosophical and scientific, some people were bound to be agnostic about the miracles though in all other respects they were godly Christian men, the Church must accept the possibility of such reverent agnosticism if it were not to cut itself off from the mind of European society. In this partial retaining of its hold upon the intellect of Europe, the Church owed a larger debt to Henson that it usually realised. Perhaps he compromised a little before his consecration, for the sake of helping an archbishop to climb out of a barrel full of gunpowder. But he vindicated sufficiently the liberty of thought which he claimed. And he could not have achieved this if he had been in truth a half-Christian. Archbishop Davidson believed in the depths of his authentic piety. To anyone who listened to him, even occasionally, this was impossible to doubt. He believed in the Christ as the Saviour of men and never wavered. That blunted the force of all the petitions, the excommunications by Weston, the circumlocutions of Watts-Ditchfield. In difficult years for the Christian intelligence, shall we exclude from the ministry in the Church a profoundly Christian man because he had to say that he did not know what happened at the birth and after the death?[17]

The 'Modern Churchmen'

The term 'modernist' has become so widespread in popular religious usage, if not as a term of abuse then as a vague label for any questioning attitude towards traditional belief, that some effort is needed to recall its specific origins and entry into the British scene. Properly speaking, 'Modernism' was initially the name of that movement among Roman Catholics, mainly in France, at the end of the nineteenth century, which sought to reinterpret Catholic dogma in the light of modern historical and scientific inquiry, and at the same time to refute the Liberal Protestant argument that the emergence of the Catholic Church was a betrayal and distortion of the original, simple gospel of the historical Jesus. The French priest A. F. Loisy (1857–1940), Professor of Sacred Scripture at the Institut Catholique, Paris, was the acknowledged leader of the movement. His *L'Évangile et L'Église* (1902) was intended as an answer to Adolf von Harnack, the leader of Liberal Protestantism in Germany, but its conception of religious truth as always in process of historical development was seen by the Vatican as an attack on the integrity of dogma. The movement was condemned by Pope Pius X in 1907 in his decree *Lamentabili* and his encyclical *Pascendi gregis*. Priests were required to take an oath renouncing all modernist tendencies, and the movement was effectively crushed as a Roman Catholic phenomenon. The tendency, however, had spread into English-speaking Catholicism, where several notable personalities and intellects made sufficient impact before the papal condemnation to ensure that 'modernism' would not easily be forgotten. Pre-eminent among these was the Irish priest George Tyrrell (1861–1909), who identified a Modernist as 'a Churchman, of any sort, who believes in the possibility of a synthesis between the essential truth of his religion and the essential truth of modernity'. Perhaps most influential in the long-term, as far as the British public was concerned, was the layman Baron Friedrich von Hügel (1852–1925), who, while not explicitly identified as a 'Modernist' (and in any case, being a layperson, was exempt from having to define his position in relation to the movement), popularized many of the movement's most creative insights, especially in terms of spirituality and religious experience.

It seems that only after its banning within Roman Catholicism did the adoption of the term 'Modernism' within Anglicanism and other groups begin. But the main Anglican group which gladly took the title to itself was already in existence, founded in 1898 as 'The Churchmen's Union for the Advancement of Liberal Religious Thought'.[18] Prolixity eventually gave way in 1928 when it became the 'Modern Churchmen's Union'. But well before then its members were happily known as 'Modernists' or 'Modern Churchmen' – certainly since 1911 when the journal *The Modern Churchman* began to appear, soon followed by the first of the many summer Conferences of Modern Churchmen, in 1914. The 'Churchmen's Union', as the original title was known in abbreviation, came about through a coalescence of Broad Churchmen who felt the need of organization to promote the 'reinterpretation and restatement' of dogma, and generally to liberalize the teaching, discipline and government of the Church. Almost immediately the group was in dispute with the Anglo-Catholic English Church Union, of which Lord Halifax was the most celebrated patron. Hastings Rashdall (1858–1924), Tutor in Philosophy at New College, Oxford, was soon in evidence as one of the leading minds in the Churchmen's Union. Saintly, tending to an austere, even ascetic, spirituality, he was formidable in the breadth of his learning. His *Universities of Europe in the Middle Ages* (1895) made his reputation as a historian of ideas, while *The Theory of Good and Evil* (1907) established him as a major and original thinker in his own right, in the Oxford idealist vein. Rashdall held to three great essentials of Christian belief: 'a personal God, personal immortality, and a unique and paramount revelation of God in the historic Christ'.[19] But much of doubtful value, in his view, had been built upon the essential Christianity of Jesus himself. 'There is a great deal of hay and stubble that has simply got to be cleared away.' The first Secretary of the Churchmen's Union was W. F. Cobb, Rector of St Ethelburga's, Bishopsgate, at first sight an unlikely choice, since until 1899 he had been an officer of the English Church Union. But liberalizing influences were at work within him, and he transmitted these to others through his involvement in the Churchmen's Union. He was considered much too moderate by some, and in 1900 he resigned, though he remained active in the Union, to be succeeded by William Manning, Vicar of St Andrew's, Leytonstone. Among names associated with the movement in these early days were George Henslow (cleric and noted botanist), Percy Gardner (archaeologist, philosopher and lay theologian of some originality) and W. R. Inge (authority on mysticism, of melancholy wit, and from 1911 Dean of St Paul's).

The Churchmen's Union might have indefinitely remained nothing more than a loose congeries of like-minded liberal Anglicans, but for the arrival on the scene of H. D. A. Major (1871–1961). Major was born in England but brought up and educated in New Zealand, where he was ordained to the Anglican priesthood. In 1903 he returned to England to continue theological study at Oxford. Here the liberalism of S. R. Driver and W. B. Sanday was in the ascendant, and Major, already seeing himself in the broad Anglican tradition, gladly followed their lead. In 1906 he was appointed to the staff of Ripon College, then in the cathedral city which bears its name. Ripon College, founded by Bishop Boyd Carpenter in 1897, was an avowedly liberal centre of Anglican theological education, and so it was to remain throughout its career (as Ripon Hall it transmigrated to Oxford in 1919, and united with Cuddesdon in the mid-1970s). During 1907–08, Major became a committed member of the Churchmen's Union, and by 1909 was addressing it with a paper on theological education. In 1911 he joined the Council of the Union, and was appointed editor of its new journal *The Modern Churchman*. This was the decisive step in Major's career, and in the life of the Union. Major found an outlet for his propagandizing energies, and the Union found an articulate public voice.

'The old never dies until this happens, Till all the soul of good that was in it have itself transformed into the practical New' – this somewhat cumbersome, and historically questionable, motto from Carlyle adorned the front cover of the new periodical, presently to be replaced by Erasmus's charge against the obscurantists of the sixteenth century: 'By identifying the new learning with heresy you make orthodoxy synonynous with ignorance.' It appeared monthly, and soon had work to do in defending J. M. Thompson, whose *Miracles in the New Testament* led, as we have seen (see previous chapter) to the withdrawal of his licence, and also B. H. Streeter and the *Foundations* team in 1912. *The Modern Churchman* under Major undoubtedly became, by the 1920s, the most articulate and popular mouthpiece of liberal Christianity in England (though some might argue the case for the *Hibbert Journal*).

Far from dampening the ardour of the Modern Churchmen, the 1914–18 War saw the strengthening of the movement, in literary expression at least, and in a manner which was to lead to some of the most violent controversy with conservative Anglicanism. In 1918 there was launched a series of books, 'The Modern Churchman's Library', heralded by M. G. Glazebrook's *The Faith of a Modern Churchman*.[20] Major acted as editor of the series and explained in his foreword the intention of presenting to educated and thoughtful people brief statements of various aspects of Christian truth, in terms of modern thought. 'The writers of these volumes will be practising members of the Church of England, who accept the main results of recent criticism, whether scientific, historical or literary. Trained scholars and thinkers, they do not undervalue tradition: but above all they are truth-seekers and desire to be truth-speakers.' This modest candour was confirmed by the familiar Erasmus quotation re-appearing on the front cover, and Tyrrell's definition of a Modernist (a label now adopted unhesitatingly by these Anglicans) on the title page.

Glazebrook v. Chase: The Battle of Ely

M. G. Glazebrook, a product of Oxford Broad Churchmanship (he was a pupil of Jowett of Balliol) was headmaster of Clifton College from 1891 until 1905, when he became a canon of Ely. Opening for the Modern Churchmen, his *Faith of a Modern Churchman* was, from the point of view of his own side, a competent performance. It offered an overview of the main items of Christian belief in liberal perspective, bearing in mind the kind of questions inquiring believers or interested sceptics were thought to be asking. The divine nature, atonement, resurrection, judgement and the life to come, the Church, Bible, miracles, creeds, prayer, sacraments and Christian ethics all received treatment. On the resurrection, for example, Glazebrook took a similar stance to Streeter, though less concerned with the nature of the actual resurrection appearances of Jesus himself as 'spiritual visions'. The resurrection life as expounded by St Paul, stated Glazebrook, was a wholly spiritual affair, though St Paul had to work his way through to this conclusion by several stages. The gospel accounts of the resurrection of Jesus betrayed the influence of the materialistic outlook of Judaistic conceptions of resurrection of the physical body. Thus:

> The Judaising Christians, especially in Jerusalem, clung to the old materialistic view of the resurrection, and unconsciously moulded the tradition of our Lord's resurrection into accordance with it. Comparing the simple narrative of St Mark with those of the later Gospels, we can see that the additions all have the same tendency to translate the spiritual into the material . . . So, in spite of St Paul's teaching, the image of belief in a resurrection of the *flesh* soon became dominant in the Church, was embodied in the creeds, and remained almost unquestioned until modern times.[21]

Judgement and the life to come had to undergo a similar revision. The treatment anticipates what a generation or so later would be recognized as akin to Rudolf Bultmann's 'demythologizing' programme. The old traditional picture of judgement as some grand assize, as portrayed in medieval wall-paintings, is obsolete but, says Glazebrook, it 'does vividly present a truth of which the human conscience is vividly aware'. He continues:

> If the world is not the sport of chance, but ruled by a moral power, each man's life must somehow be judged, not only in detail but as a whole; and judgment must in some way determine his future.
>
> The imagery is obsolete for two reasons. It implies a flat earth, which is the main part of the universe, overarched by a solid vault of heaven; it requires us to accept the belief in the reconstitution of the earthly body which St Paul had renounced when he wrote to the Corinthians; and it is closely connected in the popular mind with those materialistic views of hell, derived from pagan sources, which darkened the whole life of the Middle Ages.[22]

Glazebrook turns to the fourth Gospel, and to B. F. Westcott's exegesis of it, to suggest (and again like Bultmann, who likewise was heavily influenced by the 'eschatology' of that Gospel) that judgement is an event which happens here and now in a person's life by the very presence of God in it. The judgement is that darkness is preferred to light. The final consequences, to be sure, are future. If life has already been chosen, 'the soul rises from death in a spiritual body', though the future life can be only dimly perceived from the present as a mystery.

On miracles, Glazebrook hoes the already well-dug liberal ground, of the modern scientific view of nature as a continuum, of the tendency for natural causes now to be found for occurrences which in biblical times would have been regarded as supernatural in origin, and so on. On the virgin birth, 'the evidence is not such as to compel belief', the Matthean and Lucan narratives being barely reconcilable, and neither of them being mentioned either by St Paul or St John. Then:

> . . . it is not open to Christians to refuse belief on *a priori* grounds; and from very early times these miracles have been included in the creeds. Modern Churchmen, therefore, do not deny that these wonders happened. But they do claim that, in view of the nature of the evidence, men should not be regarded as heretics who decline to affirm them. For . . . belief in our Lord's Divine nature does not depend upon any material miracle. It rests securely upon moral and spiritual evidence which cannot be questioned – upon the wonder of His personality and upon the response which has been found in the lives of countless millions.[23]

Here was the clearest possible statement of the separation between belief in miracle *per se*, and belief in the uniqueness and divinity of Christ.

The most interesting chapter in *The Faith of a Modern Churchman* is that on the creeds and their use. We are given a potted history of the growth of creeds in the early Church, in particular the Apostles', the Nicene and the so-called Athanasian Creed. That they indeed have a history, a story of development, indicates how modern Christians should regard them. 'They are not a "deposit" given to be guarded, but a plant whose growth is to be fostered. So long as the Catholic Church was vigorous and intelligent, the creeds were continually being modified to suit new conditions of thought and life.'[24] After this, we might expect Glazebrook to call for a revision of the creeds, or a proposal for a Modern Churchman's Creed. But no such suggestion is made, no specimen given. Glazebrook is sceptical of such a project and offers a different approach:

> The younger generation claim that it is imperative . . . We who are older

> realise the hopelessness of trying to express the infinite in terms of the finite; and are therefore less confident than either modern youth or ancient Fathers in the wisdom of recasting old forms. Many of us prefer to enrich the old forms by reading into them the knowledge which is gradually being gained, without altering their outward form.[25]

In particular, says Glazebrook, 'symbolical interpretation' of items which earlier believers had taken to be literally true, was now entering in, particularly with regard to such items as heaven and hell (though not mentioned by name, Gore's authority was clearly being implied for this view). But, on behalf of the Modern Churchmen, declared Glazebrook, the same claim was now being made in the cases of the virgin birth and the resurrection.

The Faith of a Modern Churchman received a critical though polite review from J. K. Mozley in the *Church Times*.[26] The real debate took place in a different quarter, and much closer to home. Glazebrook presented a copy of his book to F. H. Chase, who had left his Cambridge chair of divinity to become Bishop of Ely. Glazebrook's solicitude for the theological welfare of his bishop was rewarded by a stern letter in reply, stating that as his bishop, Chase could *not* admit the Modern Churchmen's claim that credal items like the virgin birth and bodily resurrection could be interpreted symbolically. A vigorous exchange of open letters ensued, which spilt into the pages of *The Times* (there is something faintly ridiculous about the sight of two senior clergy, living virtually within sight of each other in the fens of East Anglia, solemnly corresponding via Fleet Street). Chase was adamant that to interpret the creeds in this way ran clean counter to the bishops' statement in Convocation of 1914 – that the historical items in the creed were indeed historical – and Glazebrook was equally certain that Gore's admission of a degree of symbolical interpretation had to be extended to the whole creed.

Soon Chase was busy with his own reply to Glazebrook. His *Belief and Creed* appeared early in 1919.[27] It displayed considerable erudition, for Chase was a specialist in New Testament scholarship, which Glazebrook was not. He was able to marshal a considerable array of evidence against, for example, Glazebrook's view that there had been progression in St Paul's conception of the resurrection, from Jewish materialist ideas of physical resurrection to a purely 'spiritual' conception of resurrection life. Perhaps it was slightly too expert a rebuke. Glazebrook had, after all, written a highly readable book for the popular intelligent market, and the general reader who has been impressed by readable error is unlikely to be easily swayed back by unreadable truth. But certain passages in Chase's reply show how the debate on the events associated with Christ was gradually forcing out into the open the real issue of the incarnation.

Glazebrook had argued that, 'As to the Virgin Birth . . . the evidence is not such as to compel belief.' Chase replied that belief – religious belief as distinct from factual knowledge – is never *compelled* by historical evidence. Historical evidence can only establish probabilities. The probability of certain events having been shown, those events then become the material on which religious faith works.

> No one can prove past possibility of intellectual doubt that Jesus Christ once lived. But the evidence makes the probability that He did once live on earth so high that it approaches as near as the nature of the case allows to absolute certainty. Then religious faith realises that the life of Jesus Christ on earth completely corresponds with faith in a living God who cares for His creatures, and that it satisfies the deepest instincts of man's nature; and so faith enables a man to say, 'I believe in Jesus Christ His only Son our Lord.'[28]

The purely *historical* evidence for the virgin birth is slight, but again there is a peculiarly *religious* ground for holding to it. Chase then moves to the heart of the matter as he sees it:

> We are not indeed entitled to have any *a priori* ideas as to the way in which the Incarnation *must* have been brought about. We are not in a position to make any dogmatic assertion as to what was *necessary* in regard to an event so uniquely unique as the Incarnation. But from the first, since the story became known to a few and afterwards was embodied in the two Gospels, it has seemed to generations of Christian people congruous and reasonable that Jesus, being what we believe Him to be, Incarnate Son of God and sinless man, should have been begotten 'not of the will of the flesh nor of the will of a man, but of God'.[29]

'Congruous and reasonable': a most significant admission by an orthodox churchman. In effect Chase was saying that belief in the divine sonship of Christ was a belief logically prior to and grounded independently of a belief in the miraculous nature of his birth, and that the virgin birth was believed because of its appropriateness to *that* truth, the truth of incarnation. Indeed, it was on this very ground that Chase went so far as to castigate Glazebrook for implying that the virgin birth was merely symbolic. A symbol for what? The incarnation and divinity of Christ? No, for that has *already* been confessed in the clause 'His only Son our Lord'. Remarkably, then, in the interests of orthodoxy itself, Chase had separated incarnation from virgin birth – and in a theologically more complete way than the Modern Churchman Glazebrook had done. The virgin birth was now seen as having a propriety of its own, and therefore in one sense had a certain credibility about it. But orthodoxy, in the person of Chase, had saved this credibility by removing its *necessity* for belief. The virgin birth could now remain in the creed only by being recognized as of quite secondary significance to the clause stating the doctrine of incarnation *per se*. Was Chase aware of how much he was conceding as the price of 'essential' orthodoxy, any more than was Gore in his admissions of 'symbolical' interpretation? At any rate, it is difficult to see how with any consistency Chase could continue to *demand* subscription to the literal historicity of the miraculous in the creed, at least as far as the virgin birth was concerned, in the light of his recognition that the historical evidence as such was slight, and that the religious ground was one of congruity with the *primary* belief about Christ. To speak of the congruity of the miraculous birth with the incarnation in fact became a typically orthodox Anglican way of describing it.

If, then, the belief in Christ as incarnate Son of God was becoming identified as the centre of belief, it was inevitable that sooner or later it would itself come under debate. Christology as such, rather than the miraculous, would be at issue. The Modern Churchmen, and Hensley Henson for that matter, were saying that they believed in Jesus as Son of God. But did traditional orthodoxy and modernism share the same understanding of the classical formulae that Jesus Christ was the only begotten Son of the Father, by whom all things were made, true God of true God, who for our sakes. . . ? The matter came to a head, and more dramatically than most people of any party anticipated, in 1921.

The Girton Conference 1921

The Churchmen's Union, under Major's instigation, had held its first summer conference at Ripon in July 1914, the year in which the controversy over symbolic interpretation of the creeds and clerical subscription was at its height. The two most outstanding speakers were F. J. Foakes-Jackson and Kirsopp Lake, at that time probably the two most radical Anglican scholars of New Testament and early church history. On the history of early Christianity both held positions nearer to Loisy and the Roman Catholic Modernists than to the Liberal Protestants (and hence to most of the Modern Churchmen). In their view, the historical Jesus was far less significant to belief than the subsequent, universal movement of religious belief and practice which he stimulated. Perhaps the engulfment in the Great War less than a month after the conference diverted public attention from the proceedings, but, as Alan Stephenson points out, the substance of much that was said at Ripon closely foreshadowed the infamous occasion at Girton, Cambridge, seven years later. Remarkably, thanks to Major's energy, several conferences were arranged during the war years.

The 1921 Conference, held during August at Girton College, Cambridge, was to be devoted to the person of Christ, and the faith of a reunited Church. The subjects were Major's choice (he was now Principal of Ripon Hall, now re-sited in Oxford), the organization of the Conference the work of Glazebrook. As at Ripon in 1914, the views of Foakes-Jackson and Kirsopp Lake would be a major item of discussion. It was therefore something of a paradox that a conference which was to become notorious for its apparently heterodox utterances was in part motivated by the felt need to counter unacceptably radical views! The subject of Christology, said Major,

> is full of difficulties today, and for responsible and practical Modernists to select it and speak about it frankly and fearlessly demands courage. Final conclusions may not be reached on many points, but the selection of the subject is neither needless nor premature in view of . . . Professor Lake's two recent books.[30]

The speakers on Christology were to be Cyril Emmet, R. H. Lightfoot, R. B. Tollinton, J. W. Hunkin, E. W. Barnes, Nowell Smith, Hastings Rashdall, H. D. A. Major, J. F. Bethune-Baker and R. G. Parsons. Foakes-Jackson was to be present, with the right of reply to his critics. Lake was not there. Hensley Henson, even from the time of the Ripon Conference of 1914, had distanced himself from the Modern Churchmen, regarding any flirtation with Foakes-Jackson and Kirsopp Lake as dangerous in the extreme, and in any case had, ever since his compromise with Davidson, been seen by the Modern Churchmen as a traitor to the cause.

Much of the input from the main speakers was indeed highly critical of Lake and Foakes-Jackson. That, however, was not the impression made by the initial reportage. Two addresses in particular caused something of a sensation outside the conference – that by Rashdall on 'Christ as Logos and Son of God', and Bethune-Baker's on 'Jesus as both Human and Divine'. Once again it was the secular national press which helped to ignite the public controversy. One of the first reports, that in the *Daily Telegraph*, in fact commended the Modern Churchmen for the interest they were arousing in religious matters. But the *Daily Express* managed to headline some extracts from Rashdall's speech which appeared to state that he denied the divinity of Jesus Christ. Rashdall was incensed, and immediately wrote to the *Church Times* in an attempt to fend off the storm of criticism that he knew would come. He was too late. His letter appeared on 19 August, but that same issue was already full of comment. 'Liberal Christianity – The Last Phase' was the title over the editorial, hailing Girton as the death-bed of liberalism. There was a long article by Canon Peter Green of Manchester accusing the Modernists of having minds 'still in the grip of nineteenth century dogma', and a shorter piece by Gore on 'Miracles and Doctrine'. 'It always seemed to me,' wrote Gore,

> to be quite a vain hope that men would cease to believe the miracles and continue to believe the doctrines . . . But it is now made quite evident by the declarations of these 'liberal' divines. They cannot believe in the Godhead of Christ. He was only a highly inspired man. So far the issue between Modernists and Catholics is cleared up, and that is a gain.

It is not clear to what extent at this stage Gore, Green and other commentators had access to the Girton papers at first hand and in their entirety. Rashdall's letter complained that the *Daily Express* had 'carefully picked out the passages in my paper . . . in which I asserted the real humanity of our Lord, while omitting those in which I spoke no less strongly of His Divinity'. Worse, the newspaper had actually attributed to him a statement that 'Jesus Christ was, in truth, man in the fullest sense, and not God'. This, declared Rashdall, was absolutely false. He maintained the Catholic doctrine that our Lord was God and man, and demanded from the editor a correction and apology, failing which he threatened legal action. (He did, apparently, successfully carry out this threat.) We shall examine shortly exactly what Rashdall *had* said at Girton. For the moment we can glance at the debate that followed. Letters, both in sympathy with and hurling anathemas against the Girtonian theology, occupied the *Church Times* for several weeks.

> . . . To put it mildly, an attack had been delivered on the fundamentals of the Christian faith; and that, not by outsiders, by men who openly and frankly accept the position of hostile critics and are eager to maintain that position, but by those of our own household, by Deans, Canons and recognized Professors and Teachers of Theology

was one typical lament, which bemoaned the fact of seeking to convert people on the fringe of religious thought and experience 'and then – the Girton Conference!'[31] William Manning, sometime Secretary of the Churchmen's Union, resigned his membership in protest. Major, who in his own conference paper had implied that Christ claimed to be

Son of God only in a 'moral' sense, was himself accused by Peter Green of heresy. Not only so, but a certain C. E. Douglas, curate of St Luke's, Southwark, actually sent a formal charge of heresy on Major's account to the Bishop of Oxford, Hubert Burge, requiring him 'in accordance with canonical precedent . . . [to] hold inquisition into the matter forthwith'. Douglas refused to lessen Burge's embarrassment by tactfully withdrawing the charge, and so Burge referred the matter to a panel of consultants drawn from Oxford professors. Major defended himself at length on both historical and theological grounds. In the light of the Oxford panel's findings, Burge informed a wrathful Douglas that he did not feel able to proceed with any charges against Major. Petitions and debates in Convocation ensued, the eventual – and positive – outcome of which was the Archbishops' Commission on Doctrine, to which we shall refer at the close of this chapter.

Bethune-Baker and Rashdall

Though Major suffered much from a would-be heresy hunter, it was probably at least as much due to his leading role in the Girton Conference and the Churchmen's Union, as to any content of his paper, that he was the target for criticism and abuse. Understandably, most concern centred around what Bethune-Baker and Hastings Rashdall had said, albeit they felt they were fighting off the even more radical teaching of Kirsopp Lake and Foakes-Jackson. In retrospect, by common consent it was Bethune-Baker's Christology which was the most speculative. Bethune-Baker was never actually a member of the Churchmen's Union, but 'Modernist' became in many eyes synonymous with what he had written in his book *The Faith of the Apostles' Creed* and with what he now said at Girton:

> I know almost nothing about God's character apart from Jesus. But I attribute to God the character of Jesus. I say my conception of God is formed by my conception of Jesus. The God I recognize is a supreme 'person' like Jesus in all that makes 'personality' . . . So Jesus is the creator of my God.[32]

As far as God was concerned, it appeared that even by the standards of our more recent process theology, Bethune-Baker was pushing divine immanence to the extremest lengths, to the point where God and man are mutually dependent. 'Neither is complete without the other. Language almost fails us, but God is always being actualized, fulfilled, expressed in man, and man only comes to full consciousness – the fulness of potentiality – in God.'[33]

To attack statements so extreme was perhaps like pushing at an open door. This was not quite the case with Rashdall, whose arguments were imbued with more ambiguity and who from the beginning defended himself with vigour. On his return to Carlisle from Cambridge, and smarting under his sensational treatment in the press, he felt compelled to preach in the cathedral on two successive Sunday evenings, in order to clarify and defend his views. These sermons, together with another address and the original Cambridge paper, were published the following year as *Jesus, Human and Divine*. True enough, journalism had misquoted, or partly quoted, or quoted out of context, a number of quite innocuous remarks on the theme of what the doctrine of Christ's divinity does *not* mean. Jesus did not claim divinity for himself. He was fully human. His human soul did not pre-exist his birth. His divinity does not *necessarily* imply the virgin birth. The human Jesus did not possess omniscience. Chase and Gore between them could have asserted most of these views (perhaps excepting the first). But to the uninitiated, heard at second-hand, and taken in themselves to be exhaustive of the matter, they could easily sound destructive of belief. But educated, orthodox opinion should have found little at which to take offence.

In fact what disturbed educated orthodox opinion (and such as Hensley Henson) much more, were those sections of Rashdall's papers which were *not* sensationalized in the secular press. That is, his remarks not on the humanity, but on the divinity, of Christ, and his attempt at a positive restatement of the doctrine of the incarnation in modern terms. Thus:

> If 'Divine' and 'human' are thought of as mutually exclusive terms, if God is thought of as simply the Maker of man, if man is thought of merely as a machine or an animal having no community of nature with the Universal Spirit who is the cause or source or 'ground' of the existence alike of Nature and of other spirits, then indeed it would be absurd to maintain that one human being, and one only, was both God and man at the same time. But such a view of the relation between God and man would not at the present day be accepted by any philosophy which finds any real place for God in its conception of the universe.[34]

Rashdall makes clear that his basic perspective is that of idealism. The rock from which his mind was hewn was – as with so many of his generation – the thought of his Oxford teacher T. H. Green. Hence the emphasis upon a community of nature between man and God, whereby all human thinking is to some degree a reproduction of the Divine Mind, and wherein the highest ideals which sway the human conscience are the truest revelation of the eternal ideal of the Divine Mind. 'All modern philosophers who recognize that the knowledge of

God is possible are agreed that we can only attain such knowledge by thinking of Him in the light of the human mind at its highest.' This idealistic tenet Rashdall equates with the essential truth of the incarnation, although a somewhat revised version of incarnation – 'It is impossible to maintain that God is fully incarnate in Christ and not incarnate at all in anyone else.'[35] Rashdall does not go so far as R. J. Campbell who, as was seen in a previous chapter, dared to say that God incarnates himself equally in all human beings. For Rashdall, it is in the conditions of the *highest* human life that God can most fully reveal himself:

> If we recognize that it is especially in the moral consciousness at its highest, and in the lives which are most completely dominated by such a moral consciousness, that God is revealed, then it becomes possible to accept the doctrine that in a single human life God is revealed more completely than in any other. If we believe that every human soul reveals, reproduces, *incarnates God* to some extent . . . then it becomes possible to believe that in One Man, the self-revelation of God has been signal, supreme, unique.[36]

In Rashdall's nutshell, the doctrine of the incarnation means that the character and teaching of Jesus are the fullest disclosure to us of the character of God and his will for man – or, Jesus is what early Christology called the *Logos* of God. Jesus displays perfectly that moral ideal which is in God eternally. Preaching from his Carlisle pulpit Rashdall summed it all up thus:

> What the doctrine of the Word, and the doctrine of the Holy Trinity, which is based upon it, should most of all teach is simply this: That God is revealed in Christ; that the character of Christ is the character of God; that we may think of God as like Christ; that the character of Christ, so far as it can be summed up in a word, is Love; and that God goes on revealing himself to human souls, especially in that society of Christ's followers we call the Church.[37]

Modernism: an assessment

There can be no doubt that Rashdall, at least, was seeking to be faithful to the formulae of the classic tradition of Christology. He was justifiably hurt by the merely careless accusations that he was *denying* what the creeds asserted. He was genuinely trying, not to amputate, but to translate those formulae into contemporary terms. The summary of his Logos Christology quoted above does not contradict any of the major credal terms relating to the person of Christ, or the mainstream doctrinal accounts of it. It is a question, though, whether it does justice to the *fullness* of the traditional doctrine. To say that Jesus presents us with a perfect example of the moral ideal in God himself, is not strictly *untrue* to the New Testament, to Nicaea and Chalcedon; but neither does it convey the primary thrust of those sources (and for that matter of the ancient heresies as well!) namely, God *doing* something utterly decisive in Christ for the human situation.

J. K. Mozley, in his review of Glazebrook's *The Faith of a Modern Churchman*, had spoken of the absence of a sense of Christianity as 'supernatural revelation'.[38] By this he did not mean a revelation of facts and doctrines unattainable by the unaided mind. But it does mean, he asserted, that Christian belief stands for 'the belief in a breaking-in of God *ab extra* into human history' – the emphasis of the New Testament being that 'The Transcendent One became immanent after a special manner through incarnation'. Mozley was accurately pin-pointing the major theological confusion at the heart of Modernism – a conflation of the specific event of the incarnation with the divine immanence in general. That, Mozley saw, had an immediate further consequence: 'The thought of God's breaking-in to history is lost, and with it is lost that deep stream of Christian gratitude and devotion which has flowed from the realization of what God did for us when He gave His Son.' Less politely, in the furore following the Girton Conference, an anonymous 'Priest of the Diocese of Peterborough' declared in the *Church Times*: 'One thing we gather the Modern Churchmen have succeeded in doing: they have evolved the dullest type of religion that has ever failed to carry conviction to man's reason or to touch his heart.'[39] Hensley Henson felt similarly, and complained of the 'cocksure modernists' who were 'forgetting that a church cannot proceed on the principles which may fitly control the procedure of a univerity'.

It was indeed a paradox that Rashdall's Christology aroused such controversy and yet, at heart, was so vapid and hardly likely to make many converts. It is a highly intellectualistic, moralistic Christ who arises at Girton and reappears to his disciples in Carlisle. It is of course the Christ of philosophical idealism, who somehow personalizes the moral ideal of the universe. It is somehow also redolent of a public-school morality, a Christ who is to be venerated as head boy of the cosmic academy, embodying all the virtues to which the academy aspires. Such a Christ might indeed be acceptable to the current philosophy – though even as Rashdall spoke idealism in Britain was being wrapped in its grave-clothes – but would it actually disturb or *enthuse* people with a vision of truth and life which they could not obtain elsewhere? Was it, in the end, anything other than idealism in Christian phraseology? Rashdall had earlier made an interesting admission concerning the relation between the Christian ethics of the New Testament and the historical Jesus. Rashdall never doubted the existence in history of Jesus Christ, but in his *Ideas and Ideals* he had written:

> The Christian ideal of life is present in the New Testament however it got there. If conscience tells us that the words of Christ are true, they would be true even if those words were wholly the creation of the Church, and none of them were really uttered by the historical Jesus.[40]

In other words, Christianity itself, at its living centre, was an ethic rather than a redemptive revelation.

'If as a system of thought it were negligible, as a prevailing atmosphere it was most influential. It had the effect of making hundreds of priests hesitate over their message.' So runs Roger Lloyd's caustic verdict on Anglican Modernism.[41] The first sentence is probably highly perceptive. The second is only partially true. Equally likely, it made many clergy and laypeople think, which is not to be discouraged in the Churches. In many cases it breathed a sense of liberation into minds otherwise ridden with guilt at the thought of even asking questions about traditional belief, and gave a sense of wider space in which questions could at least be asked. Dogmatism is not the only kind of certainty, nor, for some people, in pulpit or pew, the most persuasive. What was emerging through the Modernist controversy was the possibility of alternative interpretations of doctrine coexisting within the same Church, a possibility mooted by F. D. Maurice in the nineteenth century, but hitherto conceded by relatively few, whether Anglo-Catholics, Evangelicals or – as they appeared to others – the Broad Churchmen themselves. For while the Broad or liberal tradition presented itself in the name of openness and humility before the truth, as manifested in many of the Modern Churchmen it carried more than a whiff of intellectual superiority, with an implied dismissal of all lesser minds. This is what annoyed Henson – 'these cocksure Modernists' – and Mozley's rebuke was as pertinent as it was courteous:

> Try to understand the strengths of your opponents' case; it has more scientific value than you yet realize; it has the support – your attitude compels us now and then to point this out – of men within the Church of England, in Scottish Presbyterianism, and in English nonconformity, who are second to none for range and thoroughness of scholarship, for theological depth and penetration; it rests upon, and is developed out of, belief in one great principle – the free and gracious act of God in sending

His Son for the salvation of the world by Incarnation, Atonement, Resurrection; to that basal faith our theology is the continuation, and our devotion the tribute; our adherence to it is a thing of our minds and hearts and consciences, and we are not convinced that your position is anything but an illogical, and, therefore, finally untenable compromise between natural religion and supernatural Christianity . . . In choosing our side we believe that we can call in aid both from the science which teaches what Christianity originally was, and the experience which reveals in history the secret of its life and power.[42]

The superior style was not unrelated to the contents of Modernism. An analysis of doctrine and imagery which claims to uncover the 'actual' meaning 'behind' the language can come perilously close to a twentieth-century version of second-century *Gnosticism*, with its pretensions to an exclusive, esoteric knowledge of things spiritual, lying hidden under the apostolic teaching. It was no accident that Rashdall saw the logical possibility of dispensing with the historical Jesus, for the logic of idealism is, ultimately, to de-historicize truth, to make actual events, decisions, victories and defeats, successes and tragedies, incidental to universal and general truth which can be eternally contemplated beyond change and chance, and carried in the mind alone – a ballet of bloodless categories, to use Kierkegaard's phrase.

There was another aspect of Anglican Modernism, less often considered, but closely related to this tendency to a bland philosophical idealism. Rashdall belonged to the Christian Social Union, but there was little of the fiery prophet of social righteousness in him, certainly not as compared with Gore, who had championed Christian Socialism at Oxford in the 1880s. In fact the Modern Churchmen as a whole were socially and politically very conservative. Inge, the 'gloomy Dean', was notoriously reactionary and dismissive of the modern age. Glazebrook and Major were similarly nervous of any marriage between liberalism in theology and liberalism, still less socialism, in politics. In his paper at Girton in 1921 Major 'praised Lake for at least dissociating Jesus from political messianism'. And, comments Stephenson, 'All modernists except Brandon have here followed Lake'.[43] Percy Gardner 'did not believe in democracy or feminism. He was a Conservative in politics, a puritan in morals, and in manner a don of the old type'.[44] Of course there have been notable exceptions among individual members of the Modern Churchmen's Union down the years, notably Hewlett Johnson, the 'Red Dean' of Canterbury, and perhaps above all the pacifist Charles Raven, who during the 1930s had a sharp dispute with Major, who in turn sternly resisted any association of the Churchmen's Union with concerns other than the strictly 'theological'. (E. W. Barnes, to be considered in the next chapter, though he associated with the Modern Churchmen, and even gave a paper at the 1921 Girton Conference, was never actually a member of the Union.) Surveying the Modern Churchmen's conference programmes down the years, nothing is more striking than the virtual absence during the 1920s and 1930s, of any attention to social and political questions in the light of Christian belief, modern or otherwise. The implications for belief of historical and literary criticism, relations between religion and science, Christianity and other religions – these abound among the titles of papers given. But one would hardly judge, looking at these agendas of concern, that Church and society were living through post-war reconstruction, a General Strike, a world recession, the growth of totalitarianism and the threat of yet another world war. Only when we get to 1940 – which to say the least was leaving it quite late in the day – do we find a paper such as 'Bolshevism and Nazism' being featured, and, ironically, war prevented that conference taking place.

Was there, in much of that early Modernism, an instinctive resistance to *any* notion of incursion, disruption, discontinuity, in any sphere, natural or human? Was the dislike of 'miracle' in the natural order more closely parallel than the Modernists cared to think to their aversion to radical intervention and change in the human social order? Taking the disputants of 1912–22 in their totality, today's Christian of 'liberal' sympathies may not find it so easy to decide, after all, who is the more appealing: the intellectual *illuminati* of Girton, open and inquiring and socially bland; or Frank Weston, stubbornly refusing to enter the thought-world of the twentieth century, yet the ardent Christian Socialist, the outspoken defender of African workers' rights and flaming critic of Anglican racism? Idealism can all too easily become a way of saying 'Peace, all is well', recognizing, as the only real problem, the question of why it does not always *appear* to be an equable, harmonious universe. It is perhaps revealing, if unfortunate, that the picture on the dust-cover of Alan Stephenson's history of the Modernist movement, is neither a face, or faces, or a place, but a row of dated looking books. The Modernists who, like Inge or Raven or Johnson, were really interesting figures, were interesting mainly for reasons other than their Modernism.

Aftermath: The Doctrinal Commission

The most substantial legacy of the 1918–21 disputes over Modernism was the Archbishops' Commission on Doctrine in the Church of England. It was not wholly, in origin, a response to that controversy. The first initiative came from Hubert Burge, Bishop of Oxford, and a group of younger Anglo-Catholics following the Anglo-Catholic Congress of 1920. Randall Davidson was at first hesitant in the extreme. But the Girton incident increased the impetus for Anglicanism to discover and assert just what range of doctrinal agreement it was supposed to comprehend. Convocation, meeting in May 1922, unanimously passed a resolution much in the spirit of the 1914 statement, that is, on the one hand reasserting the necessity for the Church to adhere to the Nicene Creed – 'and in particular concerning the eternal pre-existence of the Son of God' – and on the other recognizing the gain from 'fearless and reverent' inquiry using modern historical and literary methods. It would seem that, so long as Davidson was at Lambeth, anything was allowable so long as it was 'reverent'. (Davidson's private opinion of Major was that he 'takes himself a little too seriously, and rather puts on the dress of a leader, which he is not'.)[45] The ultimate in Anglican balancing acts is to be found in the resolution's closing sentences:

> [This house] deprecates the mere blunt denunciation of contributions made by earnest men in their endeavour to bring new light to bear upon these difficult and anxious problems. At the same time it sees a grave and obvious danger in the publication of debateable suggestions as if they were ascertained truths, and emphasises the need of caution in this whole matter, especially on the part of responsible teachers in the Church.[46]

Davidson's caution about the proposed Commission was eventually overcome, not just by the arguments of others, but by his own percipient judgement, which he voiced in his own speech to that debate in Convocation: 'I believe that the harm which has arisen from some of the controversies in the last 50 years has been largely because of the lack of anything in the nature of mutual conference among the people ranged on particular sides.'[47] As an exercise in 'mutual conference', the Commission which Davidson and the Archbishop of York finally appointed in 1923, certainly was to fulfil its task. Its terms of reference were: 'To consider the nature and grounds of Christian doctrine with a view to demonstrating the extent of existing agreement within the Church of England and with a view to investigating how far it is possible to remove or diminish existing differences.' It was therefore in no sense an ecclesiastical court, or a body empowered to state what *should* be regarded as acceptable Anglican doctrine. It comprised some twenty-five theologians representing high church, evangelical and liberal opinion. Streeter was a representative of the liberal wing, Will Spens the catholic; Burge was the first chairman, succeeded on his death by William Temple.

The Commission did not exactly rush to conclusions. Its report *Doctrine in the Church of England*[48] did not appear until 1938, by which time Temple was Archbishop of York, and many of the leading figures of the original controversies were dead – Gore, Weston, Davidson, Rashdall, even Streeter. But its lengthy, even leisurely, proceedings had a symbolic effect. Anglicans were at least talking to one another, instead of at or past each other. The Introduction could say with some conviction: 'If God is love, it is only among people animated by mutual love that understanding of Him can be advanced. To admit acrimony in theological discussion is in itself more fundamentally heretical than any erroneous opinion upheld or condemned in the course of the discussion.'[49] In fact, the sharpness and acrimony of controversy lessened considerably in any case in England during the inter-war years. There was controversy in areas other than strictly theological – over Prayer Book revision especially. But also, more positively, those years saw the flowering of one of the most creative periods in British theology. The controversies of the first two decades of the century seemed to have done some of the heavy spade work in turning over the soil and exposing to the air the issues that theology would have to tackle in the modern age, by people prepared to dig still deeper and more carefully. It was the age in which flourished, as well as the mature Temple, such figures as Edwyn Hoskyns, Leonard Hodgson, F. R. Tennant, Edwyn Bevan, John Oman, H. H. Farmer, C. H. Dodd, H. Wheeler Robinson – many of them non-Anglicans but then theology was becoming an increasingly ecumenical enterprise – not to mention the brothers Donald and John Baillie in Scotland. Then too, by the early 1930s the newer, astringent note of continental neo-orthodoxy began to be heard, as the works of Barth and Brunner made their appearance in English along with Kierkegaard and Buber. 'If we began our work again today,' Temple admitted in introducing the Report, 'its perspectives would be different.'

Some have always maintained that the Report was never allowed to make its full weight felt in Anglicanism, partly for circumstantial reasons, especially of course the onset of war in 1939. Others find it too bland by half, amounting to little more than 'X says this, while Y says that, and all are good Anglicans'. But it does make certain points which, for the sake of seeing issues in longer historical perspective, will have to be made again and again. For instance, on Christology, it points out that from early times two broad approaches have coexisted in Christianity. One approach ('Antiochene'), begins with Christ's humanity (and from it came the Nestorian heresy). The other ('Alexandrian') begins with his divinity (and from it emerged the monophysite heresy). Neither school intended to deny either the divinity or the humanity – but tended to. The Church affirmed both, each in its completeness. Each approach needs the corrective of the other. On miracles, including the virgin birth, while on the whole sympathizing with the traditional view, the Report acknowledged that those who suspended belief in their historicity might well do so on *religious* grounds. Congruity – which in 1919 Chase had invoked as grounds for the historicity of the virgin birth – was thus being seen as capable of cutting both ways. Whether contemporary Anglicanism as a whole has yet conceded this point may be open to question.

Notes

1 H. Henson (ed.), *Church Problems. A View of Modern Anglicanism*, London: John Murray 1900, p. 1.
2 See O. Chadwick, *Hensley Henson: A Study in Friction between Church and State*, Oxford: Clarendon Press 1983; H. Henson, *Retrospect of an Unimportant Life* (2 vols), Oxford: Oxford University Press 1942–3.
3 Henson, *Retrospect*, vol. i. p. 80f.
4 ibid., p. 80.
5 H. Henson, *Christian Liberty and Other Sermons*, London: Macmillan 1918, p. 100.
6 Henson, *Retrospect*, vol. i. p. 179.
7 *The Times*, 20 December 1917.
8 *The Times*, 22 December 1917.
9 *The Times*, 23 December 1917.
10 ibid.
11 *The Times*, 29 December 1917.
12 *The Times*, 1 January 1918.
13 *The Times*, 5 January 1918.
14 Henson, *Retrospect*, vol. i, p. 235.
15 ibid., p. 233.
16 ibid., p. 214.
17 Chadwick, op. cit., p. 148f.
18 See A. M. G. Stephenson, *The Rise and Decline of English Modernism*, London: SPCK 1984, on which this chapter draws.
19 ibid., p. 61.
20 M. G. Glazebrook, *The Faith of a Modern Churchman* (No. 1 in the Modern Churchman's Library), London: John Murray 1918.
21 ibid., p. 28.
22 ibid., p. 32f.

23 ibid., p. 71.
24 ibid., p. 76f.
25 ibid., p. 80.
26 *Church Times*, 15 March 1918.
27 F. H. Chase, *Belief and Creed*, London: Macmillan 1919.
28 ibid., p. 77f.
29 ibid., p. 78f.
30 Stephenson, op. cit., p. 111.
31 Letter from Revd G. H. Morrell, Catford, *Church Times*, 2 September 1921.
32 Stephenson, op. cit., p. 118.
33 ibid., p. 119.
34 H. Rashdall, *Jesus, Human and Divine*, London: Andrew Melrose 1922, p. 17 (Girton Paper on 'Christ as Logos and Son of God').
35 ibid., p. 19.
36 ibid., p. 20.
37 ibid., p. 37f.
38 See note 26.
39 *Church Times*, 19 August 1921.
40 Quoted in Roger Lloyd, *The Church of England in the Twentieth Century*, London: Longmans, Green and Co. 1946, p. 80.
41 ibid., p. 103.
42 See note 26.
43 Stephenson, op. cit., p. 116.
44 ibid., p. 44.
45 G. K. A. Bell, *Randall Davidson, Archbishop of Canterbury*, Oxford: Oxford University Press 1935, p. 1142.
46 ibid.
47 ibid., p. 1143.
48 *Doctrine in the Church of England*. The Report of the Commission on Christian Doctrine Appointed by the Archbishops of Canterbury and York in 1923. London: SPCK 1938 (reprinted 1982).
49 ibid., p. 23.

5 Two Individualists: T. R. Glover and E. W. Barnes

The controversies so far surveyed have largely been 'doctrinal' in the sense that they have been arguments over statements, concepts and ideas: how much of the creed is to be accepted as literal fact, and how much symbolic; which reformulations of the classical christological statements in modern thought-forms and philosophical terms are valid, and which are not; and so forth. But on all sides in such debates, the assumption has been of the prime importance of expressing Christian belief in clearly articulated words, concepts and ideas, gathered in coherent doctrine, whether traditional or 'modern'. That assumption, at least, was largely shared by Gore and Streeter, Weston and Rashdall. But lurking beneath all such arguments, a third party has been waiting to posit an alternative approach. This is, that Christian believing is not primarily a matter of doctrinal formulae and verbalized concepts. What matters above all is the 'spiritual' or 'religious' *experience*, that which touches the heart, changes the will, uplifts the emotions and releases new moral energies. This has of course always been an important strand in Western religious life, whether in mysticism, or eighteenth-century pietism, or in the Quaker emphasis on the 'inner light'. On the Continent Schleiermacher gave it powerful impetus with his emphasis on religion as 'the feeling of being utterly dependent', and with his description of doctrines as statements having meaning only as referring to the religious consciousness and feelings. It was revived in those versions of Liberal Protestantism towards the end of the nineteenth century which emphasized the moral influence of Jesus, and his spiritual or divine 'worth', rather than his divine-human nature. In an age when historical criticism and scientific rationalism were corroding the apparent reliability of the biblical records and the credal formulae, 'experience' itself offered a kind of immunity from the acids of modernity. After Darwin, after Strauss, whatever else might be dubious as historical fact or literal truth, the actual experience of inner warmth and light stimulated by religious influences could not be gainsaid. This was the talisman with which the believer could venture into the dark, unknown and hostile world of modernity. Jesus remained the joy of loving hearts, the fount of life, the light of men, however dubious became the traditional ways of asserting and defending his unique significance. He remained an influence, an experience.

The two figures we shall consider in this chapter had at least this much in common, that each in his own way stood strongly for this assertion of 'experience' over against doctrine or dogma. That said, there may well be surprise at yoking together the Baptist layman T. R. Glover (1869–1943) with the Anglican Bishop E. W. Barnes (1874–1953). They were indeed very different personalities – to call them 'individualists' is admittedly a paradoxical way of expressing a likeness – and their very different careers gave them markedly different responsibilities. But both of them became embroiled in controversy within their respective communions, Barnes much more drastically and dramatically – and more frequently – than Glover, but in the final analysis for not dissimilar reasons. What is more, between the two figures there are actual biographical parallels and relationships of quite considerable importance. Though Barnes became an Anglican and a bishop, like Glover he too came from a Baptist home. Both men studied at Cambridge, brilliantly so, and became dons there – Glover for life, Barnes till early middle age – and for a significant period they were contempories and knew each other. For the first time, virtually, in this study we can leave Oxford and the pervasive effect of its late nineteenth-century philosophical idealism. (Neither Glover nor Barnes was affected even by the Cambridge brand of idealism as taught by J. E. McTaggart.) Each was an acknowledged authority and expert teacher in his chosen discipline, Glover in classical studies, Barnes in mathematics. Neither had any formal training in theology (a damning enough fact for some of their critics), and their approaches to theology and questions of belief were greatly influenced by the perspectives of, respectively, the classical historian and the natural scientist.

Each was a character of considerable self-will, and independence of mind. As with all 'strong personalities' each made and lost many friends by the manner as well as the content of his speaking. The temptation with all treatments of such people is to be so fascinated by their 'individuality' as to lose sight of their representative roles amid the movements in thought – social and cultural as well as ecclesiastical – of the time, and in the debates which they provoked. In standing so strongly for themselves, Glover and Barnes were also voicing what many less articulate people were wanting to say – or ask. Through their writings, both men had a following which reached well beyond the usual church readership into the public beyond. Bearing these perspectives in mind, we shall look at the careers and controversies of each in turn, and in conclusion make a further brief comparison and assessment of their significance.

T. R. Glover[1]

During the infamous 'Down Grade' controversy of 1887–88,[2] which resulted in the withdrawal from the Baptist Union of C. H. Spurgeon, prince of preachers, no one felt more strongly about the need to preserve liberty of interpretation than Richard Glover, eminent minister of Tyndale Baptist Church, Bristol. Glover's church, set on the boundary between the smart and growing suburb of Redland and the genteel 'village' of Clifton, was a prime example of Nonconformity's expansion both in numbers and confidence, helped greatly by the growing prosperity of its largely middle-class membership. Vigorous preaching and energetic involvement in the affairs of Bristol, philanthropic work in the poorer areas of the city, staunch support for Liberal politics at home and for missionary work overseas, marked this church and its ministry. Glover was an able scholar, and wrote a fair number of biblical commentaries and devotional books in a liberal theological vein. At the time and thereafter, he felt deeply wounded by Spurgeon's attack on the Baptist Union as a 'confederacy in evil' on account of its harbouring increasingly liberal theological tendencies, and was certain that he himself was one of Spurgeon's prime targets, alongside others such as John Clifford.

At the time, Richard Glover's son, Terrot Reaveley (he took the latter as his usual Christian name), was in his late teens. He was, and remained, deeply attached to his father, who was probably the single most important influence on his life. The son never forgot the pain the episode caused his parent, and ever afterwards the name 'Spurgeon' signified to him an unforgiveable sin. This deep emotional inheritance was to be a serious factor in his relationships with fellow Baptists for the rest of his days. To understand what happened later, a further consequence of the Down Grade controversy must be noted. While very few ministers actually followed Spurgeon in seceding from the Union, a significant body of Baptist opinion remained sympathetic to him, and did not feel that justice had been entirely executed. A strong body of 'Spurgeonite' Baptist life continued, wary of liberal theology and stressing the evangelical hallmarks: biblical inspiration, personal conversion, the saving power of the blood of Christ shed in the sacrificial, substitutionary atonement, and the second advent. The peculiar form of agreement in doctrinal belief among Baptists also needs to be noted. The Baptist Union is an association of independent local churches. The principle upon which this association is based is not that of subscription to a creed or any formal doctrinal statement, but rather an acknowledgement of certain beliefs held in common. By the late nineteenth century, these common beliefs were stated (in addition to those specifically referring to baptism and church order) to be 'those commonly denominated evangelical' – evangelical as distinct from either 'catholic' or 'rationalist'. For some Baptists by this time, even the word 'evangelical' had too many restrictive connotations, whereas Spurgeon had hoped that the Union might adopt a much more specific and comprehensive doctrinal declaration. In such a structure, the dynamic of maintaining orthodoxy is quite different from that in a hierarchical Church. There is no human 'authority' above the local church, to which assent must be given. The onus falls on ministers or churches, who feel that the Union or the churches as a whole are not holding to a sufficiently orthodox course, to secede and steer in what they believe is the direction of truth. Very rarely has that course been taken.

In 1888 T. R. Glover went up to St John's College, Cambridge, to read classics, and so was among the first generations of Nonconformists to benefit from the abolition of religious tests at the ancient universities. He was elected to a Fellowship of St John's in 1892, and for the rest of his days his life was centred on Cambridge, apart from a five-year spell teaching in Canada at the turn of the century. He quickly made his name as an outstanding lecturer in the university, especially in Roman life and thought, and almost to his death wrote prodigiously for both the student and the more popular market. In addition to his commentaries on Virgil, Horace and Herodotus, his better-known works included: *Life and Letters in the Fourth Century* (1901), *The Conflict of Religions in the Early Roman Empire* (1909), *From Pericles to Philip* (1917), *Democracy in the Ancient World* (1927), *The Ancient World* (1935) and *The Challenge of the Greek* (1942). In 1920 he was elected Public Orator of the University, a post he held for eighteen years. His election was in the face of some Conservative and Anglican opposition, fearing the consequences of allowing a specimen of militant Nonconformity into a position which, in its role of preparing and delivering Latin orations in honour of the recipients of honorary degrees, represents the university on its most dignified public occasions. Glover never had difficulty in providing the correct blend of erudition, style and wit, nor did he abuse the position for sectarian purposes.

That blend was the hallmark of all Glover's speaking and writing, laced though it often was with prejudice and pugnacity. 'You disagree with everybody and get on with most people, I notice,' a colleague once remarked to him.[3] Glover was larger than life, physically and in every other way. Undergraduates would flee at the sight of him emerging from his rooms in St John's, lest any of them be press-ganged into marching a mile or more with him on his homeward route, to be subjected to a welter of conversation on any topic under the sun. Reminiscences abound of his overbearing manner, yet also of his candid opinions being voiced with a playful, boyish smile on his lips even while delivering the sternest rebuke. He liked to be argued against. A young assistant minister at St Andrew's Street Baptist Church was berated by an irate Glover for his first sermon. The minister, despite his diminutive size and relative youthfulness, had the temerity next day to call on Glover and demand the chance to state his case. Glover was amused, and the two were friends for life. Violet Hedger, one of the first women to be ordained among the Baptists, found Glover affecting astonishment that she had presumed actually to attend a meeting for ministers at the Baptist Union Assembly, and asked her what St Paul would have thought about that. 'I'm not sure,' she replied, 'but I will ask him when I meet him – that is, if I ever get to heaven.' 'Perhaps it will be better for the peace of heaven if you do not,' said Glover.[4] One of the neatest thumbnail sketches was supplied by the secretary of a missionary society:

> He cannot be overlooked when he is present, for he has a way of appearing ever and anon out of the blue, making meteoric flashes, and as abruptly departing . . . His speeches are always challenging and provocative, and, as everyone knows, he has the family gift of coining phrases and introducing unexpected ideas. Also, he is altogether charming, even when devastating.[5]

Hensley Henson, after a chance meeting with him in Cambridge, wondered how such an intelligent man could be a Baptist. His university lectures were popular, and if the purpose of the lecture is to infect the audience with enthusiasm for the subject at least as much as to impart information, then by all accounts Glover's lectures were brilliant. As one student put it, he did not lecture, he talked. He talked in such a way as to bring the ancient past to life, with sympathy, flashes of humour, and constant allusions to parallels and contrasts in present-day life and issues. He was equally lively in print. Popular and academic tastes change, but half a century later *The Ancient World*, for example, still has a freshness about it, a kind of erudite mischievousness which will awaken the interest of all but the dullest reader. Here is how he introduces the history of Troy:

> Troy town, they tell us, covered roughly as much ground as New Street Railway Station in Birmingham, perhaps a little less; but, as the Greeks said, 'charm goes with the little'. Troy has meant more in History, and so far has done more for human happiness. The story is told by Homer; and men have debated who Homer was, and how many people he was; was he a guild of hereditary poets? or was he some one, perhaps a prince like Pisistratus of Athens, who collected all the 'lays' of the 'bards', and wove them rather carelessly into one story? Are there not contradictions? One wonders if people who talk so have read *Don Quixote* . . .[6]

But it was above all in the ancient literature and poetry, especially the Latin, that Glover excelled. He consciously rebelled against the standard Cambridge approach of purely philological and textual analysis. At least he refused to regard these approaches as the only or most important ways of dealing with a medium which was essentially *human*. He wanted to reach, and bring to life, the actual poet behind the poetry, thinking, feeling and willing. As T. H. Robinson put it, 'He had the very rare gift, almost amounting to genius, of throwing himself into the personality of the writer. As he read Virgil he was, for the time, Virgil, looking on life as the poet saw it, sharing his emotions and opinions.'[7] Glover was employing by instinct what he had scarcely, if at all, ever heard of: the hermeneutical approach to historical and literary texts advocated by Schleiermacher and developed by Wilhelm Dilthey, which sees historiography as the art of 'reliving' the writer's experience in one's own imagination and awareness of what living means. He had enough personality to spare for such an exercise, and one of the questions which this approach inevitably provokes, is whether Glover really brought Virgil into the twentieth century, or whether he simply put himself into the ancient world, jokes and all.

All this is no mere preamble to Glover's religious and theological contribution. For Glover, Jesus and the New Testament writers themselves belonged to the ancient world. It was as they were studied according to the same canons of historical and literary research as were employed upon their Greek and Roman contemporaries, that their uniqueness would be demonstrated and thrown into relief. This, however, is to anticipate slightly a sketch of Glover's religious and theological development, which must now be given.

Under his father's ministry and personal influence, Glover had imbibed a faith imbued with a strong sense of the need and right of private judgement in spiritual matters. During his undergraduate days, and for some years while he was a don, his faith underwent stringent questioning as it faced all the issues brought by late

Victorian scepticism: historical criticism, the scientific explanation of the cosmos in natural terms, the pure relativity of the Christian claims in face of the multiplicity of religions, and the sheer sense of the insecurity and uncertainty of knowledge. When, around 1893, he did feel able to articulate a mature faith for himself, he spoke of it in terms of faith in Jesus, rather than faith in the Bible, or even faith in God. He wrote in a letter to his father:

> [Christianity] has met the need and fulfilled the wants of mankind at its best, and as the universe seems generally well contrived with a complement for everything, it is not improbable that here too need felt and need met are in a line with things generally and therefore what commonly appeals to most men at their best is probably as true as anything else . . . Judging too from his character and personality Jesus seems more likely to be right and reliable than ordinary teachers. Where he does speak of what is beyond our proving, he does not give himself away as others do. In any case his own attitude towards the unprovable is sounder than that of any of his expositors. And it seems to me that all one can do is to take up his position as far as possible. Also his view of God, whatever he was himself, is the only thing that can make life tolerable. But . . . we have to take most things on trust from him as resurrection, a future life, his relations with God and perhaps even more. Knowing then that the Galilean saw and acquiesced in the order of the universe, in life and death and bereavement, and wished nothing changed and found nothing to regret for all his appreciation of man's mind and feeling, I think we must be content too.[8]

This was only the beginning, not the end, of Glover's personal credo which matured with the years. But the 'reliability' of Jesus himself, the impression of his 'character and personality' were to be the linchpin of Glover's belief and religious thought to the end of his days.

For a time Glover's denominational allegiances loosened. He frequently attended Emmanuel Congregational Church (and so heard P. T. Forsyth during part of his ministry there), and during the early 1900s became involved with the Society of Friends. While he deeply appreciated the Friends' inwardness of devotion, he gradually came to feel that their religious sentiment was not sufficiently anchored in the historical origin of Christianity, and above all the historical Founder himself. In addition, when the Great War broke out in 1914, while initially in some sympathy with the pacifist stance, he reluctantly conceded that to fight was the lesser of evils. He returned with more conviction to the Baptist fold and there he remained for the rest of his life. Till the end of the 1914–18 War he was a staunch supporter of the Passive Resistance Campaign, the Free Church protest against state funding for church schools, refusing to pay that portion of his rates destined for such purposes.

As was noted earlier, Glover's love of the ancient world and his devotion to Jesus were closely related. It was well said of him that what made his portrait of Jesus so fresh and appealing was that he saw Jesus through the eyes of the pagan world 'at its best', as Virgil or Horace might have done. Popular Christian apologetics has sometimes given the impression that the Graeco-Roman world needs to be seen in blackest hue in order to point up the contrast made by the coming of Christ. Glover would have none of this. If one could show that Christ and the gospel immeasurably enriched the old world even at its *best*, then the greater service would be done both to learning and the faith. It was a mature attitude.[9] There was, indeed, in Glover a real humanism, and it was an element which he knew had to be argued for in present-day Christianity (at least among Baptists and Evangelicals) as in the first centuries. Among Glover's best pieces of translation is his version of Tertullian, and it may be that temperamentally Glover was a twentieth-century version of the vexatious Christian polemicist of the second century. But whereas Tertullian had weighed in heavily against secular learning – 'What has Athens to do with Jerusalem?' – on that issue Glover felt much more at one with Clement of Alexandria, who, as he put it in *The Conflict of Religions*, 'has first of all to fight the battle of education inside the Church, to convince his friends that culture counts, that philosophy is inevitable and of use at once for the refutation of opponents and for the achievement of the full significance of faith'.[10]

By 1914, Glover was a frequent speaker at Student Christian Movement conferences, and had produced a number of biblical and historical studies for that kind of readership. He was to write prolifically for the popular religious market all his life. The book which made him famous, *The Jesus of History*, was based on material he used for a wartime lecture tour of India, and it appeared in 1917, published by the SCM Press. It carried a foreword by the Archbishop of Canterbury, Randall Davidson, which was testimony to the improving climate of interdenominational relations, but the book sold itself on its own merits. In fact it was a phenomenal – and continuing – publishing success, running through twenty-five editions and 124,000 copies in thirty years. Story has it that it was the success of this venture, more than any other single item, which enabled the SCM Press, hitherto simply the publications department of the Student Christian Movement, to be set up as an independent publishing concern. Its appeal was felt throughout the English-speaking world, and by readers of all Christian traditions and none. It is the quintessential Glover, even though he felt obliged to follow it up with

Jesus in the Experience of Men. He himself must have felt it to be so, for he dedicated it to his aged father.

Seventy years on, even the title now appears *passé*, signifying an age when it was naively assumed that Jesus 'as he was' could be directly accessible to us across the vast cultural divide between the first and twentieth centuries, and bypassing the early Christian community which modified the picture of Jesus in accordance with *its* own needs, long before we got near with our presuppositions. There is little about the eschatological element either in the Jewish background or in Jesus' own teaching. Glover was, however, versed in much of the higher criticism of the day, and had read Streeter thoroughly. He knew that the Gospels were not biographies in the modern sense, but comprised 'fragments'. Behind the fragments and reminiscences – possibly even caricatures – there was nevertheless a *personality* indelibly impressed upon the record. And it was in terms of *personality* that Glover dealt with the gospel material and its central figure:

> The central figure of the Gospels must impress every attentive reader as at least a man of marked personality. He has his own attitude to life, his own views of God and man, and all else, and his own language . . . So much his own are all these things that it is hard to imagine the possibility of his being a mere literary creation by several authors writing independent works. Indeed, when we reflect on the character of the Gospels, their origin and composition, and then consider the sharp, strong claims of the personality depicted, we shall be apt to feel his claim to historicity to be stronger than we supposed.[11]

Glover, reflecting his time, did not appreciate the extent to which the early *community* may have been creatively involved in shaping the gospel narratives. Nor, perhaps, did he appreciate how fully creative he himself may have been in depicting the Christ of *The Jesus of History*. One wonders if any of his more candid friends ever suggested to him that the 'marked personality' of independent judgement was an apt self-portrait. But there is strength and even a certain grandeur in Glover's Jesus, for:

> He is not to be trapped in his talk, to be cajoled or flattered. There is greatness in his language – in his reference of everything to great principles and to God – greatness in his freedom from ambition – in his contempt of advertisement and popularity – in his appeal to the best in men – in his belief in men – in his power of winning and keeping friends – in his gift for making great men out of petty.[12]

On the other side of the account, Glover, who was generally averse to sentimentality, verges on the coy and mawkish in his reconstructions of home life in Nazareth, and his portrait of Mary would serve as a charter for anti-feminism.

Glover's account, then, is of a human Jesus striking in his personality. How does this portrait bear on the traditional doctrinal language about Christ? It must first be recognized that Glover was typical of much Nonconformist theology in being centred on the atonement rather than on the incarnation. Not that these two can be meaningfully separated in the final analysis, but it is the case that in any one thinker or any one tradition, the centre of gravity tends to lie with one rather than the other, and, broadly speaking, Anglicanism has emphasized incarnation, Free Church theology the cross. Glover's view of the work of Christ, however, had difficulties with many of the traditional terms in which it was customarily expressed. So:

> When we look at the terms, we find that the essence of sacrifice was reconciliation between God and man . . . and that the Messiah was understood to be destined to achieve God's purpose and God's meaning for mankind and for each man . . . Reconciliation, the victory of God, the mutual intelligibility of God and man – all three terms centre in one great thought, a new union between God and man. That . . . is the common element; and that is, as men have conceived it, the very heart of the Christian experience.[13]

Atonement was for Glover less a transaction executed by Christ on behalf of God and man, than a new experience of communion with God within the human heart, wrought by attachment to Jesus.

> The change that Jesus definitely operates in men, they have described in various ways – rebirth, salvation, a new heart, and so forth. What they have always emphasized in Jesus Christ, is that they find he changes their outlook and develops new instincts in them, and that in one way and another he saves from sin; and they have been men who have learnt and adopted Jesus' own estimate of sin . . . This new life is at all events all the evidence available; and how much it means is very difficult to estimate without some personal experience.[14]

It is difficult to estimate how far Glover's subjective account of the work of Christ allowed him any Christology in the proper sense. On the one hand, Glover was too good a historian to overlook the importance of the development of doctrine in the early Church. He could wax eloquent on the significance of Nicaea where, he argued, if victory had gone to the Arians it would have meant the death of the Christian movement. On one occasion he sharply crossed swords with a correspondent in the *Baptist Times* who referred to the 'hair-splitting' of Nicaea and who continued:

> We should be grateful that the safe custody of Christianity has never been

> entrusted to learned disputants. Mental gymnastics have their peculiar value, but only to those who exercise them. It should be obvious that any word or creed that in itself brings a tear to an already stricken world must in its very nature be anti-Christian.[15]

Glover fumed against this as typical of much supposedly Christian sentiment.

> It is not obvious to me, either from nature, history or religion, that tears are the ultimate criterion of truth. But even if we take this lachrymose standard for life, have no tears been saved for mankind by the insistence of the Church that Jesus Christ was not a pagan's demi-god, a myth, a fable, bound to vanish, or a poor creature like ourselves? Do let us brace ourselves. Christ made no such fuss about tears. It is all of a piece with Christian Science nonsense about pain. The most serious fact yet known about pain is that Christ chose pain – chose tears, too, when he might have escaped them.[16]

Again, the question is answered in terms of the personality and life of Jesus rather than of an act of God through Jesus. And it is an answer which is prepared to say what Jesus is not, rather than who he positively *is*. Glover might be dismissive of Quakers as lacking any Christology, but some found Glover woefully inadequate at this point too (a standing joke among younger ministers and theological students was that, whenever Glover felt the discussion was getting out of his depth, he would say, 'Let's sing a hymn!'). For Glover God is unknown except as the Father of Jesus. But it is a God who is taught and 'shown' by Jesus rather than a God who *acts* through Jesus. It is also, to a serious degree, a God who is *limited* to the individual personality of Jesus, a personality whom Glover in turn, in *The Jesus of History* and other works, wrenches unnaturally from his most immediate historical context, the Jewish. One might have expected that from his knowledge of early church history Glover would have wished to avoid a repetition of the Marcionite heresy, which declared the Old Testament to be no longer valid for Christians, and the Father of Jesus Christ to be a quite different God from the Creator and Law-giver of the Hebrew Scriptures. Glover, however, found repellent the polemical use of the Old Testament by the early Fathers. Indeed, as time went on he found the Old Testament itself increasingly distasteful, and objected to ministers taking sermon texts from it. Arthur Dakin, reviewing Glover's *The World of the New Testament*, commended Glover for picturing paganism in its strengths as well as its weaknesses but shrewdly observed, 'One sometimes wonders whether enthusiasm for the Greek does not go a little too far, whether he was really all that was claimed for him, and whether by many writers he is not exalted at the expense of the Jew.'[17] *The Jesus of History* takes a thoroughly negative view of Judaism in relation to Jesus and his teaching. While it was clearly a tongue-in-cheek remark, nothing could be more damaging to Glover's reputation as a biblical historian, than his statement to some Cambridge students that, 'Our Lord cannot have received much benefit from the intoning of the Psalms and from the expositions of the synagogue at Nazareth, yet it was his custom to be there each Sabbath.'[18]

It would be wrong to suggest that Glover had no sense of the social, cultural and economic settings in which life is lived – his accounts of the ancient world make that clear. But the individual personality, in abstraction, takes over in both the ancient history and the Christology (or, as some might say, the Jesusology). Glover, lecturing on the famous speech of Pericles, stated that Athens was working out an ideal of humanity, which abides to this day. 'You in America, we in England, conform too much to type. Athens is the school of Hellas *because* [quoting Thucydides] "each individual amongst us can in his own person, with the utmost versatility and grace, prove himself self-sufficient in the most varied forms of activity".'[19] It is then but the smallest step for Glover, writing on the meaning of the gospel in relation to Christian reunion (which he opposed on the grounds of religious freedom) to say that

> Jesus, like Greek thinkers, and like the scholars and pioneers of Renaissance and Reformation, laid a very remarkable stress on the individual. It was the glory of the Athenian democracy that it discovered the individual . . . Athens preferred her citizens not to be of one mould; she preferred them different . . . The great funeral speech of Pericles shows what can be made of the individual, but it does not give him anything approaching the significance which Jesus gives him, as recorded in St Luke's fifteenth chapter.[20]

This emphasis upon the individual was, as we shall see, the root of Glover's problem with the atonement, and the reason why, to the annoyance of conservative Baptists, he could render a 'subjective' account of the doctrine.

The Jesus of History was well liked by liberal-minded people in all denominations. It was included in the list of recommended reading for the 1921 Modern Churchmen's Conference at Girton. Conservative Evangelicals were suspicious. What about the miracles, on which Glover was studiously silent? What about the saving significance of the death of Christ? Was salvation, peace with God, merely a matter of Jesus creating in us a new sense of God and of filial piety? The spirit of the book seemed far removed from the hymn,

Bearing shame and scoffing rude,
In my place condemned he stood;
Sealed my pardon with his blood;
Hallelujah! what a Saviour!

There were rumblings when Glover was elected to the Presidency of the Baptist Union for the year 1924–5. Even some of his friends feared that he might be a divisive influence on the denomination. However, he went to some lengths to mollify the conservative wing, or at least not to antagonize them. He took as his theme for the Assembly in 1924 'God in Christ', and his presidential address closed on a designedly reassuring note: 'As I grow older I want more and more to preach Christ without theory, to tell people the tremendous facts associated with Him – the fact of victory over sin, the changed life, and the most amazing fact of all, Himself.'[21]

Christ without theory? It sounds attractive, but nevertheless a surprising statement to hear from one who had sat under P. T. Forsyth's ministry. At the end of his presidency, there was genial laughter when, commending his successor, Glover told the Baptist throng, 'I hope you will look as well after his orthodoxy as you have looked after mine.'[22] In part, Glover owed his post-war popularity among Baptists to his opposition to any form of reunion of the Churches in response to the Lambeth Appeal, and along the lines being advocated by J. H. Shakespeare, General Secretary of the Baptist Union. That, for the moment, tempered fundamentalist criticism. Across the Atlantic, it did not save him from some quite scurrilous attacks by the self-styled Bible Baptist Union of Canada, led by a Dr D. T. Shields, when he visited Toronto in 1928 (the fact that even such a transparently evangelical saint as F. B. Meyer was *persona non grata* with Shields gave Glover little chance).

Back in England, there were signs of mounting theological tensions among Baptists during the late 1920s. The Spurgeon tradition was alive and well, led by H. Tydeman Chilvers, incumbent of Spurgeon's old pulpit at the Metropolitan Tabernacle (though neither church nor minister were in membership with the Union), and editor of the monthly *Sword and the Trowel*, the magazine begun by Spurgeon and in which the Down Grade controversy had been launched in 1887. Accusations of 'modernism' were being levelled at the Union from some quarters. A particular *cause célèbre* was that of W. E. Dalling, a candidate for the ministry who had not attended one of the denomination's colleges, but who was accepted by the Union on condition that he undertook some personal tuition and reading under the guidance of A. C. Underwood, Principal of Rawdon College.

Dalling, however, protested that neither 'the Modernist Dr Underwood' nor the books which he was recommending were acceptable to him, and demanded an alternative tutor. A minor pamphlet war was launched by Dalling and his sympathizers, alerting Baptists to 'the modernistic propaganda which proceeds and grows in Baptist Colleges'.[23]

Then, in 1931, the Baptist Union decided to mount a 'Discipleship Campaign' to combat the slow but steady decline in church membership over the previous twenty-five years or so. It was the sort of operation which, initiated in ecclesiastical headquarters, so often sounds tired before it has even begun (several years later the *Baptist Times* was reporting that the campaign was still slowly gathering momentum). Every Baptist was challenged to win at least one more person for Christ. Preparation for the campaign would involve the familiar exercise of study groups, for which notes would be supplied on basic aspects of the Christian faith. Who better to prepare a booklet on 'Fundamentals' than T. R. Glover?

Glover's notes *Fundamentals* appeared at the end of 1931. The booklet covered Sin, Punishment, Repentance, Conversion, Salvation, Atonement, Justification and Sanctification. As an example of what a Baptist of the time considered to be the 'Fundamentals' of the faith, the list is instructive. There is no mention of creation, or incarnation, or the Trinity, or the Kingdom of God, or the Church. But even in such compressed form, Glover still had the vivid touch, bringing the biblical terms to life with a deft use of his classical and historical expertise. For instance, in the section 'Repentance' he draws a parallel with other fields of human activity:

> No progress in art, or trade, scholarship or anything, is possible without self-criticism. (Plato's famous sentence should be remembered and discussed – 'the unexamined life is not worth living'; see Plato *Apology* 38A. Contrast the woman in Prov. xxx, 20, who wipes her mouth and says she has done no evil.)[24]

Throughout, Glover uses the method of 'penetrating the metaphor' in dealing with the biblical terminology. At the heart of salvation is God's forgiveness of sin. But what does it mean to speak of Christ as 'taking away the sin of the world'? Glover understands it subjectively and as a direct description of historical change. Christ has 'historically taken a great deal of sin out of society' – certain sins common in the ancient world are rarely committed today, people are more apologetic for others, new standards of conduct are accepted, and Christ has himself become the ideal, and has given a new power and motive for life.

Coming to the atonement, Glover states:

> This is constantly associated in popular religion with sacrifice and 'the Blood'; and a theology partly derived from the Old Testament, partly from Roman law, has been developed, which does not adequately represent the New Testament, or the mind of Christ as seen in the Gospels, or the views of large sections of the early church.
>
> Note that the term *atonement* may to different minds suggest very different things; it has no standard meaning; it has, in fact, had changes in meaning; and in the popular sense it is hardly to be found in the New Testament.[25]

The primitive and Old Testament concepts of 'sacrifice' are, says Glover, barely able even as metaphors to convey the meaning of 'atonement' – 'The New Testament writers only use sacrifice as metaphor and only incidentally . . . Sin is treated too fundamentally to allow a place for sacrifices . . . Christ belongs to a wholly different range of realities and conceptions from that implied in sacrifices.' As for the 'blood of Christ', this means simply 'the death of Christ', as his own will and choice and that *his* will was the revelation of God's great love, reconciling us to himself. Glover here, as elsewhere, was fond of referring to Luther's advice, to 'begin first at the wounds of Christ' for all understanding of God. The ransom theory (that Christ crucified was the price paid to the devil) was a travesty; the victim theory (i.e. 'that God punished Christ *instead* of the race') had attendant difficulties, 'but it stands that Christ's suffering has saved us from suffering'. In the end, for the New Testament atonement is reconciliation, a renewed relationship between God and man. Similarly, Glover deals with the metaphors of redemption and justification, as drawn from the ancient slave market and law-court, and as signifying a new life – 'the new righteousness is the power of an endless life (Heb. vii, 16) a ceaseless, happy development of character in a great friendship'.

In all this, Glover was concerned to open up the inner and experiential meaning of the great biblical terms to people, especially young people, to whom they had ceased to convey any sense at all. M. E. Aubrey, General Secretary of the Baptist Union, who had been Glover's minister in Cambridge and who knew him better than most, had circulated Glover's notes to a number of theologians for comment before finally accepting them for publication. Among the referees was, interestingly, Charles Raven, an admirer of Glover's earlier works, especially *Jesus in the Experience of Men*. Raven was slightly dubious about the order in which Glover took the themes – 'I cannot ever start with sin' – but even more so about Glover's congenital difficulty with the person of Christ:

> The question of Christ's relationship to God – call it the problem of his power to forgive or the doctrine of the Incarnation – cannot be shirked and these outlines shirk it . . . It is futile to think that you can have a doctrine of Atonement while your Christology is 'in the air'.[26]

Aubrey took Raven's point ('the lacunae . . . are rather appalling', he told Glover) but felt that the theological untidiness might in fact engage the layperson more readily. So the booklet was released late in 1931.

The growls from the theological right were not long in coming, and from the Metropolitan Tabernacle in particular. Tydeman Chilvers commented in the February 1932 *Sword and the Trowel* that, being an official publication of the Baptist Union, it made clear what the doctrinal position of the Union was. He continued:

> Amazement and astonishment are mild words to express my feelings after once reading. Thankfulness that the Tabernacle and its Pastor are not members of the Union were the thoughts that followed. What really practical purpose will be served by this conglomeration? It is very evident, according to the *Fundamentals*, that the Holy Scriptures of the Old and New Testaments are not the final court of appeal in matters of doctrine. There is also implied a very sad reflection upon the Evangelical Baptists of, to say the least, the last 100 years.
>
> Why does the Baptist Union go to Dr Glover for the arrangement of 'Fundamentals'? Is he the only theologian, or rather, is he *really* a theologian? I trow not. Having read most of his books I fully recognize his culture and appreciate his powers of historic and literary research, but when he takes his stand as a teacher of Bible doctrine . . . I consider he is altogether out of place. Most sincerely do I hope that the Baptist Churches will reject this publication.[27]

The next issue of the *Baptist Times* stated that Chilvers was mistaken. Such publications, while issued by the Union, carried only the authority of their authors. This in fact amounted to a disclaimer by the Union, and a sign of embarrassment at the publication. Aubrey could not help being nervous at the prospect before him, for while Chilvers and his congregation did not belong to the Union, Spurgeon's College certainly did, as did many pastors in the Spurgeonite tradition, including some who were members of the Council of the Union. One such, Thomas Greenwood, wrote to the Discipleship Campaign Committee urging the withdrawal of the booklet, on the grounds that its treatment of the atonement was an *attack* on the doctrine as taught by Evangelicals from Wesley to Spurgeon.

Chilvers returned to the fray in the March *Sword and the Trowel*, insisting that the Union could not unhook itself from responsibility for the booklet, and claiming that an injustice was being done to many true and loyal evangelical Baptist ministers – 'There is much seething and unrest amongst a large section of the Union.' And where would the Union be today but for Spurgeon's work? Was it honest, reasonable, or right to issue a booklet that cut away the very foundation of the doctrines for which Spurgeon stood? Then came the reference to the precedent which was already in many people's minds:

> Dr Glover's utterances and writings touching the Bible and theology are enough to make the good man rise from the dead and call for another *Downgrade Controversy*. Spurgeon's name is nothing apart from *his firm evangelical teaching* and his devotion to the Bible as God's Word. We must in honour to our Lord defend the BAPTIST evangelical tradition of Charles Haddon Spurgeon.[28]

As for the booklet itself, said Chilvers, what truth it contained made it the more dangerous, for it struck a blow at the evangelical and scriptural doctrine of *Atonement by Blood*. 'The old and precious idea of a personal, vicarious, substitutional sacrifice for sin, and Christ bearing sin's penalty is scouted.' According to Glover, sacrifices were a mistaken idea, and 'blood' was repugnant to modern taste, whereas 'Anyone who tampers with this great essential truth can hardly be trusted to deal with other vital doctrines; for the "blood is the life" of all the fundamental teaching of the Bible. If a man is theologically wrong at the hub, every spoke is loosened.' And what did Glover mean by 'metaphor'? In short, the book had 'not enough Gospel in it to save one soul, let alone inspire a campaign in our [*sic*] great and beloved Baptist denomination'.

By now it was indeed being asked by leading Baptists whether another Down Grade controversy was in the making. Aubrey and the Campaign Committee had clearly been wrong-footed by the reaction to *Fundamentals*. Such trouble as had been anticipated would, it had been felt, relate to the 'lacunae' in Glover's outline. In fact it was what he *had* said that was provoking the storm, for it was seen as a constrained attack on Spurgeonite evangelicalism. Nothing could be further from Chilvers' mind, apparently, than a doctrine of incarnation or Trinity. All that mattered was that the blood had been diluted if not sponged away. Glover was gently sounded on the possibility of withdrawing the booklet. He refused, insisting that the responsibility must lie with the Union and Campaign Committee, and at one point hinted that he himself might leave the Union if the pamphlet was disowned. Time was getting short, as the Council was due to meet on 7 March, and even such a moderate, and friend of Glover, as Charles Brown counselled him to withdraw the booklet as a peace-saving exercise. But too much was at stake emotionally, as well as intellectually, for Glover. If the opposition was being nerved by loyalty to C. H. Spurgeon, *Fundamentals* was charged with the sacred memory of Richard Glover and all that *he* had stood for.

The Baptist Union Council met on 7 March. Greenwood and others proposed that the booklet be withdrawn. At one point Glover himself even offered to do so rather than hurt his brethren's feelings. But a majority were clearly opposed to this. After lengthy discussion, it was finally agreed that the booklet would still be issued, but that another publication, calling attention to doctrinal interpretations not dealt with by Glover, would be made available as well. This was to be written by Percy Evans, Principal of Spurgeon's College. Glover himself magnanimously seconded the motion, and his speech in support of it brought a tense day to an agreeable conclusion. He was aware, he said, that his treatment of Christ's sacrifice was inadequate and incomplete. He knew no representation of that great fact which could be regarded as adequate and complete. To him Christ was everything. He was Saviour, Friend, and Lord. For years he had been trying to understand the meaning of Christ's death. He could sing all the evangelical hymns, but he was seeking to reach another constituency for whom that language as yet meant little. The mystery of the cross was unfathomable.[29]

Relief all round. A jubilant Aubrey sent his personal *Laus Deo* to Glover. The flammable vapours seemed to be dispersing – when within four days Glover dropped a lighted match and there was a horrendous explosion. *The Times* had been running a series of articles from various contributors under the title 'Fifty Years', reviewing developments in different fields of activity. Glover was asked to contribute a piece on the Free Churches. He had written it sometime in February, and it was sheer, if malicious, chance that it appeared on 11 March, the Friday of the week in which the Council had met. Worse, it was headlined with the title THE DEFEAT OF SPURGEON, an eye-catching but provocative piece of sub-editing. In fact the main theme of the article was not Spurgeon and his influence, but the greater involvement of the Free Churches in higher and theological education, and the mutual influence of Nonconformity and the ancient universities since the abolition of religious tests. But the article began by asking why the famous American court case on evolution held at Dayton, Tennessee, in which fundamentalism had shown its social and cultural strength, had no parallel among British Baptists or other Nonconformists. Glover went on to argue that the different attitude to modern learning among British Baptists had been both symbolized and secured by the Baptist Union's stand against Spurgeon's accusations in 1888. Of Spurgeon he said:

> He had a huge congregation which, in spite of faults of his own and constant criticisms by outsiders, he held charmed. Nature had given him a squat, ugly exterior, and made amends by adding a marvellous voice and the supreme gift of oratory. He was an untrained man, without the discipline of ordered study, but he read enormously and remembered. Every one knows how often Catholic and Calvinist have been able to live in the profoundest sense of God's love while holding tenets (or thinking they held them) which others found strangely incompatible with the central belief. Spurgeon was of this stamp. A large-hearted human creature, he maintained an orphanage and (in a rather amateur way) he trained young men for the Baptist ministry. It is, unhappily, no strange thing that a great man, who attempts too much, will prefer at least the homage and tattle of admirers to challenge from independent minds.[30]

Glover gave a racy account of the Down Grade controversy. Spurgeon alleged ('people told him so, and he believed it') that Baptists were abandoning the Bible. After his withdrawal he carried on a jihad against the Union. Then:

> I remember (for my father was personally attacked, and I was not a child) asking the aged Frederick Trestrail, who, in old age (and great girth), kept a clear head and a lively humour, if he thought the trouble came from Spurgeon's gout. No, he said abruptly, it was Satan. Well, gout, conscience and Satan make queer alliances in us all. The thing was not done in a corner: the whole Protestant world watched, and the Baptists bore the brunt of it.

The controversy and its outcome showed, said Glover, that Baptists were not the crude, unlettered ranters despised by Matthew Arnold. They had trained leaders from their own colleges, university colleges and the Scottish universities. Less famous and less gifted than Spurgeon, they nevertheless had a wider intellectual outlook than he. 'No obscurantism lost its battle of the Marne. No stronger leaders than Spurgeon, no likelier place for a victory than his own denomination, could have been thought of; and the attack failed.' The rest of the article, somewhat rambling as it progressed, surveyed the developments in Free Church life in relation to the wider movements in education.

Many of his non-Baptist friends expressed delight at this vintage Glover. Those who *were* Baptists ran for cover. Sure enough, the Sunday following, the wrathful Tydeman Chilvers ascended Spurgeon's pulpit at the Metropolitan Tabernacle to announce The Triumph of Spurgeon and the Overthrow of Glover. Every line of the article was scrutinized and found to be either historically inaccurate, or offensive to just about every virtue in the Christian canon. The name of Spurgeon was exalted:

> Spurgeon as a Calvinistic evangelical thoughtful preacher and expositor carried the day for the Evangel, established for his time the religious thought according to the Bible, and whenever the cloven foot of error in the garb of a boasted intellectualism or in whatsoever form approached him, it was glad to escape overcome and defeated before the mighty Sword of Truth that he wielded, and not until Spurgeon's voice was silenced in death did the challengers have any real courage to voice themselves, as Dr Glover has now done.[31]

Glover could no longer be numbered with Evangelicals. He had no right to say such untrue and ungracious things about so great a man. It was utterly false to speak of the 'defeat of Spurgeon', and in a mighty peroration the address concluded with an assurance that the truths for which Spurgeon stood had not been overcome by 'university intellectualism' or rationalistic thought. The Banner of Evangelism would ever float imperiously bearing the inscription VICTORY TO THE LAMB. The congregation then sang 'All hail the power of Jesus' name', and, as if in order to demonstrate that Spurgeon was indeed undefeated, at the close of the service the organist played the Hallelujah Chorus.[32]

Next morning a summary of Chilvers' address appeared in *The Times*. Aubrey, understandably dismayed, pleaded with Glover by letter, 'For the love of Mike go slow for a bit!' and wrote to *The Times* dissociating the Union from the former President's article. The *Sword and the Trowel* carried on the war for another issue or two, claiming that letters and resolutions from churches and public meetings had 'poured in upon us' in support. The Baptist Union leadership did what was probably the only thing it could do, and remained silent apart from issuing a note in the *Baptist Times* that 'the Baptist Union has no controversy on the subject'.[33] The issue died down, although for the rest of his life the sniping at Glover continued from fundamentalists in the denomination. But it was a close thing, for if Glover's article had appeared just *before* the Council meeting at which *Fundamentals* had been discussed, there is no knowing what might have happened. Glover's defence, that in *Fundamentals* he had not intended attacking anyone, would hardly have stood up in the eyes of the Spurgeonites. The article was, after all, and however kindly, dismissive of Spurgeon; and even when acknowledging his contribution and his personal qualities, somewhat condescending. It was the final avenging of Richard Glover. At the same time, Chilvers did protest a little too much. Glover had not actually criticized the orphanage (Chilvers seemed to think he had, and went to great lengths to extol its merits), nor had he cast any aspersions on the *present-day* Spurgeon's College (which again Chilvers in great detail defended), whose Principal Percy Evans was counted a personal friend by Glover.

Two points can be made in concluding our account of Glover and his controversies. The first is theological. Glover, we have seen, wanted to preach 'Christ without theory', and to speak of Christ solely in terms of 'himself', and the change, the new life, the new outlook on God and sin and everything else which Jesus Christ brings into human experience. Experience, not doctrine, should rule the day. In that sense, it is true that, as his critics alleged, Glover was not a theologian, but a historian with imaginative insight and an attractive pen. But in fact Glover *did* have a theory which, however unwittingly, governed his treatment of Christ, and he illustrates particularly well the final impossibility of the 'doctrine-free' position he claimed to occupy. He had a profoundly significant doctrine, though he would not have thought of it as such: the doctrine of the individual. As we have seen, his emphasis upon the individual or 'personality' or 'character' accompanied his treatment of the ancient world, where he derived it from Periclean Athens, and it inspired his treatment of the New Testament. Lecturing in Bristol he said:

> Does character interest you? Do you feel the difference between one man and another? Are you interested in the everything of life – the minutest thing, the little things, the big things, that make character? There were plenty of these things in Jesus, otherwise there would not have been a Christian movement. Does it appeal to you?[34]

Glover seems to have had no real concept of *community*. His Baptist contemporary, H. Wheeler Robinson, was at this time working out his concept of 'corporate personality' as an element in Hebraic thought. But as we have seen, Glover had an aversion to the first two-thirds of the Bible and is unlikely to have paid much heed to such ideas. Relationships are conceived by him in terms of the 'impact' of one 'personality' upon another, the impact being registered in terms of internal changes in attitude under the 'influence' of the other. The understanding of a *relationship between* persons seems to elude him entirely. A further consequence flows from this, with immense implications for both soteriology and Christology. Given his atomized, 'Athenian' ideal of the human individual, there seems little room, or need, in his thought for *representative* relationships. Individuality is pressed so hard that no one can, or should, stand for anybody else, or perform anything *on behalf of* another. Hence the sheer subjectivity of his view of atonement. Jesus himself makes me think differently about God, enabling me to love God, and that, for Glover *is* atonement; whereas for both catholic and evangelical classical teaching on the subject that is the *fruit* of atonement. Glover habitually spoke of Christ who 'loved me and gave himself for me'. In reality his own understanding seems to be of a Christ who 'gives himself *to* me'. Hence all sense of human solidarity, in sin and in Christ, is lost. The Christ who represents us all before God, as well as representing God to us, is not in view.

Hence Glover's dispute with the fundamentalists was bound to be sterile. Faced with Glover's 'metaphorical' interpretation of atonement, the conservatives were quite entitled to ask Glover, 'Metaphorical for what?' The biblical terms are indeed in the end metaphors, as all language must finally be in relation to God. But this does not mean they are simply to be dissolved into inward experiences. They are metaphorical for a relationship which exists from God's side, as well as our experiential side. Glover with his individualist concern with immediate experience, and the conservatives with their literalism, had little chance of fruitful discussion.

The second point is social and cultural. The issue between Glover and the Spurgeonites concerned not just theology, but an estimate of the value of education and learning for their own sakes. That particular generation of Baptists, as presumably other Free Churchmen, was still not wholly convinced in all quarters of the need or wisdom of higher education. In March 1932, without in fact alluding to the Glover controversy, A. Weaver Evans, a minister in Weston-super-Mare, complained about a missing note in the contemporary pulpit, namely the power of the blood and the substitionary death of Christ. Significantly he continues:

> The sons and daughters of our people went to college and returned home with a degree; they became so superior that the terms in which C. H. Spurgeon, Frank White, Henry Varley, Gratton Guinness, and a host of others preached the Gospel were declared to be 'vulgar'. So refined had our younger people become that Scripture phraseology must be improved upon and in so doing robbed of all its content.[35]

Glover, it has been seen, had from early days been convinced of the worth of higher learning, including biblical studies, and regarded himself as a kind of modern Clement of Alexandria with a mission to convince Nonconformity of this. Indeed he made the matter a main theme of his Presidential Address to the Baptist Union in 1924. In his *Times* article, he placed alongside the Down Grade controversy in historic significance, the opening by the Congregationalists of

Mansfield College in Oxford, in 1882. This signified in the most concrete way the advent of Nonconformity into the ancient universities, as of fact as well as of legal right.

> Some have wondered whether the Free Churches have really gained by the change. That I cannot compute . . . I think that the opening of the Universities was inevitable, and I fancy that the main currents of English life, of the world's life, do not altogether depend on Oxford and Cambridge . . . I will say this, however, that the admission of Dissenters has strengthened the Universities – and the Church of England.

But those arguing most fiercely against Glover's *Fundamentals* were also those who, like Tertullian, could see no case for tying Jerusalem to Athens. In and with the theological dispute went a different evaluation of one of the most significant trends in modern British society.

E. W. Barnes[36]

Much has been written on Bishop Barnes. It has become customary for him to merit little more than a mention as a well-meaning but wrong-headed intellectual, an obsessional, prejudiced and insensitively authoritarian bishop. A recent history of the Church of England heads the three pages given to him 'The Follies of Dr Barnes', and, contrasting him with more recent scholars who have reached similar conclusions to his views on the New Testament but whose academic integrity is to be accepted, concludes 'It is difficult to feel such respect for Dr Barnes.'[37] It is noteworthy, however, that quite apart from the biography written by his son, a work which reflects a natural filial sympathy, we have also the considered testimony of A. R. Vidler, who suffered as one of the 'rebel priests' in Barnes' Birmingham diocese, and who on the centenary of Barnes' birth felt that justice had not been entirely done to him by the conventional wisdom. In view of the material available elsewhere, we shall here restrict ourselves to a brief sketch of the controversial trajectory pursued by Barnes, allowing him to speak for himself when possible, and then raise certain questions about the assumptions lying behind some of the accusations against him, before concluding the chapter with our summary of the larger issues raised by a comparison of Barnes with Glover.

Barnes was born in 1874 in Altrincham, the son of a Baptist father and Wesleyan mother. He became an Anglican while at school in Birmingham. In 1892 he entered Trinity College, Cambridge, to read Mathematics. A brilliant student, he took a first and was elected to a Fellowship of Trinity in 1898. Pursuing research in mathematics, further distinctions fell his way, with a Doctorate of Science in 1906, and election as a Fellow of the Royal Society in 1909. As scholar and teacher he displayed exceptional clarity of mind and expression and, in the words of his son, a determination 'to use logic to distil truth and order out of part of the mathematical mash'.[38] Physically he wore a lean and hungry look, a spareness of frame matching the mental austerity within. But many who knew him, throughout his life, speak of the kindly bright eyes, the personal charm and courtesy which continually surprised those who, at second hand, had only heard of Barnes the ogre.

Barnes was ordained to the priesthood in 1902, that is, while still a young mathematical don at Trinity. He had no formal training in theology, and continued his mathematical work and teaching for thirteen more years. The significance of this aspect of his career has been insufficiently remarked upon. He was a firm believer in the tradition of combining priesthood with the secular responsibility of teaching. He counselled at least one of his undergraduates, successfully, to adopt this course,[39] and on the sad occasion in 1947, almost at the end of his career, when he stood before the Convocation of Canterbury to defend his most controversial book, he reiterated his view that 'The schoolmaster who was also a clergyman used to be a valuable influence on the community. He has almost died out.'[40] The description is suggestive – schoolmaster, *also* a clergyman. Barnes' own primary sense of identity (don, also a clergyman) while at Cambridge is conveyed by that remark and it probably never entirely left him, even when he became a 'full-time' cleric.

That happened in 1915. By the early stages of the Great War Barnes had adopted firmly pacifist views, and was strongly in sympathy with his colleague Bertrand Russell, who was deprived of his Fellowship by Trinity for his anti-war stance. Barnes took up his first full pastoral charge as Master of the Temple in London, remaining there till 1920, when he became a Canon of Westminster. From the time of his ordination, if not before, his theological views had been moving in a markedly liberal direction. His sermons in college chapel had repeatedly stressed that religious truth could be grasped only by personal, spiritual experience, and he regarded himself as indebted to the mystical approach – in which there was considerable revival of interest in the early years of the century thanks to writers like Dean Inge and Evelyn Underhill. This was at exactly the same time as Glover, also in Cambridge, was flirting with Quakerism. Barnes and Glover knew each other well, and Barnes was to think highly of *The Jesus of History*.

Barnes' strong pacifism, a comparative rarity at that stage among any clergy, had already made him a figure of some dubious repute, and it was to do so throughout his life. He first appeared as a disturber of the theological peace, however, in August 1920, when he preached the annual sermon before the British Association for the Advancement of Science, at Cardiff. Its actual title was 'The Christian Revelation and Scientific Progress', but thanks to some sensationalizing press coverage it quickly became known as the 'Monkey Sermon'. Its basic theme was the need, in view of the known evolutionary origins of man, to revise the traditional doctrine of the Fall. Excitement in the press produced a flood of correspondence, and next Sunday he returned to the theme in a sermon in Westminster Abbey, on 'Evolution and the Fall', which provoked yet more public and private comment. It is remarkable how, sixty years on from the furore over Darwin's *Origin of Species*, the public could regard as novel any theologian's acceptance and advocacy of evolutionry theory. In fact, Barnes himself was regarded as somewhat *passé* for raking over the evolutionary embers again. Hensley Henson thought he was flogging a dead horse. But the specific point which Barnes was making should be noted. He was not simply arguing, yet again, that the Genesis account of creation was not to be taken literally. He was criticizing the tendency of theologians to accept an evolutionary origin for mankind while retaining a quasi-historical understanding of the 'Fall' as something that really had happened once-upon-a-time in the distant past. Barnes, consequently, was accused by some of denying 'Original Sin'. For his part, he was seeking to locate the meaning of such time-honoured phrases, not in mythical history of the race, but in present spiritual experience. As he said in his Westminster Abbey sermon:

> Have we not all felt the power of sin? Have we not struggled for help to conquer temptation? Do we not all know the horrible strength of the rival passions within us, how hard it is to love our enemies or to do good to those who despitefully use us? Have we not all at times been so alienated from God that the words 'Blessed are the pure in heart, for they shall see God' have seemed the verdict of divine condemnation? And have we not found, in prayer and persistence, in supplication of the Lord Jesus Christ, power once again to follow him as Master, and a sense of pardon and forgiveness? This, and not some ancient piece of folklore, is the dynamic of the Christian faith, the source of its enduring claims. In the love of Jesus Christ lies our hope, in that love manifest in his life, poured out with his blood on the Cross. For his love is the love of God, the great guiding principle of the spiritual evolution of humanity.[41]

'We have recently been told,' wrote Arnold Pinchard in an article shortly after the two sermons, 'on the authority of one who is doubtless a good mathematician and equally certainly a bad theologian, that if one accepts the evolutionary theory of the ascent of man, one must therefore necessarily be obliged to deny the doctrine of the Fall and of original sin.'[42] Such a snap judgement barely accounts for what Barnes was actually saying. In any case, while the theological *cognoscenti* might murmur that Genesis versus Evolution was a burnt-out issue, for many in the public, members of the Churches or not, it was far from over, as the correspondence in the *Church Times* alone during September 1920 shows. Alec Vidler judges that 'Barnes was right in thinking that the clergy as a whole were not being nearly candid enough in the pulpit concerning the effects on Christian belief of scientific theories and also of biblical criticism.'[43] Barnes, incidentally, while mathematics was his speciality, read widely and deeply in the natural sciences, particularly the biological field, throughout his career.

Barnes never joined the Modern Churchmen's Union, though he gladly took the description 'modernist' to himself, and in fact addressed the 1921 Girton Conference. During the next two decades of his life his name was to be linked with controversy of a rather different kind, though certainly partly due in consequence to his theological beliefs. In 1924 he became Bishop of Birmingham, a position he occupied till his retirement in 1952. In the course of his enthronement sermon he referred to a 'pagan sacramentalism' in Latin Catholicism, which pretended it could create the bread of salvation by some magic rite or formula. 'Let us keep to the main tradition of the English Church', he pleaded. His target was, of course, the Anglo-Catholic theology of the Eucharist and the practice of reservation of the sacrament, a highly contentious issue during the 1920s in view of the measures to revise the Prayer Book, which met their ignominious end in 1928. The ensuing bitter disputes with his 'rebel' Anglo-Catholic clergy in Birmingham, some of them involving legal cases, have been well rehearsed in recent years, from sympathizers as well as opponents of Barnes.[44] His most provocative statement came at a civic service in Birmingham in October 1927, in a sermon on 'Sacramental Truth and Falsehood', when he asserted that a *physical* change in the bread obviously did not occur at consecration, since no chemical analysis detected any such change. 'Yet if there be a *spiritual* change it must surely be possible for man to recognize it by his spiritual perception.'[45] Belief even in 'spiritual change in dead matter' was idle superstition. On the other hand, Barnes argued, the whole eucharistic service was a medium of the Real Presence.

That same year saw the appearance of what was, surprisingly, his first book, a collection of sermons, *Should Such a Faith Offend?*[46] He was in fact extremely occupied in preparing and giving the Gifford Lectures at Aberdeen during 1927–9. The stated purpose of the Gifford endowment is the promulgation and defence of natural theology, and Barnes, with his scientific training and expertise, was a natural choice as a lecturer. *Scientific Theory and Religion* was the result, published in 1933.[47] A massive work, it was subtitled 'The World Described by Science and its Spiritual Interpretation'. Not many theological works have been produced where page after page is covered in mathematical formulae. The following year, 1934, there was a brief skirmish in his diocese over modernism. Barnes had written an approving foreword to *The Gospel of Modernism* by one of his clergy, R. D. Richardson. He was challenged at his diocesan conference as to his own acceptance of the creeds. He replied that there was a need to believe in the great doctrines of the creeds, the incarnation and the 'ever-living Christ' rather than in particular interpretations.

Barnes was rarely out of the news. Though true to his pacifist convictions, he was a popular pastoral bishop in wartime, not least because of a libel case he brought upon himself, through alleging sharp practices by cement manufacturers which prevented the speedy construction of air-raid shelters and so endangered the public. He lost the case, but so strong was local support for his moral stand that a fund was raised to pay the costs. Unknown to most people, however, he was occupied throughout the war years on another project, which he was regarding as the climax of his intellectual career. *Scientific Theory and Religion* had been criticized as strong on science but weak on theology, and Barnes felt the need to produce a companion volume to redress this imbalance. His subject was the history of Jesus and the early Church, and the result was *The Rise of Christianity*, which appeared in March 1947.[48]

The book was, in short, an account of the origins of Christianity shorn of all miraculous elements. Neither at Jesus' birth, nor after his death, was there any breach in the uniform operation of natural processes, nor was there any such interruption in the deeds he performed in his ministry, nor in those performed by the apostles. Christianity was a new, redeeming movement, changing the moral and spiritual state of the world. The world of that time was a superstitious, amazingly credulous world. It was inevitable that the first Christians should reflect their context and produce in the New Testament 'a strange mixture of spiritual insight, religious beauty and moral strength, combined with incredible stories and bizarre beliefs'.[49] Only in modern times has belief in the large-scale uniformities of nature become an 'authoritative dogma'. Science is built upon the uniform repetition of likenesses.

> The triumphant discoveries which have resulted from scientific research based upon these principles, bid fair to transform human life. Hence the principles of science and, in particular, the large-scale, or finite-scale, uniformities of nature are now understood and accepted, not merely by a restricted group of learned men, but by practically the whole community.[50]

Miracles just do not happen. Those attributed to Jesus cannot be put into a special category. The result is clear:

> Without a doubt the need to jettison the miraculous element in the New Testament has been, and still is, profoundly disturbing to most of those who accept the Christian faith. It weakens the reliability of the gospel narratives; and, in so far as Christian thinking has been built upon the power of Jesus to perform miracles and upon the miracles associated with his birth and death, it calls for a drastic refashioning of such teaching.
>
> We do well, however, to remember that a miracle proves nothing by itself. Ignore the miracles in the New Testament and Christianity remains that same way of life, lived in accordance with Christ's revelation of God, which through the centuries men have been drawn to follow: Jesus remains the one of whom it was said (2 Cor V. 19) 'God was in Christ reconciling the world to himself.' Such indwelling was a spiritual, not a physical, fact. It must be established by spiritual evidence.[51]

What then was left of the Christian movement stripped of its raiment? It was not, on Barnes' reckoning, left for dead. Here is his concluding summary of what took place:

> It is a most strange tale, which would be incredible were it not true. In the background of the story we have a succession of men, prophets who during several centuries arose within two obscure, and none too highly civilized, groups of Semitic tribes. These men fashioned ethical monotheism, the conviction that humanity is the creation of a god who is good and who demands the service of goodness.
>
> Then there emerged in Galilee a peasant artisan, profoundly convinced of the truth of the prophets' message, who felt that he knew God and was called to serve him. This man for a brief year or so taught in a remote district, speaking of God with an intimate and beautiful certainty. Finally, because of teaching which expressed his loyalty to God, he was executed as a common criminal.
>
> All memory of him ought rapidly to have vanished, but it would seem that his personality was so strong, his religious sureness so great, his moral and spiritual influence so powerful that his followers could not forget him. As they repeated his teaching they gained an unshakable certainty of his

> continuing presence. So a new religion grew up, ethical monotheism centred on Jesus the Christ.
>
> The new faith, like its founder, taught its adherents to lead clean, honourable and kindly lives. It led them to ignore many of the motives of worldly prudence by which men are normally guided. Christians believed that the Spirit of Christ bade them distrust the use of armed force, renounce the power of wealth and even forgo the appeal to established law. They lived in the conviction that, apart from such help, goodness and goodwill shown in speech and deed would in the end prevail. After being persecuted for well-nigh three centuries by the authorities of an empire to whom its tenets were an affront, the Christian faith triumphed – and forthwith its adherents began to forsake their distinctive outlook on life. The salt lost its savour. An opportunist monotheism, at its best stoic rather than Christian, remained. Expediency – the higher expediency which God may be thought to approve – became the all too common guide of the Christian in the perplexities and dangers of his earthly life.[52]

The Rise of Christianity was almost universally dismissed by reviewers. Even the *Modern Churchman* thought it jejune and adding nothing to a knowledge of early Christianity. To anyone acquainted with current New Testament scholarship the book was an embarrassment, and such as C. H. Dodd had little difficulty in pointing out its inadequacies. Barnes in fact had almost totally ignored contemporary work in the field, had not shown his manuscript to anyone else for consultation and advice, and so an amateurish impression was inevitable. There was a lack of any real historical sense, and as an anonymous reviewer in the *Church Times* put it, 'The issues which are alive today preoccupy him, and he reads them back gratuitously into the ancient Church . . . [the] book has all the confident, dogmatic air of an emancipated Victorian rationalist.'[53] Had Barnes not been a bishop, of course, the book and its reception might have remained simply a matter of academic debate. But public interest was aroused by the sound of a bishop apparently denying the faith he was employed to defend and advance (one cartoonist pictured a cleric complaining to another that whereas the Dean of Canterbury believed everything he read in *Pravda*, the Bishop of Birmingham didn't believe half of what he read in the Bible). What is slightly strange is that the official ecclesiastical reaction was relatively slow. A good two months after publication, there was no mention of it by the Archbishop of Canterbury in his speech to Convocation, which was largely occupied with canon law reform. Fisher evidently was inclined to let the matter ride, although the Archbishop of York, Cyril Garbett, is recorded as saying: 'I do not think in the whole course of my ministry anything has happened in the Church of England more likely to injure the work and influence of the Church than this miserable book.'[54] E. G. Selwyn, Dean of Winchester, also put pressure on Fisher to find some means by which Barnes' views could be repudiated as incompatible with his office as a bishop. Fisher was duly persuaded to take a tougher line, and wrote to Barnes, '. . . the holding of your opinions and the holding of your office are incompatible, and for myself I believe that you ought in conscience to feel the same.' Further correspondence ensued. The debate widened during the summer, with H. D. A. Major arguing that there were now sufficient precedents established, not to mention the breadth of interpretation recorded by the Doctrinal Commission, to warrant a liberal treatment of the Bishop.

Fisher was determined at all costs to avoid an actual trial or arraignment for heresy, such as had brought Bishop King of Lincoln to court in 1888, but some measures had to be taken to reassure feelings in the Church. He asked Selwyn and Leonard Hodgson of Oxford to prepare for him a critique of the book. Thus armed, Fisher faced the opening session of Convocation in October 1947, and made a long opening statement. He had not warned Barnes that this was going to happen until the night before. Barnes had not even brought a copy of his book with him from Birmingham, and was not able to obtain one in London in time for the session. Nor was he given an opportunity to reply to Fisher until much later in the day. Fisher spoke courteously of Barnes and his book which had caused 'both distress and indignation among Churchpeople', and cast no aspersions on Barnes' sincerity, his honesty, his motives or indeed his Christian devotion, to all of which he paid high tribute. Selwyn and Hodgson had evidently done their work well, and Fisher was well able to list the inadequacies of the book in its assumptions and in its treatment of the New Testament documents in the light of recent scholarship. The core of his speech ran:

> There is little which is new in itself in the book. In its assumptions and in many of its arguments it presents a view of Christ and of the Christian faith which has often been advanced in the last hundred years, which has been weighed and answered by scholars, and which is not accepted by the Church. But it is necessary to say further, that in so many respects the Bishop's book so diminishes the content of the Christian faith as to make the residue which is left inconsistent with the scriptural doctrine and beliefs of the Church in which he holds office. For instance, the Bishop, governed by his assumptions, reduces the resurrection of our Lord to a subjective conviction on the part of His disciples, 'that the Spirit of the Lord Jesus was with them . . .'
>
> If any man is able to believe no more than this book offers him about the

> resurrection, let him believe and Christ will be with him. But it is not the faith of the New Testament or of the Church, which hold that the first disciples saw the risen Christ and found in that objective experience a manifest act of God, and the source and the security of their conviction.[55]

Due to the omissions, distortions and understatements in the book, said Fisher, that a bishop should publish material so inconsistent with the Church's doctrine could only 'disturb and shock us'. The Archbishop would have no trial as to whether his views satisfied the requirements of church doctrine, but: 'If his views were mine, I should not feel that I could still hold episcopal office in the Church.' At the Convocation of York, Garbett spoke similarly, if more brusquely.

Barnes, replying later that day, was restrained and dignified. He did not defend the book in detail, but made clear why he thought the issues were important, from pastoral and apologetic considerations:

> For many years I have been progressively troubled at the increased alienation from our church of the young people, especially those who are trained in science. The spirit of these young people not seldom is naturally Christian, but intellectually they cannot accept the Christian faith as it is too often presented. Many of the best of them would have become clergy.[56]

Returning to his favourite theme of the value of the schoolmaster-priest, Barnes stressed the appeal to the young of Christ and his teaching:

> None the less many young men and women say to-day they cannot accept the gospel story, primarily because of the miracles embodied in it. All they have learned in their general scientific training has convinced them that God acts uniformly through Nature. They are certain that the miraculous stories, however valuable as allegories, cannot to-day be plain history, and some of them are at times led to doubt the historicity of the Cross.

There, basically, the matter ended. Barnes was an old man, by many of his critics now pitied rather than feared. The *Church Times*, in a somewhat weary leader, dealt with Barnes in what reads almost like his obituary, listing his previous misdemeanours and thinking that the Archbishops were wise not to prosecute in view of 'the acreage of spiritual barley which would have to be ploughed up in the process of eradicating the theological cockle'.[57] The *Sunday Pictorial* serialized parts of *The Rise of Christianity*. The BBC Third Programme put on a knockabout discussion between Barnes and Canon Alan Richardson in August 1948.

Barnes, it can be held, was out of date with his concern for the scientifically educated youth of the day. In the immediate post-war years, in fact, traditional forms of Christian belief were doing surprisingly well. According to one recent historian of the period, 'There never was a time since the middle of the nineteenth century when Christian faith was either taken more seriously by the generality of the more intelligent or could make such a good case for itself.'[58] It was, after all, the age of C. S. Lewis. But it *was* the case that many people continued to feel, as many still do, that the miraculous is an intellectual stumbling block in the way of accepting Christian faith. Barnes' motive was to reach such people. Unfortunately, he seemed only able to do so by being as dogmatic in his insistence on the need to jettison the miraculous, as conservative orthodoxy was in its demand for its retention. The danger facing any Church is always that of intellectual complacency, the feeling that, because certain scholars have written books which meet the sceptical argument, then the job is done. Barnes was rightly pointing out that the task has to be done over and over again, and in a secular society it will have to be continually attempted, whatever professional theologians and clerics may say about it being 'old hat'. The congruence between the religious tradition and terminology on the one hand, and the assumptions built into a scientifically dominated culture and educational system on the other, will always have to be worked at anew. There are those people for whom to accept the miraculous in total, is like being asked to believe that the earth is flat, who just *cannot* believe in miracles. Barnes' approach can be seen as a valid option for such people, an invitation to look at what the Christian story looks like minus the miraculous, and to start from there, with the law and the prophets and the serving, teaching Jesus, and see where that leads. And does Barnes' sketch of the rise of that movement, with its pacifism, its concern for brotherliness, its contentment with powerlessness and its repudiation of expediency, lack all appeal – or indeed truth? Were some of the attacks on him perhaps the reactions of those for whom a reminder of the pre-Constantinian Church was too threatening, too near the bone for a National Church still jealous of its privileges? How many bishops have risked themselves for what they believed to be right and for the good of others, as Barnes did?

Glover and Barnes: Bearers of Culture

Glover angered the fundamentalists of his denomination, and at times worried the leadership. Barnes angered the Anglo-Catholics of the Church of England, continually annoyed its leadership, and at the end dismayed it. Both men, at heart, believed that direct spiritual, inward experience of the influence of Christ was the essence of Christianity. Much else was metaphor or allegory which, in so far as it had any meaning at all, referred to that *experience*. We should not ignore the differences between these men. Barnes was a socially progressive thinker, concerned for birth control, eugenics, marriage law reform, peace and international relations. Glover, after the First World War, was increasingly suspicious of internationalism and the social gospel. It is a moot point whether his election as University Orator at Cambridge did not signify the triumph of the establishment over Nonconformity at least as much as the reverse. The one-time passive resister was increasingly socially conformist.

The most interesting point of comparison, however, is that Glover the classicist and Barnes the mathematical scientist, thrust the claims of their professional disciplines at the attention of their respective denominations. Glover argued long and hard for the value of historical scholarship and classical learning, as an ally in the vindication of Christian belief based on the New Testament record. Seen against its Graeco-Roman background, and that background at its best as well as its worst, the great 'fact' of Jesus Christ, the great change he had wrought in human affairs, would be displayed all the more clearly. Barnes, all through his career, saw himself as a professional scientist, as indeed he was. The Church, he felt deeply, had still not taken cognizance of the full implications of the scientific world-view for the way Christian belief was to be expressed and formulated in the present day. In the one case, evangelical Nonconformity was presented with the pursuit of classical culture as the perspective within which Christianity was to be interpreted, in advance of the purely biblicist tendency to which it had been prone. In the other case, the Church of England, most of whose leaders had been educated in the classicist tradition, was presented with a scientific perspective which appeared brash to the point of crudity. In both cases, where controversy broke out there was a clash of culture as well as of specific ideas. With Glover and his fellow Baptists this aspect was quite clearly articulated in the exchanges over the value, or danger, of university education and background. With Barnes, the cultural clash was not admitted. Fisher's Convocation speech just did not engage with Barnes' key question: How can we conceive of God acting within the uniformities of nature as disclosed in natural science? It is not the only question, but it was worth asking, and still is. It is the missionary question, of how the faith will look to certain people given their particular cultural perspectives and presuppositions. It might at least have been recognized, instead of being dismissed as one of Barnes' unfortunate 'obsessions'. Amid all his over-simplifications and distortions Barnes was at least reminding the establishment that outside the Church was a world with unanswered questions, and in his own work he was attempting to bring that secular perspective to the forefront of attention. Is it an unworthy role for a bishop, not simply to care for the flock of the faithful, but also to be a sign to the 'other sheep' not (yet) of his fold? Neither a Glover nor a Barnes is a comfortable figure to have around. But Churches and denominations – and parties within them – over the years and generations display built-in tendencies to become mini-cultures in themselves. They are well served, if controversially so, by those who challenge the autocracy of one single cultural mode.

Notes

1 On Glover, see H. G. Wood, *Terrot Reaveley Glover. A Biography*, Cambridge: Cambridge University Press 1953; M. E. Aubrey, 'T. R. Glover. Review and Reminiscence', *Baptist Quarterly* XV (October 1953), pp. 175–82; T. H. Robinson, *Terrot Reavely Glover, Scholar and Christian*, London: Carey Press 1943.
2 See chapter 1.
3 Wood, op. cit., p. 128.
4 V. Hedger, 'Some Experiences of a Woman Minister', *Baptist Quarterly* X (July 1941), p. 246.
5 B. R. Wheeler, 'Fifty Years in Furnival Street', *Baptist Quarterly* X (July 1941), p. 359.
6 T. R. Glover, *The Ancient World*, Cambridge: Cambridge University Press 1935, p. 30.
7 Robinson, op. cit., p. 6.
8 Wood, op. cit., p. 30.
9 Compare Dietrich Bonhoeffer's appreciation of W. F. Otto's *The Gods of Greece* – 'I could almost claim these gods for Christ' – *Letters and Papers From Prison*, London: SCM Press 1971, p. 333.
10 T. R. Glover, *The Conflict of Religions in the Early Roman Empire*, London: Methuen 1909, p. 276.
11 *The Jesus of History*, London: SCM Press 1917 (1948 edition), p. 23.
12 ibid., p. 58.
13 ibid., p. 181.
14 ibid., p. 183.
15 *Baptist Times*, 20 August 1931.
16 *Baptist Times*, 27 August 1931.
17 *Baptist Times*, 11 June 1931.
18 *Baptist Times*, 5 March 1931.
19 T. R. Glover, *Democracy in the Ancient World*, Cambridge: Cambridge University Press 1927, p. 65.

20 T. R. Glover, *The Free Churches and Reunion*, Cambridge: Heffer 1921, p. 13f.
21 Wood, op. cit., p. 21.
22 *Baptist Times*, 1 May 1925.
23 *Baptist Times*, 5 February 1931.
24 T. R. Glover, *Fundamentals*, London: Baptist Union Publication Department 1931, p. 12.
25 ibid., p. 23.
26 Wood, op. cit., p. 160.
27 *Sword and the Trowel* 806 (February 1932), p. 31f.
28 *Sword and the Trowel* 807 (March 1932), p. 68 (italics his).
29 *Baptist Times*, 10 March 1932.
30 *The Times*, 11 March 1932.
31 *Sword and the Trowel* 808 (April 1932), p. 103f.
32 *The Times*, 14 March 1932.
33 *Baptist Times*, 24 March 1932.
34 *Baptist Times*, 14 January 1932.
35 *Baptist Times*, 31 March 1932.
36 On Barnes, see esp. J. Barnes, *Ahead of His Age: Bishop Barnes of Birmingham*, London: Collins 1979; A. R. Vidler, 'Bishop Barnes: A Centenary Retrospect', *Modern Churchman* XVIII (Spring 1975), pp. 87–98.
37 P. A. Welsby, *A History of the Church of England 1945–1980*, Oxford: Oxford University Press 1984, pp. 53–6.
38 Barnes, *Ahead of His Age*, p. 34.
39 See Vidler, 'Bishop Barnes', p. 88f.
40 *Church Times*, 17 October 1947.
41 Published in *Should Such a Faith Offend?*, London: Hodder and Stoughton 1927, p. 16f.
42 *Church Times*, 10 September 1920.
43 Vidler, 'Bishop Barnes', p. 90.
44 See A. R. Vidler, *Scenes From a Clerical Life*, London: Collins 1977, chapter V, for a view from the 'rebel' side.
45 Barnes, *Ahead of His Age*, p. 193.
46 See note 41 above.
47 E. W. Barnes, *Scientific Theory and Religion: The World Described by Science and its Spiritual Interpretation*, Cambridge: Cambridge University Press 1933.
48 E. W. Barnes, *The Rise of Christianity*, London: Longmans 1947.
49 ibid., p. 64.
50 ibid., p. 66.
51 ibid., p. 84.
52 ibid., p. 386f.
53 *Church Times*, 17 October 1947.
54 Barnes, *Ahead of His Age*, p. 404.
55 *Church Times*, 17 October 1947.

56 ibid.
57 ibid.
58 A. Hastings, *A History of English Christianity 1920–1985*, London: Collins 1986, p. 441.

6 A Promising Commotion: Cambridge 1962–3

In 1961 an obscure verse from the book of Genesis became famous almost overnight: 'My brother Esau is an hairy man, but I am a smooth man.' Thus Alan Bennett, on the stage of the Fortune Theatre, began his nightly send-up of the contemporary sermon, one of the funniest items in the revue *Beyond the Fringe*. It was not only hilarious, it was also cruelly close to the truth about many pulpit performances, with its pompous delivery, bland platitudes, and meandering, inconsequential trains of thought, not to mention its innocent but disastrous *double entendre*. Along with the then Prime Minister Harold Macmillan, nostalgia for wartime heroics, royalty, and just about everything else which was taken seriously, or took itself seriously, the show also poked fun at the with-it clergyman ('Call me Dick – that's the sort of Vicar I am') as the contemporary expression of muscular Christianity.

Beyond the Fringe, a product of young Oxbridge graduates, marked the opening of the flood of satire which characterized the ethos of the 1960s. It was hardly surprising that organized religion had to take its share of lampooning, for 'irreverence' was the hallmark of the satirists, whether on stage, or in the pages of *Private Eye*, or most publicly of all, on the BBC television show *That Was The Week That Was*, which began in December 1962. Satire, however, was but one expression of the relentlessly critical and self-critical spirit of the age, and this spirit was in turn but one aspect of the social transformation which overtook Britain in the 1960s. The extent of that transformation may be debatable, but Britain in 1969 was socially, politically and culturally a very different place from Britain in 1959. Religiously and theologically it was different too.

The 1960s, it can plausibly be argued, were conceived in the 1950s. The early post-war hopes of a renewed and restructured Britain, which had swept the Attlee Labour Government to power in 1945, had faded into indifference by 1951 under the slowness of economic recovery, and the Conservatives had been returned to power in time for the Coronation of 1953 to cast a sense of traditional spendour over the ending of austerity, and they could take credit for the beginnings of what would soon be called 'the affluent society'. Eden succeeded Churchill as Prime Minister, and to those who had hoped for a new

Britain it seemed as though despite the war, despite the arrival of the welfare state, nothing had really changed since 1939. At the top the same bland assurance, the same snobbery, the same assumption of the superiority of the social order, remained. Then came 1956. The Suez crisis exploded the myth that Britain was still a major world power who could 'make her influence felt' on her own – and that assumption was one which was essential to the self-justification of those 'born to govern'. Earlier that year John Osborne's *Look Back in Anger* appeared in the London West End. In the play's central character Jimmy Porter the Angry Young Man was incarnated to express all the frustrations and resentments of the disillusioned young adults of post-war Britain. Public school, royalty, Church and all bowler-hatted platitudes were heartily reviled. The Angry Young Man also featured in Kingsley Amis's novel *Lucky Jim*, in Colin Wilson's philosophical and cultural study *The Outsider*, which became a vogue cult among the intelligentsia for a year or two, and John Braine's *Room at the Top*. In part it was all a protest on behalf of those 'below', as seen also in the British cinema, which from the mid-1950s started to move away from Ealing comedy and stiff-upper-lip war exploits to the dramas of working-class life. The Angry Young Men, in protest against everything sham and hypocritical, demanded 'a degree of openness and, if need be, a brutal honesty that would become quite unbearable after a few hours'.[1]

The later 1950s saw the emergence of what Christopher Booker[2] calls a What's Wrong with Britain school of social commentary and journalism, of which the apotheosis was Anthony Sampson's *Anatomy of Britain* (1962). What had at first been sporadic fire from the Angry Young snipers, became a widely shared attitude, though, perhaps because it *was* now becoming a fashion, with greater safety in numbers, it was not so angry. It was cooler, and more sure of its ground, ironic and unsentimental. It was typified by the new generation of television interviewers and personalities, thrusting their rapier questions at the hapless, evasive politician beneath the studio lights. To be 'crisp' in style, direct in method, to aim to *expose*, was the desired image – and for all its 'honesty' this was the age when 'image' was all-important. The media, above all television, now became crucially determinative components of the scene itself. The 1960s personality, for example, seen in the likes of David Frost, affected an air of 'classlessness', and for a while it seemed as though the old hierarchies were dissolving at the younger end. On the one hand, the new Oxbridge products were mocking the received post-war traditions. From the other end of the social scale came the new youth culture, largely of working-class origins, based on pop music and epitomized in the rise to fame of the Liverpool Beatles.

Society was moving away from deference to assumed authority. It was an experimental culture. Kenneth Tynan was calling for the wholesale relaxation of censorship on stage and screen – and largely succeeded. In the 1962 Reith Lectures G. M. Carstairs was querying the traditional strictures of sexual morality and so was hailed as the archpriest of 'permissiveness'. Students became more highly politicized than ever, for as the Campaign for Nuclear Disarmament faded from the scene, the protest against the Vietnam War intensified from 1965 onwards, and in 1968, as elsewhere in Europe, student sit-ins and demonstrations marked the rejection of paternalistic authority. It was a society on the way to mass participation. Or so it felt. At least it was a society in which everything, in just about every sphere, from sex to drugs to music to violence to politics, was *open to question*. 'Was nothing sacred?' asks Bernard Levin.

> Nothing was sacred. The restlessness of the decade, the dissatisfaction with what existed *because* it existed, took many forms but was unmistakable in them all . . . Whatever was, must not be; whatever was not, must. It was like a kind of gigantic national game of spiritual Postman's Knock, with General Post being called every time, so that it sometimes seemed as if everybody was rushing from one place to another, or one attitude to another, or one mood to another, only to rush on, or sometimes back, as soon as they had arrived.[3]

Given such a context, the temptation is almost irresistible to describe the 'radical theology' and the accompanying controversies of the 1960s as merely the religious and theological versions of this overall social and cultural trend. In the cases of both the 'Cambridge theology', to be considered in this chapter, and the 'Honest to God debate', to be dealt with in the next, the critical, questioning attitude is real enough. 'Living with questions' certainly became a characteristic 1960s theological mode. But to suggest a social and cultural determination as the sole explanation of the 'Cambridge' and 'South Bank' theology which emerged during 1962–63, is too hurried to be the whole truth. For one thing, while the public response to such writings certainly reflected the spirit of the times, especially in student circles, that response must be distinguished from the theologies themselves. For another, concurrence in time does not by itself prove a dependence of one development upon another. In the case of the Cambridge theology, at least, we shall note that it can be seen in terms of antecedents as much as of contemporary influences, and that its real parallel and origins must be sought in wartime twenty years earlier.

In 1960, few could have imagined that within three years the Church of England would be embroiled in one of the most heated disputes for years, and that in the spring of 1963 a small book by an Anglican bishop would convulse the whole religious scene in Britain. By and large, organized religion in Britain seemed in a reasonably comfortable and active state. Theology was continuing on its way with a measure of confidence. 'Biblical' theology was in command and there was much being done in the philosophy of religion to counter the claims of positivist philosophers that not only did God have no existence, he had no meaning either. In 1961 the *New English Bible* (New Testament) appeared, the fruit of years of labour by the most able scholars of all the non-Roman denominations in Britain. In the summer of 1962 in a blaze of publicity the new Coventry Cathedral was consecrated, a testimony to the renewed possibilities of Christian-inspired art and architecture, and, no less significantly, to the new awareness of the Church's ministry of reconciliation in the aftermath of the Second World War. Some excitement was being created in Rome, too, as the Second Vatican Council, called by Pope John XXIII in 1958, assembled. But, by and large, the main concerns of the Churches prior to the autumn of 1962, with the exception of certain individual theologians, were with the *presentation* of Christian belief, 'getting the message across'. The substance of belief, or its doctrinal expression, was not felt to be an issue by most of the leaders or recognized communicators of the Church. Early in 1962 the Archbishop of York, Dr Donald Coggan, appeared on the BBC Sunday evening religious television programme *Meeting Point*, in conversation with Adam Faith, an idol of the pop music scene. Yes, agreed the Archbishop, he was all for modernizing the language of hymns and sermons for the sake of the younger generation. 'Religion is jolly relevant to this life.'[4]

True, there were some who were by no means so sure or complacent about the jolly relevance of Christianity. Notably, the mood of astringent questioning had begun earlier in Scottish circles. George Macleod had been instrumental in founding the Iona Community just before the Second World War, with the declared purpose of seeking to relate Christian mission to the urban and industrial scene. His *Only One Way Left* (1956)[5] was an impassioned call for the gospel to be stripped of pious abstractions, and, both theologically and practically, to be re-clothed in humanity. It was a Scottish theologian, too, who made the first creative attempt at a 'secular' reinterpretation of the faith. Ronald Gregor Smith's *The New Man* appeared in (again!) 1956,[6] and in large measure was a succinct transposition of Buber,

Tillich, Bultmann and Bonhoeffer into the British context. Heavily critical alike of ecclesiastical authoritarianism and pietistic individualism ('an emasculated Jesusology'), it called for a new self-giving of the Christian communities to the enterprise of human history where, according to the biblical faith, God is to be met. Some of the leading radicals of the 1960s were to hail that book, in retrospect, as the pioneer blazing of the trail which they felt to be extending.

Since the year 1956 seems to recur so persistently in charting the developments, both in society and theology, leading to the 1960s, there is much to be said for locating a significant event in the prehistory of the Cambridge theology then as well. For it was in the autumn of that year that A. R. (Alec) Vidler left St George's Chapel, Windsor, where he had been a canon for eight years, to become Dean of King's College, Cambridge. On arrival in Cambridge he found that a small group of younger theologians in the university, led by Howard Root, Dean of Emmanuel College, were keen to form some kind of discussion group with a view to possible publication – 1960 would after all see the centenary of *Essays and Reviews*, which had so alarmed and stirred Victorian religion into an awareness of biblical and historical criticism. There was good reason for these dons to look at Vidler for encouragement and leadership. He already had an established reputation as a modern church historian – he was the leading authority on F. D. Maurice and on the Roman Catholic Modernists – and he was the editor of the monthly *Theology*, the most widely read and influential Anglican theological journal in the country. In addition Vidler had a well-developed instinct for this kind of enterprise, a propensity for decidedly strong views combined with an ability to work with others. A glance at his previous career makes the eventual appearance of *Soundings* in 1962, and his own provocative utterances which accompanied its publication, unsurprising.[7] Any element of surprise there may have been, was as eloquent of the state of Anglicanism in the post-war years, as it was of Vidler's own attitudes.

Alec Vidler: a trajectory of inquiry

When Vidler (b. 1899) graduated from Selwyn College, Cambridge, in 1921 he was a firm Anglo-Catholic. After ordination training at Wells he served as curate in a slum parish in Newcastle-upon-Tyne, and then, from 1923 to 1931, in the parish of St Aidan's, Small Heath, Birmingham. This Birmingham period largely coincided with the first years of E. W. Barnes' episcopate (see chapter 5). St Aidan's was in the forefront of the Anglo-Catholics' resistance to (as it seemed to them) Barnes' high-handedness, and Vidler himself became one of Barnes' *bêtes-noires*. When in 1931 Vidler informed Barnes that he was leaving Birmingham he received a curt note from the Bishop urging that in future 'you should carefully keep the pledge which you make in taking the oath of Canonical Obedience'. Long after his Anglo-Catholicism had waned, even to his later Cambridge days, the letter stood framed on Vidler's mantlepiece, a gentle reminder of the improper authoritarian tendencies to which prelates are prone – or (if one wished to view it so) the independent-mindedness of the recipient.

From 1931 Vidler lived and worked in Cambridge as a member of the Oratory of the Good Shepherd, an Anglican community of celibates devoted to academic research and pastoral work among undergraduates. Vidler acquired a reputation both as an able historian – his prize-winning Norrisian essay *The Modernist Movement in the Roman Catholic Church* was published in 1934 – and as a writer and preacher with a flair for commending Christian belief in lucid and reasonable terms. Towards the end of the 1930s his theology responded to the changing climate of the times. His Anglo-Catholicism had never been narrow or rigid, and he had always recognized the importance of evangelicalism and liberalism within the Church of England, not to mention the non-Anglican traditions. (No one in Cambridge knew more of the Nonconformist history of the city and its environs than he.) Now he welcomed the new winds blowing from the Continent in the neo-orthodox theology of Karl Barth and Emil Brunner, with their stress on the primacy of God's self-revelation in his Word, and from the United States in Reinhold Niebuhr's sternly realistic Christian social ethics. Vidler was particularly affected by Niebuhr, the more so as war with Nazi Germany loomed nearer, and liberal optimism and pacifism looked increasingly facile as answers to the human predicament. That Christians had to live with proximate tragedy while believing in an ultimate hope, was the Niebuhrian note that now sounded through Vidler's preaching and writing.

Then in 1938 there opened up one of the most creative phases in Vidler's career, when he moved to St Deiniol's Library, Hawarden. The original reason for this move to North Wales lay in the suitability of St Deiniol's, being a centre for private study, as a base for editing *Theology*, to which task he was now appointed. That certainly proved to be the case, and it was largely through his editorship of the journal that Vidler acquired his description as a 'theological midwife', seeing into print the work of both established and aspiring theologians and reviewers for the next twenty-five years or so. The circulation of the journal had been falling for some time. Under Vidler it notably revived in all ways, not least because of the air of discussion which it prompted both in articles and letters. It was typical, too, that Vidler made his editorship a collaborative exercise with a team of advisers and helpers.

In 1939 Vidler also became Warden of St Deiniol's, which suddenly acquired a new kind of importance. The years just before, during and immediately after the Second World War saw some of the liveliest discussion of what might loosely be called 'applied theology' ever to take place in Britain. A better description might be 'current issues in theological perspective'. There were important stimulants towards this discussion, first in the Conference on Politics, Economics and Citizenship (COPEC) in the 1920s, of which William Temple was chairman (and in which Vidler himself had been involved as a regional secretary in Newcastle); and then in the ecumenical 'Life and Work' Conference on Church and State in Oxford in 1937. But the sense of impending catastrophe hanging over Western civilization quickened and widened the debate. J. H. Oldham, a Scottish layman of extraordinary vitality and determination (despite severe deafness), played a key role. In 1938, just after the Munich crisis, he made a considerable impression by a letter to *The Times*, asking whether British society had any spiritual foundations left, or any clear alternative to totalitarianism, and calling for a re-examination of Christian faith and the possibilities it offered for the regeneration of 'our sick society'. In part his plea was answered by his own bulletin, the *Christian Newsletter*, which he began and edited from the beginning of the war, and which appeared every week or fortnight. Through its agency a wide variety of writers were drawn together to focus attention on specific issues of social, national and international life in the light of Christian insights. Vidler was drawn in and joined the editorial board which included such notables as Philip Mairet and T. S. Eliot. The latter's *Idea of a Christian Society* (1939) was another response to Oldham's inquiry. Vidler edited an associated series of books on Christianity, the war and the future of Europe, including Karl Barth's *A Letter to Great Britain from Switzerland*.

Vidler, never one to make the plain truth more palatable by platitudes, stated his own attitude to the war in his *Theology* editorial for October 1939. With strong echoes of Niebuhr it warned against any easy moralizing of Britain's 'cause':

> The devilry of Hitlerism does not automatically transform us into angels of light nor prophets of the Lord . . . The Church best serves the nation not by uncritically endorsing the pure idealism of its professed war aims, but by proclaiming the Word of God, which shows even the noblest human purposes to be shot through with sin.

This caused something of a flurry in the editorial board at SPCK, and an anxious Lowther Clarke, the editorial secretary, told Vidler 'we cannot permit anything to be published which can be interpreted as anti-British propaganda or as tending to weaken the national will for victory'. Vidler in reply made clear that while he was willing to discuss matters of content at proof stage he would not brook interference with what he might say about the war and related issues. The matter died down, and there were no more complaints about Vidler's editorship – especially as the journal was widening its readership so effectively – apart from a relatively minor one over an article on Freemasonry in 1951.

That early editorial in fact conveys well the *critical* spirit, in such great contrast to 1914, with which many thoughtful Christians entered the Second World War. For such, publications like Oldham's *Christian Newsletter* were a lifeline. It was an attitude combining despair and hope, an anticipation that much in civilization would be destroyed, yet already seeking to probe the possibilities for a new order. At the higher levels in the Church of England, celebrated wartime writings responding to this mood were William Temple's best-selling *Christianity and Social Order*, and G. K. A. Bell's *The Kingdom of Christ*. But much else was happening in ways less publicized than either these or the important Malvern Conference of 1940. Right on the outbreak of war, Vidler set up his own unofficial, almost clandestine, network of discussion and correspondence, the 'St Deiniol's Koinonia', numbering about fifty members and meeting periodically at Hawarden and elsewhere. It aimed for all kinds of reform and renewal in what Vidler called *ecclesia moribunda*, and included folk as diverse as the Oxford economist Denys Munby, and the theologian Alan Richardson. Circular letters were sent out every month or so, containing 'frank and often provocative statements of opinion about questions that were exercising our minds and were under discussion among us: statements that were not ripe for publication, but that contributed to a continuing and lively interchange of thought'.[8] In fact it was to continue afterwards as the 'Windsor Correspondence', and even later as the 'Cambridge Correspondence'. Some of the views expressed were thought, both by the members and others who got wind of it, to be quite radical for those days, for on one occasion Vidler was invited by William Temple (himself the last person to be averse to the renewal of Church and society) to Lambeth Palace, to discuss the 'gulf' between older and younger theologians.

Critical, frank, even 'radical': this was how it all seemed, and a good twenty years before the 1960s! One of the smallest, but to its members probably the most important, of the many cells of Christians and socially committed sympathizers that met during the war, was J. H. Oldham's 'Moot'. About a dozen members met for a weekend four times a year to consider prepared papers on philosophical, ethical, political, economic and theological issues of the time. Some of the papers proved to be the germs of books and papers published later. Vidler, again, was a member, along with such creatively contrasting people as T. S. Eliot, John Baillie, Karl Mannheim and Walter Moberly.

Alec Vidler, then, was deeply involved in this wartime scene of diverse, overlapping and interconnecting networks which were questioning, criticizing, speculating and planning in just about every area of social life, in the light of Christian theology. Naturally the specific role of the Church entered into all this at many points, but one of the outstanding features of these wartime forums was the decisive role accorded to *laypeople*. Oldham was a layman, and many of the younger people in the *Newsletter* circles emerged in the post-war world as significant figures in education, politics, broadcasting and the civil service. Another of Oldham's projects fostered this emphasis, namely the Christian Frontier Council, which sought to encourage and help laypeople, in any position of responsibility in secular life, to reflect on the ethical and social implications of their work in the light of Christian faith. Vidler was strongly supportive of this aim, and after the war he was to become directly involved in the Council. For the moment one of his most significant contributions to the issue of secular responsibility was his short book on the law of God, *Christ's Strange Work* (1944). And all the time, there was Hawarden itself, where visitors as different as D. R. Davies, Melville Chaning-Pearce, Ronald Gregor Smith, John Baillie, J. H. Oldham and even Martin Buber could meet, mix and think.

In 1948 Vidler left St Deiniol's for St George's, Windsor. His canonry provided yet another base for creative work, for as well as continuing with *Theology* he became Executive Officer of the Christian Frontier Council in succession to Oldham. It meant an immersion with industrialists, civil servants, educators, scientists and planners in the search for ethical guide-lines in their responsibilities.

At the same time his Windsor home became a kind of theological college in itself, when he was given the responsibility of preparing for ordination a number of men in middle life – nicknamed the 'Doves'.

The new dean who arrived at King's in 1956 was therefore anything but a tame ecclesiastic. For the whole of his ministry he had been deeply engaged in facing the 'frontier' questions in Church and society, and his professional academic discipline had given him an unrivalled historical awareness of the modern Church. Outwardly in some ways he did cut a suitably dignified figure for the charge of a college chapel whose architecture and music represented the traditional liturgy to perfection, with his neatly trimmed (as it was then) white beard and his formidably deep and resonant voice, which was liable to be heard in undergraduate mimicry all over King's. At the same time the nonconforming streak was symbolized in his eschewing of the clerical collar (a late Romish innovation, in his view) in favour of a black shirt and soft white tie – a mode of dress he had adopted many years before. Nor could King's, despite its high choral tradition (which Vidler left untouched) be considered a safe clerical hideaway. Its dons enjoyed a reputation for humanist criticism allied to good living, and Vidler's immediate predecessor Ivor Ramsey had, so some maintained, been driven to suicidal depression by the sceptical and irreverent atmosphere on high table. Be that as it may, intellectual integrity was even more highly valued than wit, and Vidler's theological version of this virtue quickly became as respected and appreciated as anyone else's in King's.

Soundings – *A Cambridge Moot*

By now it should be no surprise that the Vidler who arrived in Cambridge would have welcomed the possibility of a fresh theological circle being formed. To those of his generation who, like him, had tasted the bracing intellectual sharpness of the wartime debates, and the theological engagement with the secular issues of the time, the church ethos of the 1950s was coming to seem bland, boring and complacent. It would be quite unjust to say that it was the difference between Temple's archiepiscopate and Fisher's. But, in all honesty, what had happened to a Church whose leaders could say little more than that Christianity was 'jolly relevant' to this life? It sounded, and felt, to be lacking any concrete content, and just too easy to be true. The world outside the Church was simply not being taken with seriousness in its own right. It was as though the Joe Oldhams of this world had never existed. Vidler's view of the mood in the late 1950s is recorded in a lecture he gave in 1964:

> . . . often during those years I used to say to my friends that I was disconcerted by the fact that theological students, the younger clergy and the like, when I conversed with them, never seemed to shock me by coming out with any startling novelties or disturbing thoughts: on the contrary. I could shock them by the things I said much more than they ever shocked me by anything they said. It should have been the other way on, as I was now a fuddy-duddy who should be allergic to new ideas. *I found much more openness to the need for some fresh and fundamental theological thinking among the laymen of the Christian Frontier Council . . . than I did in professionally theological or ecclesiastical circles.*[9] (emphases mine)

In Vidler's view, even *Theology* was showing the same tendency towards the end of the 1950s. Judging by the articles being submitted to the editor, the interest in questions of ministry, church order, sacraments and the like was boundless. Basic matters of belief and the interpretation of doctrine for the contemporary world apparently did not exist. Vidler himself began to take a more detached view of the neo-orthodoxy he had espoused in the late 1930s. It had had very important things to say, but the earlier questions raised by liberal theology and the Roman Catholic Modernists still remained on the table. As he said later of neo-orthodoxy:

> While it had undoubtedly been a shot in the arm for theologians and for theological students and given them a fresh zest for their subject, it had at the same time, and perhaps for that reason, led to their cultivating a language, and, one might say, a jargon that prevented them from being able to communicate with interested people outside their enclave. This is a fatal condition for theology to get into, since by definition what it is supposed to be talking about is a matter of concern for all men. It must no doubt have its specialists but it must never become a mere specialism. When theologians are on speaking terms only with themselves they are doomed to frustration and indeed to damnation.[10]

In view of the last sentence it may be thought strange that when the 'Soundings' group was eventually formed, it consisted entirely of theologians, although once the philosopher R. B. Braithwaite was invited and spoke at length on his conversion and baptism into the Church of England. On the other hand, as well as sharing the sense of need for critical inquiry into basic issues of belief and practice, the group embraced a surprising diversity. They could not even as a group be termed Angry Young Theologians, for they included such established names as George Woods, who migrated from Downing College to a chair at London, and John Burnaby, Regius Professor

Emeritus at Cambridge. J. S. B. Habgood of King's was a young physiologist-turned-theologian; Ninian Smart was becoming well known as a specialist in world religions; Geoffrey Lampe as a New Testament scholar. J. N. Sanders and Hugh Montefiore likewise tended towards New Testament studies. Neither youthfulness nor intellectual ability were in themselves sufficient qualifications for membership. J. A. T. Robinson, then Dean of Clare College, and Donald Mackinnon, Norris-Hulse Professor of Divinity and the leading philosophical theologian in Cambridge, were not invited.

What is more, intensely theological though the group was, a highly original note – and in one or two members' eyes it was barely a theological note – was struck by H. A. (Harry) Williams, Dean of Trinity. Twenty years younger than Vidler, he too had come through an early Anglo-Catholic phase into a broader outlook, though not without acute mental and spiritual anguish. A graduate of Trinity, he returned there as Dean in the early 1950s and lectured in divinity. The outwardly undramatic donnish existence was not matched, however, by the turmoil within as he underwent a shattering mental and emotional breakdown, an experience he has recently described in his autobiography.[11] In retrospect he attributed the crisis to a religious origin, the strain imposed on his real self by a demanding, moralizing and guilt-inducing religion, in which God had become indistinguishable from a tyrannical idol demanding obeisance. He sought and received help from a Cambridge psychoanalyst, and thereafter for Williams Freudian and Jungian psychology were essential accompaniments to any theological understanding of human motivation, and to the doctrines of sin and salvation. Above all, the theologian had to be aware of his own humanity. He later wrote of what that experience had taught him:

> I had begun to apprehend my own personal identity. I was disillusioned with thinking as a purely cerebral activity, a mere accumulation of ideas and a juggling with them . . . Under the veneer of catholic orthodoxy it had left me in the clutches of guilt-feelings which were pathological because unrelated to reality . . . I had imagined that I was ransomed, healed, restored, forgiven, because Christian doctrine as intellectual theory asserted that I was. But in actual fact I was sick unto death and little more than a slave. This contrast led me to see that Christian truth, to be really possessed, must become part and parcel of what I was. A doctrine, to be fully appreciated, had to be knit into my personal identity. I saw that I could not truly say 'I believe' unless it was another way of saying 'I am'. And the 'I' here was the total one, which included the unconscious self as well as the conscious.[12]

A Christian interest in psychotherapy was not new, but psychological and emotional disorder tended to be seen, by Christians, as the problems which belief and prayer could cure. That customary forms of belief and practice might themselves be the problems, as repressive enemies of the real life of the soul, had scarcely been recognized. Williams, out of his own experience, could now open up this issue and did so with both passion and wit, as the dons and students who heard him preach in Trinity Chapel discovered in the late 1950s, notably the first sermon he preached while recovering from his breakdown, 'Life Abundant or Life Resisting?'[13] Closely related to his new understanding of life and doctrine was the discovery, acceptance and fulfilment of his own sexual nature, as he has since frankly told in his autobiography.

Soundings: the essays

The group met regularly in Vidler's rooms, and occasionally spent a weekend away together, discussing each other's papers until they felt confident enough for publication, in 1962. Cambridge University Press, of whose board of syndics Vidler was a member, agreed to publish. The title *Soundings* derived from a saying of Miles Smith, Bishop of Gloucester in the seventeenth century, which was discovered by Vidler and aptly conveyed the mood of the essayists: 'Man hath but a shallow sound, and a short reach, and dealeth onely by probabilities and likely-hoods.' It also alluded to the story (Acts 27.28f) of St Paul's shipwreck when the sailors, feeling themselves to be nearing shore, took soundings of the depth. The cautionary note was underlined by Vidler in his editorial introduction:

> The authors . . . cannot persuade themselves that the time is ripe for major works of theological construction or reconstruction. It is a time for ploughing, not reaping; or, to use the metaphor we have chosen for our title, it is a time for soundings, not charts or maps. If this be so, we do not have to apologize for our inability to do what we hope will be possible in a future generation. We can best serve the cause of truth and of the Church by candidly confessing where our perplexities lie, and not by making claims which, so far as we can see, theologians are not at present in a position to justify.[14]

It was thus out of a mature sense of history – its future no less than the past – that Vidler was speaking and the book was written, not out of a wilful, passing iconoclastic impulse. The time would come, but was not yet, when theology could reassert itself with confident answers. But the present was a time for questions 'which are not yet being faced with the necessary seriousness and determination' and 'are not likely to receive definitive answers for a long time to come'.[15] Take away this long-term view, and it might indeed appear as though the authors were simply celebrating the permanent demise of constructive theology.

So to the essays themselves. Howard Root in 'Beginning All Over Again' argued the case for a new attempt at a natural theology; not a rehabilitation of the old abstract metaphysical arguments, but an exploration of the implications of the real contemporary experience of being human. His essay expressed superbly the spirit of new inquiry, and carried a dire warning about the sharpness of the challenge it would bring to a comfortable and complacent Church:

> We shall have to contemplate and absorb the disturbing visions of human nature which find expression in serious modern literature. We shall have to come to terms with a world in which old patterns of morality no longer direct or inspire because they no longer have life. We shall have to admit that we have no ready answers to the questions people ask because for so long we have insulated ourselves against their questions. Christian faith has been an ark of retreat . . . Our first lesson will be to learn that our greatest ally is not the dying establishments but the hungry and destitute world which is still alive enough to feel its own hunger. The starting-point for natural theology is not argument but sharpened awareness. For the moment it is better for us that the arguments have fallen to pieces.[16]

John Habgood warned about 'The Uneasy Truce Between Science and Theology'. In one of the most penetrating essays, 'The Idea of the Transcendent', G. F. Woods in fact went further than diagnosis, by not only pointing out the problems with the old concepts of transcendence, but also clarifying just how speaking of God as 'beyond' could, and could not, be used with meaning. Ninian Smart in 'The Relation Between Christianity and the Other Great Religions' called for an end to the 'isolationist' attitudes introduced by Barthian theology which, whatever its strengths, had not only dichotomized faith and reason, but had insulated Christianity from hearing the voice of God in other religions, a hearing that could shed light on the heart of Christianity itself. Again, discomfort was predicted – 'Reading the Buddhist scriptures may sometimes be a cure for anti-religious feelings, but it doesn't always conduce to Christian orthodoxy.'[17] J. N. Sanders wrote on 'The Meaning and Authority of the New Testament', distinguishing between the infallible religious authority of Christ himself, and the fallible, mediated authorities of Church, Scripture and conscience. 'We ought to acquiesce in uncertainty in those matters which Our Lord has left ambiguous, instead of flouting his one clear law of charity in making them matters of division.'[18]

Hugh Montefiore's 'Towards a Christology for Today' sought to translate the intention of the Chalcedonian definition into meaningful contemporary terms, despite the 'metaphysical impasse' which was now obstructing theology, and saw a way forward along the lines of dynamic, functional terms rather than static essences (reminiscent in some ways of Temple's *Foundations* essay of 1912). Geoffrey Lampe covered already well-trodden ground in criticizing the penal theories of atonement ('The Atonement: Law and Love') and instead suggesting the ultimacy of love in redemption – 'The Cross is the ultimate sign of man's hatred; and in that very focal point of hatred the love of God accepts him despite the worst that he can do, in his most extreme sinfulness and bitter enmity.'[19] Woods contributed a further essay on 'The Grounds of Christian Moral Judgments', and John Burnaby wrote on 'Christian Prayer', seeing the essence of prayer as union with the will of God, and expressing criticism of those elements in traditional worship which accord ill with the spirit of Christ, such as the psalms of complaint 'animated by a temper which even the most reckless allegorizing can scarcely baptize into Christianity'.[20]

Some of the essays, certainly those by Lampe, Burnaby and Montefiore, could have been written by almost any liberal Anglican from the time of *Foundations* onwards (and were not necessarily the worse for that). The fresh note was struck by the sharp challenge to the assumption that lip-service could be paid to orthodoxy while continuing to ignore the questions which, coming from the contemporary world, had an integrity of their own, and in the call, expressed particularly well by Howard Root, to look at theological questions from the human sphere outside the camp. Certain things, however, always need saying in every generation, and crucial now as always was the issue of authority and freedom of interpretation. Vidler appended a note on these questions to Sanders' essay on the New Testament, and it stands as an admirably succinct statement of how faith in the unconditional authority of God himself, can be combined with adherence to the human, mediating authorities found in the Church and its traditions. Those traditions, because historical and contingent, can never claim that absoluteness which is ascribable to God alone. The Church may claim *adequate* but not *absolute* authority, and hence doctrine must be open to revision in the light of new discoveries. We walk by faith, not by sight, and 'The craving for an absolute authority on the human plane is a craving to escape from this condition.' To allow opennesss to the further guidance of the Holy Spirit and to prevent fossilization, 'the greatest possible amount of liberty of speculation and play of mind be allowed to the members of the Church, not least to theologians. Otherwise the Church's authority becomes like that of the scribes.'[21] The greater the Church's trust in God's absolute authority, the greater will be its readiness to see its received doctrines under re-examination. Vidler concedes that on occasion the Church may feel the need to exclude those who advance unacceptable opinions, but liberty of thought should remain paramount. 'While there is a proper pastoral care in the Church to avoid scandalizing simple believers, there should be an equal care to avoid scandalizing the erudite and the educated.'[22]

Vidler's own essay with which the book concluded, 'Religion and the National Church', was shorter than most yet was to provoke considerable comment. He began by asking whether 'religion', which the Church was commonly supposed to supply, was so self-evidently a good thing as eager apologists assumed. Was the Church in any case primarily here 'to encourage and develop the pious feelings of its members', as one recent Anglican writer had put it? Vidler brought forward three witnesses to argue that if religion meant something partial, sectarian and inward, it was neither as beneficial nor as Christian as was being assumed.

The first witness was F. D. Maurice, the seminal figure of mid-nineteenth-century Anglican theology and social thought, on whom Vidler had written much. The Maurician contrast ran thus –

> Religions separate men from one another and tempt them to boast of what they possess and other men do not; the Gospel is the proclamation that they already belong together as children of the one God and Father of all, and the Church is the Kingdom or Family in which their unity is to be realized . . .[23]

The second was Dietrich Bonhoeffer, whose remarks on 'Christianity without religion' had been known in Britain ever since the publication of his *Letters and Papers from Prison* in 1953, but who had yet to make his full impact. Vidler himself had a few years earlier explored a not dissimilar theme, 'holy worldliness' as he called it,[24] and as might be expected he warmed to Bonhoeffer's perception of the need for silence. 'Christians,' warned Vidler, 'should restrain their spate of words, their pious and theological jargon, and keep quiet until they have proved in their commerce with the life of the world which of their words ring true.' Ronald Gregor Smith's *The New Man* was also quoted approvingly. The third witness was an Anglican missionary, given by Vidler the pseudonym 'Tertius', who queried whether the organized forms and institutions of religion were necessary for the practice of Christianity.

In all three, Vidler detects a prophetic discernment of the possibility of quite new forms of the Church, where the Church serves the world so as to help the world become more truly itself, instead of standing over against the world and demanding that it become 'religious'. This is spelt out in terms of a new attitude, rather than a new structure: 'The qualities mainly called for are openness to the future, a willingness to travel light or in the dark, patience and imagination in experiment, a large toleration of variety and diversity based not on indifference but on trust in the continued guidance of the Holy Spirit.'[25] One might expect Vidler then to launch an attack on the present state of the Church of England, lambasting it for its archaism and smug isolationism. But the restraint continues, and it is questions, not accusations or solutions, which continue to come:

> What prospect is there that the Church of England may have a continuing mission in a society where the traditional forms of religion are being outgrown? Does this church look like being able to welcome and foster new ways of discovering and nourishing the life in the Spirit? Is it a closed or an open church, backward-looking or forward-looking, in bondage to legalism or a school of freedom?[26]

Paradoxically, Vidler sees a peculiar advantage in the 'archaism' of the Church of England, for at least no one could imagine it to be 'anything like the final embodiment of the kingdom of God or of the Christian movement in history'. That, at least, should enable a readier acknowledgement of the need for radical change. Nor is Vidler disposed to strip the Church of its 'National' character, for it is that which enables it to relate to every aspect of life, and its ill-defined membership ensures an openness which is inclusive of those on the very boundaries of belief. But the Church has no monopoly of agencies governing or serving people's lives, nor should it claim any. 'Rather, its task is to represent, to stimulate and to defend all those agencies – however little ecclesiastical or religious they may be – that minister to the freedom and fullness of man's spiritual life.'[27]

A detached observer might suggest that Vidler's picture of an open Church in a secular society simply reflected the position of King's Chapel in a humanist King's College. It would be more accurate to say that it was the maintenance of a trajectory which had been followed throughout Vidler's career. Always, ecclesiastical and clerical (even episcopal) pretentiousness had drawn his ire. Always, there had been concern to give higher priority to the problems faced by laypeople in their secular responsibilities, than to the anxieties of clerics over good order in the Church. COPEC, Modernist and Maurician studies, the

St Deiniol's Koinonia, the *Christian Newsletter*, the Moot and the Christian Frontier Council all lay along that trajectory. The Vidler of *Soundings* was not essentially any more 'radical' than the Vidler of twenty years earlier. If he suddenly sounded 'radical', that was more a reflection upon the state of the Church of England, and the other Churches, after a decade or more of complacency in which few realized that however 'jolly relevant' religion thought it was, the world was asking questions which churchmen had scarcely begun to register.

That brings us to consider one more essay, the one which was to provoke probably more comment than any other and which stamped the whole collection with a rebellious image. Harry Williams wrote on 'Theology and Self-Awareness', an exposition of Christian belief and ethics in the light of depth-psychology. It was, of course, though not stated explicitly so at the time, wrought out of his recent experience. Just as theology had had to come to terms with Copernicus and Darwin so now, Williams argued, it had to face the immense implications of the picture of the human self revealed by Freudian and Jungian analysis. The self that we know, the conscious self, is but the tip of the subconscious iceberg. A growing awareness of this larger submerged self will inevitably affect one's knowledge of God and one's attitude towards God, and this will have important results for the restating of Christian doctrine. But this growth in awareness will be painful. 'It involves a costly surrender of what we imagine or hope or fear we are, to what in our fullness we really are.'[28] If the incarnation means that Christ involves himself fully in our human predicament, and if it is through Christ that we come to know God, then to know God must fully involve our coming to know our inner energies and conflicts more fully. But that exposes us to the fear of the implication that we may be psychotic or neurotic ourselves:

> And this is why we are tempted to forsake Christ and flee, concocting for our flight the most convincing reasons possible. We cannot bear to put ourselves in the same class as the afflicted. Yet this is also the road to resurrection, to fuller, richer life. For it is our hatred of what is buried within us, our fear of it and guilt about it, which keeps it excluded from our awareness. And it is precisely this exclusion which maintains it as an enemy felt to be working against us. When received into awareness, it loses its power to hurt or destroy, and, in time, contributes positively to the well-being and depth of the personality.[29]

All our knowledge of God, Williams reminds us, is analogical. We use human images to conceive of God, images which are necessarily of imperfect people. But imperfect people provoke our resentment, and thereby we are led to harbour resentment, albeit unconsciously, against God himself for never satisfying our demands for ease and security. The anger, when it attempts to break out, we suppress as 'unchristian', but this deep-seated demon needs to be released. 'We use a great deal of energy keeping him in fetters. What follows is the dullness and deadness of many good Christian people.' In the light of this Williams then dares to attack the very centrepiece of Anglicanism, the Book of Common Prayer:

> . . . God . . . seems sometimes to be a merciless egocentric tyrant, incapable of love, and thus having to be manipulated or cajoled into receiving his children. It is one thing to make a straightforward confession of sin as is done in the *Confiteor* at the beginning of the Roman Mass. It is another thing altogether to harp continuously and at length upon our utter unworthiness to approach God, as is done in Cranmer's Communion Service. The general confession, with its repeated and elaborate protestations of guilt, looks like a desperate attempt to persuade God to accept us on the score of our eating the maximum dust possible. Even after the absolution we are uncertain whether we have succeeded in our project. We must be reassured by four quotations from Scripture. The words of our Saviour Christ are not enough. They must be reinforced by what is said by St Paul and St John. This repeated affirmation of what is claimed as a certain fact indicates, and must often produce, doubt of its truth. One would not, for instance, in an airliner feel very comfortable if an announcement that all was well was made twice by the pilot, then by the wireless operator, then by the stewardess.[30]

In face of such a 'celestial Mr Pontifex' Christians are unable to presume anything good about themselves, and thus the life abundant is blocked.

All this has clear implications for the moral evaluation of human behaviour. Christians, believing that God is love, ascribe ultimate moral value to generous, self-giving love. But that, states Williams, means that actions cannot be judged as right or wrong as observed outwardly. Actions are good when in them I am giving myself to others, and bad when I am refusing to give. A man who steals to feed his starving family could be acting in love, and conversely conventional morality could be a disguised means of withholding such self-giving. So we come to the one page which was to mark, or damn, the whole essay in the eyes of many, and the whole book in the opinion of some. For Williams went on to suggest that the criteria for acceptable sexual relations consisted in whether or not they were a means of exploitation of one by another. As for extramarital intercourse, 'it may be often, perhaps almost always, an exploitation, unilateral or mutual. But there are cases where it need not be and isn't.' Two recent films are cited to illustrate this point, the Greek *Never on Sunday* and the British *The Mark*. In both, an insecure man had, through the experience of extramarital sex (in one case with a prostitute) been liberated from fear of others and of relations with them. The men had been made whole. 'And where there is healing, there is Christ, whatever the Church may say about fornication. And the appropriate response is – Glory to God in the Highest. Yet each of the men in these two films might have disguised his fear by the cloak of apparent morality.'[31]

It was almost as if R. J. Campbell's Piccadilly roué, on his blundering quest for God, had found his way to Cambridge. The rest of the essay reinterprets faith as the 'trust' in the whole of one's self as accepted by God, and therefore acceptable to oneself. It reflects upon the seven deadly sins and, in some striking passages, which could only have been written by one who had descended as he himself had done into the pit of self-knowledge, relates the doctrines of Christ's incarnation, cross and resurrection to an individual's experience of inner abandonment, desolation and renewal. But it would inevitably be the odd, and peripheral, remark about fornication, not the novel and arresting insights into atonement, which would attract people's attention.

Soundings appeared in the bookshops in November 1962. Immediately prior to its release, however, something else happened which, whether by accident or design, raised the profile of the book, and of 'Cambridge theology', immeasurably. Theological controversy entered the television age.

Vidler in media

On Sunday evening 4 November 1962, the BBC religious programme *Meeting Point*, chaired by Ludovic Kennedy, devoted itself to 'The C. of E.' The slot had already on occasion been provocative, not least when Harry Williams had spoken frankly about belief in the resurrection and about sexual ethics. This particular evening the studio guests were Paul Ferris, an agnostic who had recently written a book on the Church of England, and Alec Vidler, in his normal non-clerical jacket and tie. Those viewers who had opted out of evening service and were hoping for spiritual uplift and reassurance from the Dean of King's were rudely disappointed for, far from defending the Church against the sceptical outsider, Vidler finally cast all caution to the winds and delivered a series of broadsides against *ecclesia anglicana moribunda*. It was, he said, a mistake for the Church to concentrate on 'religion'. Its true mission was to help people in the whole of secular responsibility 'and not all this business about religion and these ghastly hymns and all these things that go on in Church'. Would not the boundaries between humanist and Christian become blurred, asked Ferris? Vidler's reply was, in effect, that the more agnostics and questioners there were in the Church, the better for the Church, which was far too conformist and complacent. Kennedy asked Vidler what the clergy should then occupy themselves with. Vidler replied gruffly that he was 'bored with parsons', and wanted to see *everybody* in the Church becoming articulate over the issues of faith and responsibility instead of the 'endless chatter' from the clergy. In fact, the Church could do with far fewer 'professional' clergy, congregations could produce their own leaders, and the 'clerical caste' should be broken down. There was too much suppression of thought and intellectual integrity in the Church, and a lot of leeway to make up. Then came a question about Christian sexual morality and Vidler's comment: 'I don't think the ordinary people in the Church have thought through the implications of abandoning a very legalistic type of ethics and regarding moral laws as rigid things that you have to obey.'

The trajectory had completed its course, and there was an explosion as Anglican tempers were detonated. Earliest into the fray was the *Church Times*, whose front page next week splashed the headline CAMBRIDGE PRIEST'S ATTACK ON CHURCH over the story. Inside, its current affairs page complained bitterly:

> From Dr Vidler, who after all is a priest of the Church (though it was hard for anyone seeing and hearing him on this programme to realise it), viewers might reasonably have expected some clear exposition of the Church's real nature and condition. Instead they were given the impression that the Church was an outmoded organisation in a helpless muddle. His sweeping criticisms suggested that everything was wrong with the Church (except the Establishment), and nothing right. He had no use for sermons . . . nor for hymns, or indeed, it seemed, for any form of worship. Worship should give place to unfettered discussion. In the current Cambridge fashion, he seemed averse to the idea of 'moral laws'. He gave no hint of understanding the Church or its authority, its mission or its Lord. He did not mention God.[32]

Then, with an innuendo hinting at conspiracy, the report concluded:

> The BBC could easily have found an effective spokesman for the Church . . . if it wished. It did not so wish. This is not an isolated incident, but part of a pattern. It is high time that the Archbishops took a long, hard look at the damage which, however unintentionally, is being done to the

good name of the Church, and to the cause of truth, by some aspects of the present policy of the Religious Broadcasting Department of the BBC.[33]

All of which merely underlined Vidler's point, as did, by a glorious irony, the front page of that very issue of the *Church Times*, which seemed to have been laid out precisely to illustrate the torpor of the Church. Among the articles surrounding the report of the broadcast was a note on the new Dean of Chester, 'an eminent scholar who is known chiefly for his work in connection with canon law revision' and who was secretary 'of the Commission responsible for the report which provided the framework with which the Convocations have been working for the past fifteen years' and 'an acknowledged expert on Cathedral life'; a report on the new Archdeacon of Cardiff whose chief claim to fame, apparently, was his captaincy of the St David's diocesan cricket team which shared the *Church Times* cup with Sheffield six years previously; a report that the Bishop of Oxford was moving into an ancient house in Cuddesdon; and, rather unfortunately in view of the *Meeting Point* furore, the story that a Sussex vicar was experimenting with a Sunday evening service two hours earlier than customary hitherto, in deference to the lure of evening television.

But torpor there certainly was not at the Church Assembly which met that week, presided over by the Archbishop of Canterbury, Dr Michael Ramsey. During a debate on the activities of the Church Information Office, a woman member from Ely Diocese angrily raised the matter of the broadcast, under the fond impression that it had been sponsored by the Office. (That in itself was revealing of how unprepared was the Church for the new media age. The idea that the Church might be subjected to examination by anything other than its own propaganda ministries and dragged into the secular market-place of debate, was not only unfamiliar but totally alien.) That public criticism might be offered from within its own ranks was a betrayal of Anglicanism. 'It was irresponsible that it should have been produced, and it is an insult to ask us to pay for it.' Another woman, from Southwark, said she had already written a furious letter to the BBC: 'I don't know what we can do to stop these young men talking like this.'

Sir Kenneth Grubb, Chairman of the House of Laity, counselled a rational attitude and suggested that the best way of handling misrepresentations was for everyone to set about correcting them. Mr George Goyder, Chairman of the Church Information Office, had read the script of the programme and appeared to think that Vidler's main point had been to direct young people towards fornication, 'This was not the way to present a broadcast to the nation on the moral law.' Loud applause.

'CONTROVERSIAL TV SCRIPT GOES TO DR RAMSEY' proclaimed the front page of the *Church Times* on 16 November. What Dr Ramsey thought of it is not clear, but little was heard of him in this episode apart from this non-event of his receiving the script (which almost anyone who was anyone could get anyway). Meanwhile the BBC Religious Broadcasting Department came under fire, with its Head, Canon Roy McKay, defending 'A good, objective discussion without bias, which brought out many important points.' The matter was referred to the Central Religious Advisory Committee for discussion in December, but that body dealt only with broad policy in religious broadcasting, not particular programmes. The fact was that 'The C. of E.' had been good television and had provoked debate in a way that no conventional piety could have done. All that the anguished could do was to write letters to the church press or to Vidler himself. The *Church Times* on 16 November carried two whole pages of letters on 'Dr Vidler's Broadcast Attack on the Church'. A. J. Watts, Director of Education in the Diocese of Oxford, headed the list with a personal attack on Vidler's credentials:

> Dr Vidler may wear whatever he likes – black shirt, white tie, as he pleases, in his protest against clerical dress; but, on consulting . . . *Crockford's Directory*, I notice that Dr Vidler withdrew from the hard but rewarding grind of parish life (where he appears never to have held the full responsibility for a parish) as long ago as 1931, in order to betake himself to the quieter waters of St Deiniol's Library and the private chapels of two royal foundations – all doubtless spheres of work in which he has made his distinguished mark, but hardly parochial experience.[34]

Vidler's apparent lack of parochial experience was cited by several correspondents. 'Could someone in authority convince the Dean that there is a world outside the University of Cambridge where some people are not bored with their parsons. . . ?' pleaded one. 'One expects knocks from the enemies of the Church, but not from those who (presumably) felt a call to serve her as "priests of the Lord" . . .' complained another. 'Whilst a few of us were engaged in praising God in exactly the same form as that followed in King's College Chapel, Cambridge, Dr Vidler . . . was . . . busy dragging the Church in the dirt before some millions of TV viewers.' Hardly any of the letters got beyond these outbursts of hurt feelings. One scorned Vidler as 'an obtuse and ageing Angry Young Man' and asked, 'has he never faced the need to justify, to oneself let alone anyone else, the corporate ordered worship of the church with most of its customary elements, if one is to go on being involved in it?'

There was also support, however. Even at this stage, J. A. T. Robinson, the Bishop of Woolwich, was joining in to point out that Vidler had *not* criticized worship as such, but was posing Bonhoeffer's teasing question, 'What is the meaning of worship in the entire absence of religion?' The hysterical reaction, observed Robinson, merely confirmed Vidler's opinion of the intellectual state of the Church. 'I know that what he said was dangerous, perhaps damaging, but I believe that in the long run what the world – not to mention God – most wants from the Church is honesty.' Other letters appeared in support, including one from Lincoln which suggested that instead of looking at the BBC Religious Programmes Department, the Archbishops would do better to find out why so many laypeople *preferred* to stay at home on Sunday evenings to watch *Meeting Point*. 'Here at least we are saved from quaint hymns and endless sermons preached from "six feet above public opinion" and with an assurance which many layfolk suspect.'

What anxious conservatives really needed, of course, was a hierarchical condemnation. Addressing his diocesan conference, the Archbishop of York, Dr Donald Coggan, said that sniping at the Church was not entirely to be regretted. When the sniping came from outside, it was a sign that the Church was being salt and light in the world. When the sniping came from inside, the situation was quite different:

> No man should criticise his mother, especially before those who are outside the family circle, unless (a) he loves her so dearly that he is convinced his silence would damage her; (b) he has some very clear and cogent remedies, which he can offer her, at cost to himself, for her healing. Even so, he will think long and hard before he criticises her in the presence of those who know little or nothing of her greatness, of her care and of her love for her children.[35]

These tender sentiments (no one of course bothered to ask whether condition (a) just might be fulfilled by Vidler or any of his colleagues) were regarded as significant enough to make the front page of the *Church Times* under the rather despairing headline SNIPING AT THE CHURCH SHOWS THAT IT IS ALIVE. Eventually the issue of 30 November was able to announce BISHOP HITS AT 'HURT AND SCANDAL' ON TELEVISION with the all-too-true subtitle 'Dons' High-Table Talk can be Misunderstood'. The Bishop was W. Glyn Simon of Llandaff, who was addressing his own diocese on the 'considerable stir' created by the Vidler programme (and earlier by Harry Williams). Despite his episcopal office, however, he had nothing to add to the already hackneyed criticisms of the remoteness of the dons' life from 'the humdrum life of the parish ministry' (for, he said, birth and marriage, sorrow and death 'occur with comparative rarity in academic circles'), beyond commenting on Vidler's plea for 'dialogue' in the Church: 'The clergy would be more than ready to try this kind of thing, and other experiments too, but again and again they are confronted by the reluctance and opposition of their people.' But he did at least reach a new level of banality by confessing 'that I am old-fashioned enough to wish that clergymen appearing on television, and on other occasions for that matter, were not so ready to abandon clerical dress and to appear in a variety of fancy ties and jackets'. Meanwhile back in Cambridge Vidler was losing no sleep over the fuss, for much of the correspondence he was getting was highly appreciative. With every word of protest from his critics, every expostulation of the *Church Times*, his diagnosis was being confirmed. The *Church Times* continued to protest at the 'projection of a false image of the Church's work and worship and contradiction of the truth of Christ' in this 'deplorable incident', and called for BBC religious television to note that 'the Church at large is becoming sick and tired of the choice of unrepresentative broadcasters to present the Church to the public'.[36] Nothing could be more eloquent than that last sentence, of the prevailing clerical presumption that the media, like the rest of the world, existed for the benefit of the Church, or, more specifically, for the benefit of clergy. That the world, in the form of the media, might have its own genuine and serious interest in the Church, and that this interest might be healthy for the Church itself, was as yet inconceivable.

What the controversy did provide, of course, was splendid publicity for *Soundings*. An immediate interest was in any case created by the book in its own right. For all those who were alarmed there were many, especially at the younger end, who were relieved that theologians were asking themselves and their Church some awkward questions, and being prepared to listen to other people's questions, instead of parading confident answers to this and that. People began to sense a mood of honesty breaking in upon the Church. Not least, the questions being raised by these academics were not just academic. Rarely, if ever, had the sacred shrine of traditional Anglicanism, the Book of Common Prayer, been so savagely accused of being pathologically morbid as Williams' essay argued it to be; not to mention his querying of the whole assumed ground of Christian ethics. Likewise Vidler's questioning of the national Church's preoccupation with 'religion', however tentatively phrased, touched some acutely sensitive nerves at a time of increasing insecurity as to the role of organized Christianity in modern society. The sheer virulence of the outburst against him was a useful register of that inner anxiety and self-doubt that needed catharsis.

Objections to Christian Belief

On Christmas Eve 1962 the Christmas carols from King's College Chapel sounded as reassuringly sweet as ever. Perhaps, after all, the 'Cambridge theology' and its attendant arguments would disappear with the new year. But, in that exceptionally bitter winter, the first two months of 1963 were to thrust the Cambridge questioners even more to the fore. For a number of years it had been customary for the Cambridge Divinity faculty to put on a series of lectures during the Lent or Easter terms. The subjects had been important, and even challenging. 'God, Sex and War', the theme for 1962, was nothing if not ambitious. The series advertised for the Lent term 1963 had the title 'Fundamental Objections to Christianity', and the advance publicity made clear that far from rushing to meet the objections with fluent answers, the main concern of the speakers would be to recognize the force of the objections and to state the gravity of the issues facing any Christian apologetic – to become 'atheists for the sake of the Kingdom of God' as the writer recalls Alec Vidler telling a beginning of term party in King's. The series was planned quite independently of the *Soundings* project. Two of the lecturers, D. M. Mackinnon and J. S. Bezzant, had not been involved in that book. Alec Vidler and Harry Williams made up the foursome.

The lectures were held in the large Examination Schools and the first notable feature about them was the extraordinarily large attendance. For many of the 1500 or so undergraduates who attended each of the four lectures, there was standing room only. That was a clear sign of the interest already stimulated by the 'Cambridge theologians' the previous term, but it also registered that the theme of the lectures was touching a real nerve among the young and educated, whether attached to Christian belief or not (and, as far as one can recollect, all shades of belief and unbelief attended). The buzz of interest continued long after each evening's prolonged applause died down, in college discussion groups, in impromptu discussions over coffee, and in reports in the religious and national press. The lectures were published in a matter of weeks.[37]

Donald Mackinnon opened the series with 'Moral Objections'. Ironic, at times acerbic, he exposed the ways in which 'Christian morality' is sometimes less than honest in its partiality and prejudices:

> It is impossible to escape the impression that, to certain sorts of clergy, the effective exclusion from sacramental communion of divorced persons who have remarried is the highest form of the Church's moral witness. The cynic might well be tempted to say that the heartless zeal frequently displayed in the bearing of this particular testimony, is a way in which ecclesiastics compensate for their unwillingness to engage with other besetting moral issues of our age, for instance the moral permissibility of nuclear weapons.[38]

What is more, Mackinnon asked, is there not the possibility of a moral flaw at the heart of Christian belief, if Christians did not seriously and honestly ask how much weight of moral truth could be borne by a historically uncertain gospel record?

That question was pursued by Alec Vidler in his lecture on 'Historical Objections'. He drew attention to the inveterate tendency to bias in Christian historiography, and even queried whether those who at Cambridge taught Christian origins should be, as at present, almost without exception committed members of Christian Churches. Christian history, in its origins and in its later course, was riddled with ambiguity and uncertainty. 'I often find myself,' said Vidler, 'more in sympathy or *en rapport* with non-Christians who have a sense of the strangeness and incertitude of our world and of the duty of a large measure of agnosticism than I do with Christians who are cocksure about their beliefs.'[39] Not that Vidler was commending agnosticism instead of faith, for in the end faith was not dependent upon historical certainty. It should be called a 'participation in the Christian mystery as a present reality' in the shared experience of the community of believers.

J. S. Bezzant, Dean of St John's and a product of Ripon Hall Modernism in the school of Major, supplied a good old liberal knock-about in the fourth lecture, 'Intellectual Objections'. Literal historical fall, physical resurrection, penal substitutionary atonement, second advent – 'There can be no doubt that the demolition squad long ago did its work on all this'. He called for a new natural theology to be embarked upon as the only responsible way forward through the intellectual wreckage of orthodoxy left after the impact of modernity. In advocating this he brought his lecture, and the series, to a close with a moving statement of the integrity required in the search for truth at a time when there were no assured answers:

> For myself, I cling to the hope that it will, in time, become possible. Meanwhile I think there is nothing that can be called knowledge or reasonable belief that there is or can be anything in the human mind that

> can possibly justify the passing of such a colossal condemnation on this inconceivably vast and mysterious universe as is implied in the judgment that it has no meaning or enduring value. Further, I think it is entirely reasonable for any man who studies the spirit of the facing of life as Christ faced it, and his recorded teaching, to decide that by him he will stand through life, death or eternity rather than join in a possible triumph of evil over him. Whether or not any church will regard such a man as a Christian is nowadays wholly secondary and manifestly unimportant: any church which refuses so to recognize him may be harming itself; it cannot harm him, and he should accept the refusal with regret but with equanimity.[40]

Once again, however, the most immediate impact was made by Harry Williams' lecture, 'Psychological Objections'. Partly it was a more popular version of his *Soundings* essay. It was also more personal – just how much so was not revealed until the publication of his autobiography nearly twenty years later. Williams made clear that he was not aiming any particular psychological *theory* at Christianity, but was attempting something more basic and more subtle: exposing the ways in which in theology and religious discourse, as in all intellectual pursuits (including psychology!) hidden human motives and drives are at work. Indeed much in Christianity is used as an escape from, or camouflage for, that in us which we dread knowing. Altruism, 'loving service', often outwardly appear as 'serving God' when in fact they are using God to serve ourselves. 'Behind the consciously sincere generosity there is often an egotism which is disturbing because it is unrecognized, and so, underhand. It is as though their Christianity were not more than a Merovingian Emperor. Behind stands the Mayor of the Palace whom they are too frightened to meet.'[41] But the tyranny lies deeper still:

> The weapon with which the churches bludgeon me on to the broad way is that of inflating the feelings of guilt which lie latent in us all. Make a person feel guilty enough and he will do what he is told. This latent guilt-feeling is a non-rational sense of a harshly authoritarian figure who judges and condemns us. It is as though the external authoritarian figures we have known all our lives have been injected inside us like a virus and have in this way become part of ourselves . . . Even if . . . a man is a Christian Theologian of the highest calibre, it is still possible for him to feel the inner Juggernaut, and in his feelings to confuse the Juggernaut with God.[42]

Blake's Nobodaddy has taken over – 'The Nobodaddy aloft farted and belched and coughed' – and has to be placated. Spontaneous love and creativity get suppressed because they appear in unconventional, seemingly immoral ways, and are replaced by religious and virtuous contrivances, from ritual penance to singing 'Just as I am, without one plea' (by now of course Anglo-Catholics and conservative Evangelicals alike were shifting uneasily). 'We have shown the white flag and capitulated to Him. But the peace is bought with a price. And the price is my destruction. For what I am and what I do is no longer the activity of a free agent.'

The high-point of the lecture was an eerie account of a very able Cambridge theological graduate, a High Anglican who one night had a terrifying nightmare:

> In his dream he was sitting in a theatre watching a play. He turned round and looked behind him. At the back of the theatre there was a monster in human form who was savagely hypnotizing the actors on the stage, reducing them to puppets. The spectacle of this harsh inhuman puppeteer exercising his hypnotic powers so that the people on the stage were completely under his spell and the slaves of his will – this spectacle was so terrifying that the man awoke trembling and in a cold sweat. After several months he gradually realized that the monster of the nightmare was the god he was really worshipping in spite of his having got a First in the Theological tripos. And to this god he had painfully to die.[43]

After a breakdown, the man found a new beginning by recovering a sense of proper selfhood and hence the ability to love genuinely, 'for without a self one cannot give'. Two years later, said Williams, the dreamer was seen 'drunk among the bars and brothels of Tangiers', rejoicing at the words of Jesus, 'The publicans and harlots go into the Kingdom of God before you.' (The man was, in fact, Williams himself.) The worst evil is the disguised slavery to hidden corruption in religious guise – far worse than external and obvious vices. Once again, sensitivities were roused, and it was Williams' lecture which aroused most comment, annoyance, glee or bafflement, in Cambridge at the time.

Cambridge theology – an assessment

The 'Cambridge theology' was a disparate movement, united only in a shared belief in the necessity to question, more seriously than had been done for decades, and in the name of spiritual and intellectual honesty, the received formulations and practices of belief and theology. The disparity in specialisms and emphases between the contributors to *Soundings* and the *Objections* lectures created difficulties for any properly critical response, that is, any comment which tried to get beyond what Donald Mackinnon called 'the Philistine anti-intellectualism of the *Church Times*'. That response was not lacking, however. Alan Richardson, then Professor of

Christian Theology at Nottingham (later Dean of York), replied to *Soundings* with a booklet, *Four Anchors From the Stern*, accusing the authors of unnecessarily panicking in the storms of liberalism. The most thorough and constructively critical statement came from E. L. Mascall, Professor of Historical Theology at London, whose *Up and Down in Adria*[44] continued to exploit the nautical metaphors suggested by *Soundings* and Acts 27. Mascall, a leading Anglo-Catholic theologian and philosopher in the Thomist tradition, was by no means sweepingly dismissive of the essays. He especially welcomed Woods' writing on transcendence (though here, as with some of the other essays, pointing out that creative lines of advance were already being explored by a number of scholars). He was trenchantly critical of Williams ('Pumping Out the Bilge' he called the relevant chapter) for being overly dependent on Freud at the expense of other depth-psychologists, and for wantonly redefining faith as trust in the worth of one's larger self, rather than in the objectively gracious God. Vidler's view of the National Church he saw as naively romantic. Overall his verdict was that where Cambridge was asking the right questions, it seemed to be unaware of who might already be providing suggestive answers. For some months during 1963 Mascall engaged with Williams in a lively correspondence in the pages of *Theology*.

In one sense the actual views expressed in *Soundings* were less significant than the fact that the book represented the right to ask questions and to be honest about uncertainties. This gave it a kind of *pastoral* significance, as was perceived by Henry Chadwick in one of the earliest reviews of the book. Chadwick concluded his article by a comparison with A. E. J. Rawlinson, who, as an Oxford college chaplain, was frequently visited by undergraduates beset by religious doubts: 'but they soon discovered that their puzzles and uncertainties were but a drop in the bucket compared with his, and accordingly departed much reassured and strengthened'.[45] This was even more the case with the *Objections* lectures which were published in April 1963, that is, barely two months after their delivery. William Barclay, the popular New Testament expositor of moderately evangelical views commended the collection as an 'intensely important book'. 'Any thinking Christian who reads it will be better able to face himself, the world, and God.'[46] Interestingly, while Barclay devoted most of his attention to Vidler's lecture, he identifies Williams' as 'the most searching'. Of course there was scorn from other quarters. The review in the *Listener* thought the lectures a suicidal exercise – 'the resident firemen of Christianity acting as incendiaries, cutting their own hoses, in order to demonstrate how well they understand the human condition of arson'.[47] T. E. Utley in the *Church Times* had virtually nothing to say about the content but everything to condemn about the style of what he called the 'Four Doubting Dons': 'We are led discreetly to expect something in the nature of a striptease show inserted in the middle of a vicarage garden party; all we get is a little gentle swearing in the vicarage drawing-room.'[48]

But it was the Warden of Keble College, Oxford, Austin Farrer,[49] who most succinctly parodied the four Cambridge Objectors, in the same poetic vein in which Ronald Knox, half a century earlier, had satirized the *Foundations* essayists (see p. 58). His tribute to Williams could almost have been written by Auden:

Press not hypocrisy so far
As to be better than you are
Nor by confession of your plight
Wallow in obscene delight.
The phrases of the Common Prayer
Are steps in hell's descending stair.
The bars and brothels of Tangier
Make the inward vision clear.

While Bezzant's demolition and tentative reconstruction were compressed into:

Objections to the Christian creed
Ought not, in logic, to succeed –
Flat prejudices, favoured by
Our out-of-date cosmology.
But don't imagine you can clear
The cobwebs out in half a year;
Our abstract nouns hypostatized,
Our dogmas undemythicized
Will keep religion to the few
Another century or two.

By the time the *Objections* lectures appeared in print, still more disturbance was being created by John Robinson's *Honest to God*, and the 'Cambridge theology' was being subsumed under the wider 'radical theology' movement which some saw as a Cambridge–Southwark conspiracy (see next chapter). But Cambridge continued to enjoy a reputation of its own as a centre of Christian radicalism in Britain. Vidler discovered that an interest in theology was blossoming anew all over the country, as manifested in invitations to lecture on the current debate. Academic visitors from abroad made Cambridge a place of pilgrimage. Within a year or two one could say paradoxically that a radical 'tradition' had been established, when Hugh Montefiore, now Vicar of the University Church of Great St Mary's, could publish a book of sermons *Truth to Tell: A Radical Restatement of Christian Faith*.[50] Ved Mehta, an Indian philosopher, wrote a book, *The New Theologian*, on the radical movements in Britain, Germany and the United States, and included interviews with Vidler, Mackinnon and Williams.[51] The impact spread even beyond Christian circles when a group of humanists followed suit with *Objections to Humanism*.

Vidler's own first opportunity to take stock of the 'ferment' came early in 1964 when he gave the Robertson Lectures at Glasgow University, published in 1965 as *Twentieth Century Defenders of the Faith*.[52] Its subtitle, 'Some Theological Fashions Considered', conveyed a note of detachment or, one might say, a sense of history. Vidler examined five 'fashions' – Liberal Protestantism, Roman Catholic Modernism, English Liberal Catholicism, Neo-Orthodoxy, and finally, the contemporary Christian Radicalism. Despite his involvement as midwife to this last fashion, he was characteristically cautious, conceding that for the moment theology seemed to have more to learn from the 'subjectivists' like Robinson and van Buren, than from the 'objectivists' of the preceding neo-orthodox generation. But all these are *fashions*. Pendulums swing. Church, theology, spirituality move on; continuity exists through change. That sounds like a Roman Catholic Modernist view of truth, and indeed Vidler confesses that it is with Modernists like Loisy that he feels most kinship. There is a need for openness, flexibility and comprehensiveness in the Churches, 'though I do not think that a completely "religionless" Christianity is possible or desirable'. For this reason, concludes Vidler,

> I am glad that there are the beginnings of a promising commotion in the churches, and that windows and sluices are being opened which twenty years ago seemed to be pretty closed. I find it encouraging that, though there have naturally been expressions of alarm, churches do not at present seem to be trying to suppress their radicals.[53]

Soundings went through several editions, and sold far more than the authors had envisaged. Something *was* happening in English theology. Earlier in this chapter, we argued that the genesis of *Soundings* cannot, without gross and simplistic distortion, be attributed to a falling in with the irreverently critical mood of the 1960s British cultural scene. It was allowed, however, that the public responses to the Cambridge theology might well reflect the mood of society. It was a tenet of the early 1960s that the most suspect things were those which were apparently beyond question. Henry Chadwick summarized the situation by referring to 'the general climate of uncertainty about past tradition that characterizes the mood of our age'.[54] 'Tradition' in the broadest sense, whether social, political, cultural or religious, was under suspicion. For many Christians, the 'Christian tradition' was no longer *their* tradition, it was an alien, heteronomous code from an age far removed from contemporary Britain. It stood no chance of eventual acceptance *unless* it was prepared to be questioned to the very roots. For many who wished in some way to remain identified with Christianity it is hard to see how they could ever have done so, without denying and suppressing their deepest instincts of freedom and identity, if the Churches had not been open to question. Otherwise the tradition could never be 'owned' in freedom. In the summer of 1963 Howard Root expressed the hunch that the new, radical voices from Cambridge and elsewhere 'are in touch with deeper feelings widespread in Christendom, with a deep and inarticulate longing for liberation from all the religious and intellectual paraphernalia which have encased the gospel for centuries'.[55] In retrospect, the aspirations of that time may seem to have had more romance than reality in them, and it is easy to dismiss the Cambridge theology and radical Christianity as a passing fad. If it passed, it was at least partly because it did its job. It made people realize that the Christian tradition would not survive by a mindless, unexamined repetition, the sort which says, 'The temple of the Lord, the temple of the Lord.' From time to time the tradition has to be tested to breaking-point in order that its true strengths may be identified for a new generation. It has to be set at a distance, temporarily dismissed, in order to see what are those elements in it which insist on returning with the power and creativity of truth for the contemporary scene. It has to be rejected in order that it may be embraced with a new, authentic love by today's Christians, *their own* love which values what the tradition says to *them*, instead of merely a reverence which acknowledges what it said to their forebears. That is what was happening in the early 1960s, and above all in the Cambridge theology. It was the first, negative-sounding phase in the essential dialectic of attaining to a new, mature relationship to the tradition. Nor in fact was the Cambridge theology by any means just a passing phase. One has only to look, for example, at much writing on spirituality, both academic and popular, of more recent years to see how Harry Williams' utterances during 1962–3, while wounding to many at the time, contributed greatly to what might be called a movement towards a spirituality 'from below', in which people are encouraged and enabled to open up what they really feel and fear and love, as essential elements in prayer and community. And of course Williams has continued to write widely read books on spirituality himself.

When in the spring of 1963 Cambridge suddenly became caught up in the wider controversy emanating from the London South Bank, no one was more surprised than the Cambridge theologians themselves. For when Alec Vidler, Howard Root and the others had started meeting early in 1957, they did not seriously consider including Dr John Robinson, then Dean of Clare College. He was thought to be far too conventional.

Notes

1 D. E. Cooper, 'Looking Back on Anger', in V. Bogdanor and R. Skidelsky (eds), *The Age of Affluence 1951–1964*, London: Macmillan 1970, p. 262.
2 Christopher Booker, *The Neophiliacs*, London: Collins 1970, esp. p. 163f.
3 Bernard Levin, *The Pendulum Years: Britain and the Sixties*, London: Jonathan Cape 1970, p. 327.
4 Booker, op. cit., p. 185.
5 G. M. Macleod, *Only One Way Left: Church Prospect*, Glasgow: Iona Community 1956.
6 R. Gregor Smith, *The New Man: Christianity and Man's Coming of Age*, London: SCM Press 1956. See also K. W. Clements, *The Theology of Ronald Gregor Smith*, Leiden: E. J. Brill 1986.
7 See A. R. Vidler, *Scenes From a Clerical Life*, London: Collins 1977, on which this chapter draws.
8 ibid., p. 110.
9 A. R. Vidler, *Twentieth Century Defenders of the Faith*, London: SCM Press 1965, p. 102 (italics mine).
10 Vidler, *Scenes*, p. 117.
11 H. A. Williams, *Some Day I'll Find You: An Autobiography*, London: Collins Fount 1984.
12 ibid., p. 213.
13 ibid., p. 189.
14 A. R. Vidler (ed.), *Soundings: Essays Concerning Christian Understanding*, Cambridge: Cambridge University Press 1962, p. ix.
15 ibid., p. xi.
16 ibid., p. 19.
17 ibid., p. 121.
18 ibid., p. 138f.
19 ibid., p. 190.
20 ibid., p. 236.
21 ibid., p. 145.

22 ibid.
23 ibid., p. 242f.
24 *Essays in Liberality*, London: SCM Press 1957, pp. 95–112.
25 Vidler (ed.), *Soundings*, p. 254f.
26 ibid., p. 255f.
27 ibid., p. 263.
28 ibid., p. 73.
29 ibid., p. 74.
30 ibid., p. 79.
31 ibid., p. 82.
32 *Church Times*, 9 November 1962.
33 ibid.
34 *Church Times*, 16 November 1962.
35 *Church Times*, 23 November 1962.
36 *Church Times*, 30 November 1962.
37 A. R. Vidler (ed.), *Objections to Christian Belief*, London: Constable 1963.
38 ibid., p. 14.
39 ibid., p. 77.
40 ibid., p. 109f.
41 ibid., p. 43.
42 ibid., p. 50.
43 ibid., p. 52f.
44 London: Faith Press 1963.
45 *Theology* LXV (November 1962), p. 446.
46 *Expository Times*, June 1963, p. 288.
47 *Listener*, 27 June 1963.
48 *Church Times*, 5 April 1963.
49 *Theology* LXVI (August 1963), p. 317f.
50 London: Collins Fontana 1966.
51 Ved Mehta, *The New Theologian*, Harmondsworth: Pelican Books 1968. For the Cambridge theologians, see esp. pp. 77–89.
52 London: SCM Press.
53 ibid., p. 122.
54 *Theology* LXV (November 1962), p. 446.
55 *Theology* LXVI (June 1963), p. 224.

7 Radical Ambiguity: The *Honest to God* Debate

> To tell you the truth, I was doing nothing more strenuous than bending down to tie my shoelaces, and I got a strained back. I simply stayed in bed for three months and wrote most of the book.[1]

Never can a displaced vertebra have ever had such dramatic consequences, certainly not in British theology. Wiseacres made much of 'slipped disc-ipline', but the fact remains that the appearance of *Honest to God* in 1963 provoked the most public, the most widespread and the most contentious theological controversy in twentieth-century Britain. It concerned the fundamental Christian doctrine of God, and led to charges that Bishop John Robinson was an atheist. It sparked off debates and exchanges within the Churches at every level, from archiepiscopal pronouncements to parish magazines, and caused comment in anything from learned journals to popular newspapers and, not least, on radio and television as well. For several weeks in the spring of 1963 it suddenly seemed as though everyone was talking theology – or at least had an opinion on 'that bishop who says there's no God'. At a serious level the debate was to continue for many months, and in retrospect *Honest to God* can be viewed as a crucial landmark in post-war religious thought in Britain. It was significant not only in what John Robinson said (not all of which was original to him), nor even simply in the fact that he was a bishop who said it (highly important though that was), but in the imprimatur which it gave to a kind of theological debate which had been gathering momentum for some time. Overnight, people at all levels in the Churches, or on the fringes of organized religion, realized that the agenda for discussion of belief was quite open. Theology need no longer apparently be on the other side of the fence from critical questioning, but was itself adopting the critical style. 'The *Honest to God* discussion,' wrote a young minister in the summer of 1963, 'is an exhilarating, liberating breeze of sincere enquiry into the perplexing questions.'[2] It was a style which labelled itself 'radical', and some weeks before *Honest to God* appeared Robinson himself described in a radio talk what he understood 'radicalism' to mean:

> Radicalism represents the built-in challenge to any establishment, any institutionalism, any orthodoxy: and it is an attitude that is relevant to far more than politics. Indeed, the essence of the radical protest could be

> summed up in the statement of Jesus that 'the Sabbath is made for man, and not man for the Sabbath'. Persons are more important than any principles.[3]

Of course, to a degree Robinson was reflecting the growing movement of questioning within the Churches, especially the Church of England, during 1962–63, which was sketched in the previous chapter. But his own contribution in *Honest to God* was to be the most effective symbol and catalyst of Christian radicalism in Britain.

Just why this should have been so is still a matter of debate among both theologians and sociologists of religion. Nerves were touched at a number of sensitive points. Obviously the theological issues themselves were fundamental: an attack on a God allegedly 'out there' to be replaced by a God who was the 'depth' or 'ground' of being could hardly be expected to be allowed to pass without comment, not to mention that man having 'come of age' no longer needs religion. Questions of authority within the Church were also involved. And of course in the climate of the early 1960s, when the trade in new ideas was a burgeoning media interest, a bishop expressing novel and possibly heretical ideas suited exactly the heavier Sunday papers and the middle-brow television discussion programmes. But amid all the curiosity which still surrounds the controversy, one fact is utterly indisputable: it was the theological publishing success story of the century. The SCM Press later innocently disclaimed any intention of launching a sensation on the market. The initial print-run was of 6,000 copies, a reasonable estimate for a smallish book on what was thought to be 'serious' theology. It sold out in days. By the autumn 350,000 copies were in print throughout the English-speaking world and it was being translated into six European languages and Japanese. David Edwards, Editor and Managing Director of SCM Press, could justly claim: 'The book appears to have sold more quickly than any new book of serious theology in the history of the world.'[4] By 1966 its sales had reached nearly a million. Twenty-five years later it is still in print.

The initial impact admittedly owed much to a front-page article in the *Observer* on 17 March 1963, two days before publication of the book. The paper had been approached with a view to a feature on the book, but the subject-matter was thought by the editor to be too 'theological'. Instead, Robinson himself was asked by the paper to write an article summarizing his ideas. So appeared on the front page the notorious banner headlines (chosen by the editor, not Robinson himself): OUR IMAGE OF GOD MUST GO. Both Robinson and Edwards claimed to be slightly embarrassed by this negative-sounding, if eye-catching, slogan. But doubtless in the following weeks the accountants and directors of SCM Press must have happily reflected that there is indeed no such thing as bad publicity, even for theology.

There was in fact understandable reason for SCM's surprise at the phenomenal sales success of *Honest to God*, since from an editor's point of view it was just one more on a list of books exploring the newer trends in theology which had been appearing under the SCM label for several years. Indeed, it was David Edwards' predecessor as Editor, Ronald Gregor Smith, who in 1956 published his own study *The New Man*. Like *Honest to God* this explored the meaning of 'God' in a world where traditional religious belief seemed alien to modernity, and, no less than *Honest to God*, was heavily dependent upon the thought of Rudolf Bultmann, Paul Tillich and (particularly) Dietrich Bonhoeffer. *The New Man* can be regarded as the pioneer of the theological track leading to the radicalism of the 1960s, and indeed Robinson in *Honest to God* acknowledges a debt to it.[5] Others followed right down to Daniel Jenkins' *Beyond Religion* in 1962, subtitled 'The Truth and Error in "Religionless Christianity" '. *Honest to God* thus seemed to be following what was already a well-worn path.

What had probably not been recognized, however, was that, beyond a relatively select circle of academics, theological college teachers and bookish clergy, the thought of the three theologians on whom Robinson was most dependent in *Honest to God* was little known or appreciated, and therefore how much *Honest to God* was to act as a publicity agent for them. A good deal of the book's impact was due to the gobbets from these figures' writings, often at their most provocative, tossed by Robinson at his readers.

Dietrich Bonhoeffer and his attack on 'religion' we have met in the previous chapter. Rudolf Bultmann (1884–1976) was one of the outstanding New Testament scholars of modern Germany. During the Second World War he began his own controversy with other Protestant theologians on the question of how the 'mythological' elements in the New Testament – such as the out-dated pre-scientific cosmology of a three-decker universe (heaven, earth and hell), demons, spirits and miraculous supernatural events – were to be interpreted today. The New Testament message itself, Bultmann claimed, had to be disentangled from this first-century mythology, otherwise the true 'offence' of the gospel would be obscured and confused with an unnecessary intellectual offence to modern man whose world-view was totally different to that of the ancient world. So Bultmann embarked on his famous programme of 'demythologizing' the New Testament – in some ways a misnomer since he did not believe that the message of Christ, the 'kerygma', was itself a myth. Good Lutheran that he was, the gospel always remained that of the forgiving grace of God which comes as a Word from God into the actual life of man, freeing him from self-reliance and bringing a new order of existence in trust upon God and utter openness to the future. This faith did not need the trappings of a first-century cosmology, but it did require expression in thought-forms meaningful to contemporary man – a reclothing if not a remythologizing. Bultmann found the new clothes for the gospel message in the existential philosophy of Martin Heidegger (1889–1976), for some time a university colleague of his at Marburg. Where Heidegger saw man displaying 'inauthentic' existence, refusing to take responsibility for himself and living in continual retreat from the future and death, Bultmann saw a close parallel with the New Testament picture of life apart from faith. Where Heidegger saw the possibility of a new or 'authentic' existence, a life freed from anxiety because death was recognized, faced and accepted, Bultmann saw a picture of what was actually realized when the gospel message of grace is accepted in faith. Bultmann's works began to appear in English soon after the war, and provoked lively discussion especially among New Testament scholars on the issue of his allegedly extreme historical scepticism. On the wider theological issue of demythologizing, the debate was most intense north of the border, for at Edinburgh the theology of Karl Barth, Bultmann's chief continental opponent, held full sway, while Bultmann had a lively following at Glasgow University throughout the 1950s and 1960s. It was a debate, after all, most pertinent to communities, like the Church of Scotland, which had affinities with the continental Protestantism of 'the Word'.

Paul Tillich (1886–1965), like Bonhoeffer and Bultmann, was a German Lutheran, but emigrated to the United States shortly before the Second World War. Like them, he also was deeply concerned for the communication of faith for the contemporary world. His approach, however, differed in important respects. Whereas Bultmann, for example, clung very closely to the typical Protestant concept of the Word of God in Christ as a unique revelation of God, Tillich searched for an understanding of God which could have a universal expression. He sought a total vision of human life, knowledge and experience, in which theology, philosophy, culture and all intellectual and artistic pursuits could be seen as a whole. And whereas Bonhoeffer in his last years developed a criticism of religion as a phenomenon which man was outgrowing and which was in fact a hindrance to an apprehension of the biblical faith, Tillich sought to uncover what he saw as a religious depth to all existence, in every aspect. God was indeed not a supernatural being removed from the world of experience. He was the ground or depth of all being. Nor was God an irrelevant distraction from man's human concerns – rather he was the ultimate concern, that sense of claim and call which grasps a person unconditionally. Tillich's works began to appear in English just before the Second World War, but it was not until the late 1940s that his presence really began to be felt, not least through his small volume of sermons, *The Shaking of the Foundations*, which SCM Press published in 1949. His three-volume *Systematic Theology* was to follow.

The effect on many readers of meeting these figures at first hand and for the first time was electrifying – that is, either shocking or thrilling. But, to many people who had hitherto regarded themselves as *cognoscenti* of the theological scene, not the least surprise in *Honest to God* was whence it came. If it had appeared anonymously and shorn of personal references, few would have guessed that it came from the pen of the Suffragan Bishop of Woolwich.

The man

John A. T. Robinson seemed to have been born, bred, groomed and polished for the Anglican academic establishment. He was born in 1919, not into the world as such but into the cathedral precincts at Canterbury, where his father was a canon. Two uncles, J. Armitage Robinson and Forbes Robinson, were biblical scholars of high repute. John himself could never remember a time when he had ever doubted the essential truth of Christianity, or did not feel called to the ordained ministry. After public schooling at Marlborough he read classics and theology at Cambridge, and studied for the ministry at Westcott House. In 1946 he was awarded a Cambridge doctorate for a thesis on the 'I–Thou' personal relation in religion as expounded particularly by the Jewish philosopher Martin Buber. This early excursus into the philosophy of religion was not obviously reflected in his life's main work, however, which lay in New Testament studies. Perhaps this change of direction was already a sign that, even if he were to play a set tune, it would be with some quite independent variations. Another hint of this lay in his first curacy at Bristol, for his senior priest there was Mervyn Stockwood, already acquiring a reputation as a progressive churchman with an outspoken left-wing political slant. There followed a period teaching at Wells Theological College, and in 1951 he returned to Cambridge as Dean of Clare College.

Here, as teacher and writer, his reputation as a New Testament scholar was made. The 1950s saw the peak of the 'biblical theology' movement in Britain, that is, an approach to the Bible which sought to uncover the leading ideas of the Old and New Testaments in all their distinctness – sometimes with the implication that their contrast with other religious notions, whether ancient or modern, was somehow an indication of their truthfulness. For example, the New Testament concept of the 'Kingdom of God' was set out over against modern religious and cultural ideas of 'progress', as the 'breaking in' of God's own power and rule into human history. Robinson slid into place as an able and imaginative scholar within this movement, making his mark with such titles as *In the End, God* (1950), *The Body, A Study of Pauline Theology* (1952, and perhaps his most influential book of that period), and *Jesus and His Coming* (1957). But ability and intelligence do not necessarily imply radicalism. Even within his chosen field of study Robinson was, especially on points of historical criticism, relatively conservative, and was always to be so. By the later 1950s the 'Soundings' group (see previous chapter) was meeting in Cambridge, but Robinson was never a member. He was deliberately not invited, says Alec Vidler, 'because he seemed then to be still an apostle of biblical theology and of the liturgical movement.'[6] That reference to liturgy indicates where, in Cambridge, Robinson was most overtly innovative: in the Chapel of Clare College and especially at the Sunday Eucharist. Utilizing the relative freedom of a Cambridge dean, he was a pioneer of eucharistic worship as a much more obviously corporate act, and one which related communal worship to the total community life of the college. His *Liturgy Coming to Life* (1960) was based on the experience and experiments of the Clare time, and was an important stimulus to that rethinking of Anglican worship in the 'Parish and People' movement, which was to bear some fruit in the Alternative Services of more recent days. Furthermore, his 'biblical theology' was not to be kept a thing apart. He was deeply concerned that theology should engage with the social and political scene, as may be seen from the sermons and papers published as *On Being the Church in the World* (1960): 'Just as this Eucharistic action is the pattern for all Christian action, the sharing of this Bread the sign for the sharing of all bread, so this Fellowship is the germ of all society renewed in Christ.'[7]

The Cambridge religious scene in the 1950s was considerably revitalized by the ministry of Mervyn Stockwood, Robinson's old Bristol mentor and now intimate friend, at the University Church of

Great St Mary's. Stockwood left to become Bishop of Southwark in south London in 1959 and if one is to speak, as some were prone to during and after 1963, of a connection between Cambridge and the 'South Bank', it was probably no more and no less than the Stockwood connection, for it was at Stockwood's own invitation that Robinson in turn left Cambridge in 1959 to become his suffragan at Woolwich. Robinson chose not to follow the counsel of friends who could not contain their surprise at his choice of a sprawling urban diocese to administer, in exchange for the relatively tranquil life of a Cambridge scholar. Robinson, however, for some time had been wanting to do more than write. He was wanting to change things in the Church, and at first sight, at least, a bishop has more opportunity of doing so than a don. And if what he had written in *On Being the Church in the World* had any substance, Southwark would prove it.

It was not long before the mitred John Robinson became a public, indeed national, figure of some controversy. In the autumn of 1960 came the bizarre court case of *Regina v. Penguin Books*. The publishers had deliberately brought prosecution on themselves as a test case of the limits of censorship in relation to the pornography laws, by putting on sale D. H. Lawrence's novel *Lady Chatterley's Lover*, hitherto banned from British bookshops. The case itself stands as a kind of historic *rite de passage* of British society into the 'adult' world of the 1960s. Robinson appeared as a witness for the defence, affirming that in his view Lawrence saw sex as having sacred significance, as it also had (on different grounds) for Christians. The reports of an English bishop seemingly giving his blessing to pornography naturally shocked, puzzled or entertained many people. A public rebuke by the Archbishop of Canterbury, Dr Michael Ramsey, turned the spotlight on Robinson even more sharply. Ramsey's remarks, delivered at a Canterbury Diocesan Conference early in November are worth recalling as they register the then prevailing attitudes to episcopal pronouncements – and conversely the attitudes to the laity – on the part of the Church of England hierarchy, which were to be very significant during the *Honest to God* debate. The Bishop, said Ramsey, had every right to appear in the witness box, but it would obviously cause confusion between 'his *individual right to judgment* and the *discharge of his pastoral duties*' (my italics). He continued:

> Inevitably anything the Bishop said would be regarded as said by one whose chief concern was to give pastoral advice to the people committed to his charge . . . Anyone must know that in this sexually self-conscious and chaotic age, to speak pastoral wisdom in public on particular questions is

> *extremely difficult and dangerous*. The Bishop exposed himself to this danger . . .
>
> In my judgment the bishop was mistaken to think that he could take part in this trial without becoming a stumbling block and cause of offence to many ordinary Christians, and I think I ought to say so here, since I am a pastor and your chief pastor.[8]

From a later time, and from another tradition, an observer may perhaps be pardoned for wondering just what, on such a view, the nature of the episcopal teaching office amounts to. The prime duty of the bishop, it appears, is not to upset the faithful. The chief criterion of what is to be taught is what the people already think they know and believe, in which case it would seem that a bishop, let alone one who is a former Cambridge don, is hardly necessary. Concomitant with this is an assumption about an agreed consensus on what Christian morality comprises. It was precisely this view of the matter in the Church which Robinson was to challenge even more forcefully through *Honest to God* – above all the notion that his individuality of perception and his pastoral office were to be kept apart. But to give him his due credit, Ramsey himself, as we shall see, in the midst of the furore over *Honest to God*, played an important role in helping to change the starchy attitude he had embodied in the autumn of 1960.

The *Lady Chatterley* controversy died down but was not forgotten, and Ramsey's 'stumbling block and cause of offence' might forever have hung round Robinson's neck as a pectoral albatross, but for what was to come. He was not without public support. Canon Ronald Preston preached in his defence in Manchester Cathedral, as did Dr Donald Soper at Speaker's Corner. Soper wished that 'a few more bishops would step into the limelight instead of hiding their thoughts'.[9]

Things continued relatively quietly in Woolwich. In 1962 another collection of scholarly essays, *Twelve New Testament Studies*, appeared. Then came the momentous stoop to reach a shoelace, the enforced idleness, time to reflect and write, and the book. As was said earlier, however, the controversy really broke with the *Observer* article of 17 March 1963 under that truly iconoclastic headline, OUR IMAGE OF GOD MUST GO. The phrases that followed were, depending on the reader's standpoint, either brilliantly illuminating or irresponsibly incendiary: 'Few people realise that we are in the middle of one of the most exciting theological ferments of the century'; 'New ideas about God and religion, many of them with disturbing revolutionary implications, are breaking surface. If Christianity is to survive it must be relevant to modern secular man, not just to the dwindling number of the religious'; 'Men can no longer credit the existence of "gods" or of a God as a supernatural Person, such as religion has always posited'; 'Not infrequently, as I watch or listen to a broadcast discussion between a Christian and a humanist, I catch myself realising that most of my sympathies are on the humanist's side.'

The rest was largely potted Bonhoeffer, and it was scarcely less startling to the uninitiated to be informed that the age of religion was over, that man has come of age and has to get along without God. *Honest to God* was therefore a sensation even before it was published – thanks, as with Campbell's *New Theology* fifty-six years earlier, to a secular newspaper opening up the debate. This time, however, apart from the headline, the article in question was all the theologian's own work, and Robinson could not plead loose reportage in mitigation. His boats were well and truly burnt.

The book

At first sight it should be a simple matter to summarize *Honest to God*. It is after all a small paperback of only 143 pages. In fact it is extremely difficult to do so satisfactorily, and in fairness it should be read for oneself – or re-read after the passing years. Put another way, to an unusual degree as compared with most books, a summary of *Honest to God* turns into instant review, commentary and interpretation. That is what happened from the beginning in the debate itself. There seemed to be almost as many *Honest to Gods* as there were readers. The reason is twofold. First, as David Edwards put it, Robinson was 'thinking aloud', and in a highly personal way. He was airing his own questions, hopes and fears in a way that was hitherto unusual in a serious theologian, let alone a bishop. In their time, Henson and Barnes had certainly upset people by their opinions, and Robinson in turn trailed his coat with hints that what he was saying would be thought heretical by some. But he was also baring something of his own soul and revealing where his own perplexities lay. The reader's response, whether positive or negative, could not help being scarcely less personal. Second, and more importantly, the book is marked by ambiguity, which is the surest guarantee of provoking controversy. To do the book justice, one feels again and again that one extended quote has to be balanced by another – until virtually the whole book has been reproduced. Partly this ambiguity lay in the sources he was using, or rather his use of them. The paradoxes and dialectical methods of Bonhoeffer, Tillich and Bultmann, unless their respective contexts are stated clearly, and their own use of language appreciated, collapse into sheer contradiction or confusion. Partly it was due, as we shall argue later, to Robinson's own lack of a clear conceptual framework.

It is an ambiguity one meets almost immediately in the Preface. Robinson acknowledges his own teaching office as a bishop, and recognizes as 'indispensable' the work of those apologists for the faith who feel called to reiterate, in the best contemporary language, the classic doctrines. On the other hand we are being called to 'far more than a restating of traditional orthodoxy in modern terms', and what is demanded is a much more radical 'recasting'. Was the former line just an episcopal sop? Or was the latter 'radical' call more than rhetoric? Reiteration and recasting hardly seem compatible if the need for the latter is so urgent. It was an ambiguity which was breathed when Robinson spoke in public. This youthful-looking figure ('the rosy-cheeked Bishop of Woolwich', chuckled Karl Barth[10]) calling himself a radical yet in his slim straight figure fitting so well the episcopal purple – was he really questioning the establishment whose uniform he was wearing? That calm, almost monotonous nasal voice with the cool turn of phrase – was it really prophesying? That half-smile playing over his features, was it signalling reassurance for the nervous, or hinting at another outrageous idea up his cassock sleeve?

Appropriately, therefore, the first chapter in *Honest to God* is entitled 'Reluctant Revolution'. The Bible speaks of a 'three-decker universe', of earth set between heaven above and hell beneath. Ever since the Copernican revolution in astronomy, however, the idea of a God 'up there' has been impossible to take literally, that is, spatially. We can use such language only because subconsciously we transpose it out of its literal meaning: 'For in place of a God who is literally or physically "up there" we have accepted, as part of our mental furniture, a God who is spiritually or metaphysically "out there".'[11] No wonder that older minds were reminded of R. J. Campbell and his attack on what he considered to be the outmoded 'dichotomy' between God and the world.[12] Robinson, however, ran together history of Christian doctrine, social and cultural history, and psychological theory into a form of criticism of the tradition, which made it hard to see which discipline would put things right for belief. Thus:

> Every one of us lives with some mental picture of a God 'out there', a God who 'exists' above and beyond the world he made, a God 'to' whom we pray and to whom we 'go' when we die. In traditional Christian theology, the doctrine of the Trinity witnesses to the self-subsistence of this divine

> Being outside us and apart from us. The doctrine of creation asserts that at a moment of time this God called 'the world' into existence over against himself. The Bibical record describes how he proceeds to enter into contact with those whom he has made, how he establishes a 'covenant' with them, how he 'sends' to them his prophets, and how in the fullness of time he 'visits' them in the person of his Son, who must one day 'come again' to gather the faithful to himself.[13]

The ambiguity lies in what, if anything, transcendence can now mean to Robinson, having rounded on so much of the doctrinal and biblical tradition in this way. It is not clear whether, in criticizing the God 'out there' and the whole idea of 'apartness' from the world, Robinson still wishes to preserve the distinction of God from the world. Robinson, however, proceeds with his own questions: Suppose such a God 'out there' is, as the Freudians say, only a projection, is there nothing else? Suppose the atheists are right, and that 'God', a 'Super Being' out there, is only an idol, what then? Tillich and Bonhoeffer make their entry as those who, from the theological wings, have begun this questioning already.

Chapter 2, 'The End of Theism?', begins with an unqualified assertion: 'Traditional Christian theology has been based upon the proofs for the existence of God'. To any student of the history of Christian thought that should be a highly debatable point, but Robinson's main concern is that the attempt to 'prove' the existence of God as a separate being is a doubtful enterprise. For how can God be 'proved' to exist without making him like anything else that might, or might not, exist?

> Rather, we must start the other way round. God is, by definition, ultimate reality. And one cannot argue whether ultimate reality exists. One can only ask what ultimate reality is like – whether, for instance, in the last analysis what lies at the heart of things and governs their working is to be described in personal or impersonal categories. Thus, the fundamental theological question consists not in establishing the 'existence' of God as a separate identity but in pressing through in ultimate concern to what Tillich calls 'the ground of our being.'[14]

Tillich, says Robinson, has shown that much talk about 'God' is not about the ultimate reality, but about 'a being beside others', not 'being itself', or the 'ground of being': a modified deism, in fact. God thus becomes dispensable, as Sir Julian Huxley, the biologist and evolutionary humanist, had argued. Equally, as Bultmann had shown, Christianity must be freed from its 'mythological' entanglements; and as Bonhoeffer had argued, in a world 'come of age' Christianity needed to be freed from 'religion', that is, dependence on

God as a working hypothesis, the *deus ex machina*. Such conceptions of God and transcendence have to be questioned, for if the God 'out there' is not actually an irrelevance, he is the enemy of human freedom and adulthood. Again, however, we are left waiting to know how, if God is not to be allowed to exist in any way 'apart' from the world, he is to be a reality at all.

We move to chapter 3, 'The Ground of Our Being'. Here it becomes clear that whereas Bonhoeffer and Bultmann have been conscripted to do the demolition work on the discredited 'God out there', it is Tillich who has been contracted in to erect the new theological building. Like all sound building, it goes downwards before anything appears on the surface. 'Depth' rather than 'height', says Robinson, conveys best the meaning of God, since the latter denotes apartness and lack of involvement. For Tillich, God is not another being (or Being) at all, but 'the infinite and inexhaustible depth and ground of all being'. In what may be considered to be the most significant paragraphs in the entire book, Robinson states that this is quite different from speaking of God as 'a Person':

> But the way of thinking we are seeking to expound is not concerned to posit, nor, like the antitheists, to depose, such a Being at all. In fact it would not naturally use the phrase 'a personal God'; for this in itself belongs to an understanding of theology and of what theological statements are about which is alien to it. For this way of thinking, to say that 'God is personal' is to say that 'reality at its very deepest level is personal', that personality is of ultimate significance in the constitution of the universe, that in personal relationships we touch the final meaning of existence as nowhere else. 'To predicate personality of God,' says Feuerbach, 'is nothing else than to declare personality as the absolute essence'. To believe in God as love means to believe that in pure personal relationship we encounter, not merely what ought to be, but what is, the deepest, veriest truth about the structure of reality. This, in face of all the evidence, is a tremendous act of faith. But it is not the feat of persuading oneself of the existence of a super-Being beyond this world endowed with personal qualities. Belief in God is the trust, the well-nigh incredible trust, that to give ourselves to the uttermost in love is not to be confounded but to be 'accepted', that Love is the ground of our being, to which ultimately we 'come home'.
>
> If this is true, then theological statements are not a description of 'the highest Being' but an analysis of the depths of personal relationships – or, rather, an analysis of the depths of all experiences 'interpreted by love' . . . A view of the world which affirms this reality and significance in personal categories is *ipso facto* making an affirmation about the ultimacy of personal relationships: it is saying that God, the final truth and reality 'deep down things', *is* love.[15]

Here, aided and abetted by Feuerbach, John Greenleaf Whittier and Gerard Manley Hopkins, the ambiguity is at its height, or should one say its full depth. To speak of the ultimacy of personal relationships might mean something like 'there is nothing more real than the personal relationships we experience'; or, with less novel implications, that it is in our personal relationships that we receive our clearest intimations of the nature of ultimate reality, or 'God', which transcends those relations as such but is reflected in them. Having quoted Feuerbach, Robinson seems to be saying the former. But Robinson was far too aware of where that road would lead, and the remainder of the chapter is largely taken up with an admission that in the New Testament it is not asserted that 'love is God', but rather that 'God is love'. In other words, theology cannot simply be reversed into anthropology. Theology is about human experience, but 'in depth'; theological statements are affirmations about human existence – 'but they are affirmations about the ultimate ground and depth of that existence'. How far this is more than just an assertion devoid of a rationale is not clear. Why should we retain the word 'God' at all? Because, says Robinson in discussion with the Scottish philosopher John Macmurray, 'our being has depths which naturalism, whether evolutionary, mechanistic, dialectical or humanist, cannot or will not recognize'. Yet, after still more dialogue with Tillich, and with an Anglican layperson John Wren-Lewis (a scientist heavily into theology at that time), we are still left hovering tantalizingly on the edge of an answer to the question: Is God a reality in any way 'other than us' or not?

> God as the ground, source and goal of our being cannot but be represented at one and the same time as removed from the shallow, sinful surface of our lives by infinite distance and depth, and yet as nearer to us than our own selves. This is the significance of the traditional categories of transcendence and immanence.[16]

Later on the same page we are told that the 'Spirit of God' of which St Paul speaks 'is nothing alien to us but the very ground of our own true being' (note the sudden entry of 'true' here), and we are urged to read Romans 8.26–28 in the New English Bible (though oddly, that passage begins: 'In the same way the Spirit *comes to* the aid of our weakness . . .' and earlier in the book the language of 'coming to' has been criticized as tarred with the brush of 'out thereness'). Once again we are being teased. The old theism won't do, but it seems to insinuate itself back in – note the theological sleight-of-hand in elevating 'love' to 'Love'.

The remainder of the book – just over half – maintains its course with some fairly sharp tacking. Chapter 4, 'The Man for Others', deals with the person of Christ. It is arguably the most constructive chapter in the book, but the effect was somewhat nullified by just two notorious paragraphs near the beginning which lent the whole chapter – and to some eyes the whole book – an air of wilful parody and caricature. Robinson alleges that 'most popular supranaturalistic christology' effectively denies the real humanity of Jesus – repeating the old 'docetic' heresy. This

> almost inevitably suggests that Jesus was really God almighty walking about on earth, dressed up as a man. Jesus was not a man born and bred – he was God for a limited period taking part in a charade. He looked like a man, he talked like a man, he felt like a man, but underneath he was God dressed up – like Father Christmas. However guardedly it may be stated, the traditional view leaves the impression that God took a space-trip and arrived on this planet in the form of a man. Jesus was not really one of us; but through the miracle of the Virgin Birth he contrived to be born so as to appear one of us. Really he came from outside.[17]

Robinson admits this is parody but feels it is 'perilously close' to what most people have been brought up to believe. But if ever there was a case of a phrase too far, it came in his next few sentences:

> Indeed, the very word 'incarnation' (which, of course, is not a Biblical term) almost invariably suggests it. It conjures up the idea of a divine substance being plunged in flesh and coated with it like chocolate or silver plating. And if this is a crude picture, substitute for it that of the Christmas collect, which speaks of the Son of God 'taking our nature upon him', or that of Wesley's Christmas hymn, with its 'veiled in flesh the Godhead see.'[18]

Robinson's Christology utilized, to quite some effect, Bonhoeffer's description of Jesus as the 'man for others', the one in whom love (or Love) took over completely in his life and death, and so was completely transparent to God. Through participation in his life for others, we are reunited with God, or in Tillichian language, reunited with the ground of our being from which we were estranged.

Having fought shy of 'incarnational' language, however, Robinson in the next chapter, 'Worldly Holiness' tacks back towards orthodoxy in one sense, by wishing to utilize the concept of incarnation in the interests of a spirituality which is united with the whole of life and with worldly responsibility. So George Macleod is quoted approvingly: 'In the light of the Incarnation nothing is secular'. It is in this section that Robinson is also at his most personal, in confessing his own difficulties, since student days, with the traditional pattern of prayer as requiring some kind of 'withdrawal' from the world. With

Bonhoeffer, the holy is not what is beyond life, but is the beyond in the midst of life.

> The purpose of worship is not to retire from the secular into the department of the religious, let alone to escape from 'this world' into 'the other world', but to open oneself to the meeting of the Christ in the common, to that which has the power to penetrate its superficiality and redeem it from its alienation. The function of worship is to make us more sensitive to these depths; to focus, sharpen and deepen our response to the world and to other people beyond the point of proximate concern . . .[19]

Thus to pray for another is 'to expose both oneself and him to the common ground of our being'. It is as likely to take place with that person as in his absence.

The penultimate chapter, 'The New Morality', attacks moralities based on unchangeable commands given by divine fiat, 'laws which never shall be broken'. The teaching of Jesus – and here the New Testament scholar was on his own specialist ground – is not another legalism, but the vision of the transforming, unconditional will of God (love):

> Love alone, because, as it were, it has a built-in moral compass, enabling it to 'home' intuitively upon the deepest need of the other, can allow itself to be directed completely by the situation. It alone can afford to be utterly open to the situation, or rather to the person in the situation, uniquely and for his own sake, without losing its direction or unconditionality.[20]

Nothing is prescribed, except love. This 'situational ethic' was being powerfully enforced at the time by the writings of the American theologian Joseph Fletcher. It is, says Robinson, 'a highly dangerous ethic and the representatives of supranaturalistic legalism will, like the Pharisees, always fear it. Yet I believe it is the only ethic for "man come of age".' Once again we are left in an ambiguous position. Can we then decide for ourselves what 'love' actually is? Robinson cites the case of the young man who would like to sleep with his girl-friend. The man, says Robinson, should be challenged not with a cast-iron 'Thou shalt not', but should be asked whether he truly loves and respects her. The implication is that if he does so regard her he will not wish to treat her in this way. But if this is so, is 'love' quite such a purely intuitive matter as was stated earlier? Or are not certain 'moral imperatives' or even principles being infiltrated into the scene?

The final chapter, 'Recasting the Mould', is substantially a recapitulation of the previous arguments. The ambiguity lasts until the very end. No, he is not promoting pantheism or sheer immanentism, says Robinson, for biblical faith 'grounds all Reality in personal freedom – in Love', not in deterministic or mechanical relations.

> We are not like rays to the sun or leaves to the tree: we are united to the source, sustainer and goal of our life in a relationship whose only analogy is that of *I* to *Thou* – except that the freedom in which we are held is one of utter dependence. We are rooted and grounded wholly in Love.[21]

But if the analogy is that of one personal relation to another, does not that imply distinctness between the partners? If not, is the freedom not illusory? Or if the freedom is not illusory, is it anything more than our own loving, exalted to Love, which we are worshipping and calling 'God', in which case there is no 'God' beyond this activity of ours? Robinson's final word on this is as ambivalent as any other:

> It is this freedom built into the structure of our being which gives us (within the relationship of dependence) the 'distance', as it were, to be ourselves. What traditional deism and theism have done is to 'objectivize' this distance into the pictorial image of a God 'out there'. But the projection of God from the world as a super-Individual is no more necessary an expression of transcendence than is mileage upwards from the earth's surface. They are both but objectifications in the language of myth – in terms of 'another' world – of the transcendental, the unconditional in all our experience. The test of any restatement is not whether this projection is preserved but whether these elements are safeguarded. And that I believe I have tried to do.[22]

The book lives up to its title. Ambiguity does not imply dishonesty or insincerity. *Honest to God* is a deeply sincere book, but not always a very clear book. The lack of clarity could be because it is trying to express in words what will always defy verbal expression in the very nature of the case. Or it could be because the author was still searching for the conceptual and linguistic tools to express what he wanted to say. Robinson had wanted to safeguard something of the element of 'transcendence', but to dissociate it from notions of spatial or metaphysical detachment from the world. The final and crucial question, then, is whether his Tillichian notion of God as 'ground of being', or Love as 'ultimate reality' has expressed both the transcendence and the relation between God and man. He had tried. It was now over to the readers.

Reactions 1: Vox pop

Honest to God may or may not have been an arrogant tower of speculation but it certainly unleashed a whole Babel of voices. The simplest way of sorting them out is a threefold classification into 'popular' opinions, the response of ecclesiastical authority in the Church of England, and of more considered reflections by reviewers and theological writers.

Even more strikingly than with the New Theology controversy of 1907, the *Honest to God* debate, thanks in measure to the secular press, short-circuited the academic and hierarchical channels and was instantly a people's debate – to the consternation of some. The electrical metaphor was neatly employed by Gerald Downing:

> Normally in this country, theological currents pass through many transformer stations before they reach 'lay' homes; and in many places, such stations have never been built, or if built, they have fallen into disrepair. And there are many Luddites who applaud this state of affairs, for currents are very dangerous things, and people should be insulated from them, if not by design, then at least by accident. If you try to by-pass the transformer stations you may get a very exciting short-circuit: there is a bright flash, and then all goes dead. On the other hand, you may find many of the lay homes and the local churches have all along been wired to stand very high tensions indeed, and your dangerous act may by-pass the natural and artificial resistances, and produce a glad and warm light.[23]

With the initial switch having been thrown in the Sunday *Observer*, and the book being published the following Tuesday, the national (and some local) dailies stole a march on the religious weeklies. Of course much of the immediate reaction could only have been to second-hand accounts of what Robinson was said to have said. Heresy and hearsay are close cousins. But on any terms the public debate was far more intense and more prolonged than any could have anticipated, as feature articles, editorials and correspondence columns in both secular and church papers showed for many weeks and months. There was, too, a huge correspondence addressed to Robinson personally, from the public, mostly from within the Churches. Those who took the trouble to write were presumably those who felt particularly strongly, one way or another. Treating negative reactions first, the following was typical: 'I always thought it was a parson's job to get people to go to church, but if there are many like you, nobody will go . . . The parsons have always spoken of a God up there, but now the parsons are contradicting everything they have said.'[24] One archdeacon spluttered:

> I want you to know that I speak for many clergymen besides myself . . . when I say with the utmost force at my command that I deplore the way you are damaging the Christian cause and particularly the church in which you are serving as a bishop. I fully allow your right to your own opinions and to the expression of them, but I do not think you are justified in taking advantage of your position in the way you have.[25]

The correspondent suggests that it would have been better for Robinson to have stayed in Cambridge, where he would have been 'less of an embarrassment to those who have more experience of ordinary pastoral work in the Church at home and overseas'. Such clerical anger was at least matched by a representative of that splendid English phenomenon, the Anglican colonel, who might have been crying God for Harry and St George as he wrote:

> Groping as so many of us, including yourself, obviously are for enlightenment to cure our lack of Faith and moral fibre, it seems to me incomprehensible that anyone who has attained to your high clerical office should go out of his way to offend so many by such objectionable outpourings as your latest effort *Honest to God*. This book does little more than to quote from the heretical outpourings of Bonhoeffer, Tillich and other alien agnostics. What little more it contains serves only to express in arrogant and often incomprehensible language your own pitiful lack of Faith and to undermine the Christian Ethics and beliefs of those who are unfortunate enough to read it and ignorant enough to be impressed by it.[26]

The alarmed voice from the pew was also expressed by a leading member of the House of Laity, Mr Ivor Bulmer-Thomas, who was probably conveying a widely felt concern at the threat to good morals posed by *Honest to God*:

> Dr Robinson says that in 99 cases out of 100 it is probably wrong to have sexual relations before marriage but in the 100th case it may not be so. This seems to me very dangerous. You are bound to get a lot of people convincing themselves they are the 100th case.[27]

Again and again, it was the fact of a *bishop* apparently questioning the received faith which evoked so much bewilderment and anger. Equally, however, those who welcomed the book expressed a sense of liberation for the very same fact, for it validated, as little else could, their own sense of the need to rethink just what they believed and how those beliefs were to be expressed. A woman wrote:

> I personally found the chapters on prayers and church-going in particular removed a vast load of guilt and misery. So many of one's repeated efforts merely ended in failure and a despairing effort to do better next time, and then more failure and guilt.
>
> Unlike the medievals we are now educated to think for ourselves and cannot help thinking about, questioning, and reading about all aspects of our belief, and finding things which strike with an inner certainty of truth. It is just so marvellous to have all this coming from a bishop of the church, and having one's thoughts and hopes confirmed, not rejected, from inside the Church.[28]

Others expressed sheer gratitude at having been introduced to a whole new realm of theological thinking they had never – to the shame of their clergy – known existed:

> . . . you would be surprised to know how much we have learnt from your book, and how deeply it has been discussed and appreciated on all sides, even by those who cannot as yet adopt all you say. We had never heard of the names Tillich and Bonhoeffer and Bultmann: but in the last weeks they have become almost household words.[29]

As might be imagined, the interest among Christian student circles in the universities was very strong indeed. An Oxford undergraduate told Robinson: '. . . your radical reinterpretation is just what is needed to make Christian religion dynamic and viable. Overnight it has been reinfused with life, and tremendous power unleashed.' Certainly there was intense debate among students, as one recalls from vigorous encounters in church porches and tortuous discussions over coffee cups into the small hours, in that summer of 1963.

A vicar's wife rejoiced at the discovery that she could now make sense of 'the divine and the human in Christ' – 'what you have helped to remove is my constant annoyance that Christ always had an unfair advantage'. But on the whole, even the most fulsome of letters refer to comparatively very little of what Robinson actually said in the book. As usually happens with eager listeners, some managed to project on to Robinson their own revisions of belief rather than comprehending his particular thought – 'I think that the ultimate reality is consciousness in every stage of evolution in a living universe and harmony which is Love between all the parts of that universe, and that as we are conscious we must be eternal . . .' Such readers, no less than the objectors, were seeing a symbolic significance in *Honest to God*, a raising of the curtain on a freedom of exploration and inquiry. Few in fact gave the book a 100% endorsement. One Anglican priest reported: 'Younger clergy almost unanimously *feeling* with it, if not always agreeing with it. It expresses what we all feel. I think probably only among the Conservative Evangelicals could one find a blank wall of resistance.'[30] What, however, might have troubled Robinson and the SCM Press a little more than it apparently did, was that despite all the massive publicity, despite the fact that Robinson was even now writing for the *Sunday Mirror* as well as the 'heavies', and despite all the stated aspirations for a new dialogue with 'secular men', very, very few reactions – positive or negative – were coming from people outside the Churches, that is, those people whose obstacles to belief Robinson was avowedly trying to remove. That there was interest in the public at large was clear enough. But the representatives of 'non-religious man' did not seem to be particularly impressed. A few agnostics and socialists wrote to the papers saying that the Bishop was at last dropping superstitions they themselves had discarded years before. A. J. Ayer, the Oxford philosopher whose positivist approach to truth had long since ruled out belief in God as meaningless, similarly stated: 'It seems to me he is coming round to a position a number of us have held for some time.'[31] Even Sir Julian Huxley, epitome of the humanism Robinson most admired, was politely dismissive of *Honest to God* as simply trying to retain an unnecessary religious garment for beliefs about human possibilities.[32] The real troubling of the waters, then, was taking place inside the ecclesiastical lagoon, though ripples were spreading outside. It was undoubtedly stimulating and helping many Christians who were troubled over the need for a relevant expression of their faith, and found that the book articulated for them some of the alternatives to a sterile package of doctrine. It was even helping some half-believers on the fringes of the Churches to identify with the fold again, at least for a while longer. The effects were oddly parallel to those of Billy Graham's evangelistic campaigns, which likewise have been observed to affect mainly those already influenced by the Churches in some way.

Reactions 2: Lambeth Palace

In some eyes, Robinson had clearly disqualified himself from episcopal office by his views which were heretical, blasphemous or simply atheistic. One rural dean after reading *Honest to God* wrote to Robinson: 'There is only one course open to you, honest to God, and that is to resign your bishopric and get out of the Church of England. So long as you remain, you are a stumbling block and an offence to all who have not your intellectual pride.'[33] That phraseology was of course redolent of the rebuke to Robinson delivered by the Archbishop of Canterbury after the *Lady Chatterley* episode. It was a note heard quite loudly. The Sunday after *Honest to God* appeared, T. E. Utley declaimed in the *Sunday Telegraph*: 'What should happen to an Anglican bishop who does not believe in God? This, I hold, is the condition of the Bishop of Woolwich . . . and it raises, I maintain, a question of Church discipline which cannot be shirked without the gravest repercussions on the whole Anglican Communion.'[34] To Utley, *Honest to God* was a sheer contradiction of the plain meaning of the Creed and its 'crude and precise historical statements', substituting instead a belief that 'there is something "sacred" at the bottom of human existence, that [man] should love his neighbour and that he should be indisposed to make absolute moral judgments such as are implied in the orthodox view that fornication is always wrong though often difficult to avoid'. The Church of England could not, in the name of intellectual liberty, allow its bishops to use their authority in this way. However, that same morning the voice of the SCM Press itself was heard from the pulpit of Westminster Abbey: 'Free speech is what the Church of England needs, not a heresy trial,' proclaimed David Edwards.[35]

Those who did not share the high churchmanship of the *Church Times* of those days, were provided with some slightly sadistic entertainment, for the paper was clearly undergoing an agony of frustration. Three days after *Honest to God* appeared, an editorial declared stiffly: 'There is nothing surprising about the publicity which the book has received. It is not every day that a bishop goes on public record as apparently denying almost every fundamental doctrine of the Church in which he holds office', and accused Robinson of simply succumbing to 'a particular fashion in continental theology'.[36] The *Daily Mail* was quoted with approval for having the courage and the common sense to ask if Robinson should continue as a bishop. Embarrassingly, however, the *Church Times* had sent *Honest to God* for review to no less respected a person than the former Bishop of London, J. C. Wand, and his article, carried by that same edition of the paper, while not uncritical, was certainly not dismissive and indeed welcomed it from certain angles:

> . . . the Bishop's protest is valuable because it will help us to recognize that we have not yet penetrated to the ultimate meaning of God. There is still much to be learnt, and a humble agnosticism is the mark of the greatest Christian thinkers. It will help us also to exercise greater charity in our application of conventional rules.[37]

The *Church Times*, however, was less interested in charity than in reproof. The letters page the following week was largely occupied with *Honest to God* correspondence, both for and against, and a wide variety of views were reported. The Bishop of Wakefield, Eric Treacy, regarded the book as 'dangerous'. Mervyn Stockwood was supportive of his suffragan. But on the whole episcopal comment was muted. The real question was what would come from Lambeth Palace.

It was nearly a fortnight before Michael Ramsey made any public statement, though the *Church Times* on 22 March hungrily detected what might have been a passing allusion to *Honest to God* in an address which the Archbishop gave at Slough College earlier that week. His first pronouncement, when it came, was in a medium in which he was rarely at his best, television. On 3 April he was interviewed on the Sunday evening Independent Television programme *About Religion*. He told Kenneth Harris of the *Observer* that Robinson had caricatured the ordinary Christian's view of God:

> When the ordinary Christian speaks of God as being up there or of God being beyond, he does not literally mean that God is in a place beyond the bright blue sky . . . He's putting in poetic language, the only serviceable language, that God is supreme.
>
> I think he is right when he is trying to find whether some new model of the image of God may be going to help some of the people who are right outside Christianity and the church. But it is utterly wrong and misleading to denounce the imagery of God held by Christian men and women: imagery that they've got from Jesus himself, the image of God the Father in heaven, and to say that we can't have any new thought until it is all swept away.[38]

The heresy hunters took some comfort from this, though the Archbishop, it could be observed, was more corrective of the theology than condemnatory of the theologian. The most that the *Church Times* could make of it was to put as its headline the rather tame 'Dr Ramsey gives his views on Bishop's book'.[39] Meanwhile it was the satirists of the press who were enjoying themselves the most. In one cartoon a scowling Ramsey was to be seen surreptitiously reading *Honest to God* – inside the covers of *Lady Chatterley's Lover*.

For a while, indeed, it seemed that the old attitude that bishops were not to tell their people anything that might offend them, was to prevail. However, Ramsey's most considered response came in the form of a pamphlet *Image Old and New* published in April, and it reads as if from a rather different person than the Archbishop who had spoken on television. It is, to use that word which seems a prerogative of archbishops at their dignified best, sagacious: scrupulously fair to Robinson, not inaccurate in summarizing the thrust of his argument, and above all educative in trying to place the current debate in some kind of perspective for the uninitiated. Cautious, yes, but not simply reactionary: 'It should be the mark of Christian faith to learn from the shock of new ideas, but it is also necessary to see where such ideas may be misleading.'[40] Tillich and Bonhoeffer are presented as succinctly as practicable within the compress of a pamphlet, and criticism is only offered after a careful appreciation of the positive value in whatever Robinson is saying at any stage of his argument. Ramsey's critique of Robinson's Christology is finely stated:

> I have said that [Robinson's] presentation of Christ's deity and the Cross is

> near to St John's presentation. Yet there is a significant difference . . . In the Gospel of St John we see signally the divine glory revealed in humility, not least in the scene of the washing of the feet of the disciples. In St John there is again and again that 'deep down' apprehension which has been one of the secrets of his power to elicit the sense of God in many generations. But is it possible to tear apart the 'deep down' realization and the imagery of the Beyond, of heaven, of coming and going, which is part of the fabric of the story? . . . It is in the imagery of that dimension that we see the depth of the divine humility, the humility of Bethlehem as well as of the foot-washing of Calvary.[41]

Ramsey's concluding summary – challenging his readers 'to see how and where "religion" may be a thing far less than Christianity, far less than the living God, and often too far off from the hungry world in whose midst where Christ is to be found' – was an eloquent and indeed moving testimony to the impact of *Honest to God* on himself, and indeed it could not be denied that Robinson had set people thinking and talking about the fundamentals of belief in a way that no churchman had done previously this century.

> We need to see if there are some who are helped by thinking not about God above us in heaven, or even God around us and near, but about the deep-down meaning of human life in terms of love. There may be those who find there the heart of the matter; and this is God, even though a man may not be able to cry with Thomas, 'My Lord and my God'.
>
> As a Church we need to be grappling with the questions and trials of belief in the modern world. Since the war our Church has been too inclined to be concerned with the organizing of its own life, perhaps assuming too easily that the faith may be taken for granted and needs only to be stated and commended. But we state and commend the faith only in so far as we go out and put ourselves with loving sympathy inside the doubts of the doubting, the questions of the questioners, and the loneliness of those who have lost their way.[42]

This statement was one of the most significant in the whole debate, and marked a kind of Rubicon-crossing, however reluctant, by the leadership of the Church of England. Robinson was not going to be treated to sheer rebuke as Barnes had been, and indeed as he himself had been over the *Lady Chatterley* affair. Whatever might be said about *Honest to God*, one of its main tenets was conceded – that there was a need to reformulate belief in terms of contemporary thought and experience. With that admission by the Archbishop, Robinson was safe from any form of heresy trial, or indeed, other kinds of serious harassment. The *Church Times* might huff and puff, and did. *Image Old and New* was a severe disappointment to those who had hoped for a clear archiepiscopal summons to toe the orthodox line or else . . . An editorial icily described the pamphlet as impressive – as an academic exercise. The Archbishop, said the writer, had gone further than many thought justified in discovering some good in the new view of faith and morals.

> The urgent question remains whether the Church of England's rightful claim to be Catholic can co-exist with acquiescence in the holding of episcopal office by a man who, in all honesty, finds himself apparently quite unable to hold the Catholic faith expressed in the Bible and the Creeds. This is a question which unhappily calls for something more than academic treatment.[43]

There was some consolation for this point of view when, early in May, the Archbishop in addressing the Convocation of Canterbury spoke of the book – or more especially the preceding article – having caused 'much damage' with its appearing to reject the concept of a personal God. But again, the rightness of raising questions, and the nature of the book as tentative and exploratory, was conceded. Ramsey was offering protection with his criticism, although the *Church Times* made the most of this temperate utterance by a somewhat misleading headline: 'Primate Publicly Rebukes Bishop of Woolwich.'[44]

In effect, freedom of theological inquiry with the stated objective of reinterpreting the faith of the Bible and Creeds for the present age, was secure. Robinson, we have seen, legitimated the groundswell of theological questioning in English Christianity and the Archbishop, though keeping his distance, to a degree – enough to annoy the conservatives – had validated the inquiry if not the results. Ramsey's role in facilitating the new atmosphere of openness in the Church deserves greater acknowledgement than it has generally received. But if Robinson was safe, he was not necessarily right, and to the theological responses to his work we now turn.

Reactions 3: The theologians

By 'theologians' are here meant those who wrote reviews, articles or books on *Honest to God* from a theological or philosophical standpoint, whether or not they were 'professional' theologians. *Honest to God* not only broke sales records; in terms of comment and review it must have been the most closely examined theological book of its time, both in Britain and overseas. That means, too, that the debate was the most widely ecumenical of modern theological controversies. Thus two days after publication of *Honest to God* the Free Church *British Weekly* carried an exuberant review by Erik Routley, the Congregational church historian, musician and hymnologist. 'I can see no point at which [Robinson] comes within ten miles of heresy. But there is no paragraph here which does not demand revolution – the revolution of clear thinking, of shameless honesty, of what I have called before in these pages mental chastity.'[45] The *Baptist Times* the following week put out an anonymous review, which was cautiously approving. 'It will be a pity if the heretical extravagances of the Bishop's book mislead readers to a rejection of the growing movement towards reality – encounter with the love of God in Christ at the centre of everyday life.'[46] But the reviewer also made some rather trite remarks about the Bishop needing to carry his 'nonconformist' tendencies all the way to the point of accepting believers' baptism – a note which angered an Oxford postgraduate student (now a Professor of Modern History) as merely illustrative of the smug parochialism of a denomination in decline.[47] There was, in fact, among some older Free Churchmen an element of gloating at the sight of the Anglican wrangling, as may be seen in the Baptist editorial which said, with a touch of malicious glee: 'Truth to tell, the bishop's book is not only controversial; it is untimely. It appears just when Anglicans are trying to convince Free Churchmen of the value of episcopacy as the guarantor of sound doctrine in the Church.'[48] But as the pages of the Baptist and other denominational journals over the following weeks show, the theological argument within the Free Churches was every bit as intense as in the Church of England. The issues were too fundamental for it to be otherwise, although in the *Methodist Recorder* the controversy had to compete for attention with the Anglican–Methodist conversations on unity.

Theological debates, like Parliamentary ones, involving participants with known stances, can be all too predictable. There was little surprising in some of the set-piece responses to *Honest to God*, particularly from the conservative evangelical side, as witnessed by O. Fielding Clarke's *For Christ's Sake*[49] and J. I. Packer's *Keep Yourself from Idols*.[50] Some people, already certain they were living in the last times, needed little persuading that the scoffers of religion, signs of the latter days, had arrived and that Antichrist was seated just south of the Thames. One of the most intelligent evangelical responses came from Leon Morris, who in *The Abolition of Religion*[51] tried to grapple with Robinson's sources, especially Bonhoeffer, in all their unpalatability. But there was also a measure of awkward reserve in some of the early notices, reflecting the evident uncertainty on the part of editors as to quite which category the book fell into (systematics? philosophy or religion? academic? popular?) and thus some uncertainty as to who was the appropriate person to review it. The 'Yes, but . . .' kind of response was typified by that of F. A. Cockin, former Bishop of Bristol, who commented in his review in *Theology*: 'I have very great sympathy with the motives which . . . impelled the Bishop to write it . . . Personally I find it hard to think that the difficulty of spatial metaphor "up there", "out there", is as great as he seems to suggest.'[52] The root question, suggested Cockin, was whether what was left after the removal of 'supranatural' imagery could in any sense be regarded as 'personal'. C. S. Lewis, the plain man's lay theologian, offered some comments which read like a donnish jotting on a rather clever but superficial undergraduate essay:

> His heart, though perhaps in some danger of bigotry, is in the right place . . . If I were briefed to defend his position I would say, 'The image of the Earth-Mother gets in something which that of the Sky-Father leaves out . . .' I shouldn't believe it very strongly, but some sort of case could be made out.[53]

In fact, for someone with an eye to the many-faced character of 'Christian theology', the response of theologians to *Honest to God*, spanning as they did the ecumenical spectrum and covering all approaches from conservative to radical, the controversy could have been an enriching theological education in itself. For example, G. R. Beasley-Murray, an evangelical Baptist, New Testament scholar of repute and Principal of Spurgeon's College, denounced the book as a 'calamity'.[54] His was not simply blind prejudice, however, for he pointed a telling criticism at the impersonality of Robinson's whole approach, and of his evident neglect of the role of *address to* God in religion, as distinct from third-person discourse about him. Robinson does indeed at one point quote Martin Buber's famous dictum that the Eternal *Thou* is met in and through every finite *Thou*. In fact hardly anyone, it seems, lighted upon the extremely odd fact that Robinson's postgraduate work on Buber's thought and the I-Thou relation is scarcely reflected at all in the book, not to mention that a decade earlier Buber had himself been wrestling with the very same phenomenon as was now engaging Robinson, the 'eclipse' of God in modern Western thought and experience.[55]

From a very different wing of Christian thought, Herbert McCabe, an Oxford Dominican, brought to bear the insights of the Thomist inheritance in philosophical theology.[56] Not surprisingly, McCabe makes hay of Robinson's blithe assumption that 'Traditional Christian theology has been based upon the proofs for the existence of God' – and not by suddenly adopting a pseudo-Protestantist guise but simply by referring to none other than Thomas Aquinas himself.

Robinson's final ambiguity concerning the language of 'distance' between man and God as simply referring to the 'freedom' in 'utter dependence' of man in relation to God – in other words in what sense God transcends man if he is not 'out there' – is similarly dissected:

> In the first place, what are we to say of creatures which are not free? Are they simply to be identified with God? If it is our freedom which gives us our distance or distinction from God, then clearly freedom is something which belittles us. The unfree creatures are the rays of the divine sun, the leaves of the divine trees; they simply *are* God whereas we are less than he. This theology which should issue in the call to find divinity by abdicating our freedom and personality, by losing ourselves in the instinctive life of nature can hardly be congenial to the Bishop. In the second place, to speak of man as independent of God through his freedom is to make God 'metaphysically out there' in a particularly emphatic way. To say that I can be independent of God is really to say that God and I inhabit side by side a common world, and it is precisely this that the Bishop so rightly wishes to deny. Moreover it is not enlightening to add a parenthesis about 'utter dependence'; either our freedom serves to make us distinct from God in which case it simply cannot be reconciled with 'utter dependence' upon him, or it does not, in which case some other ground must be found for our distinction from him . . . For traditional theology we are indeed free and utterly dependent on God, but our freedom does not make us free from God, it makes us free from other creatures . . .[57]

Reviewing *Honest to God* for the *Sunday Times*, F. W. Dillistone (then Dean of Liverpool) welcomed 'a brave, scholarly and deeply sincere book' whose very passion showed 'to put it crudely . . . that Dr Robinson is on to something terribly important.' But, like McCabe, Dillistone felt that the basic conceptual spadework had been done inadequately:

> He has not been sufficiently radical in his treatment of *religion*. What did Bonhoeffer mean by religion? What is the social significance of religion? He has not been sufficiently radical in his treatment of *the personal*. Is it possible to conceive of personal relationships in the abstract, independently of concrete images, of personal relationships in society? I find it difficult to attach meaning to the phrase 'personality is of ultimate significance in the constitution of the universe.' . . . I am not convinced that the image of depth and the method of existential reduction can alone suffice to meet the crisis of our time. We need also an image, or images, of personal coherence and the method of conceptual integration if we are to build up a new structure to symbolise that reality which is so obviously the object of Dr Robinson's ultimate concern.[58]

F. Gerald Downing, then a lecturer at Lincoln Theological College, warmly welcomed the book but confessed it a failure 'because it tries to pit only the strongest sectors of Paul Tillich's new religion against only the weakest sectors of traditional Christianity'.[59] There was more immanence in the Christian tradition of thought and spirituality than Robinson seemed to recognize, said Downing: again, shades of Gore's counsel to Campbell.

There was one particularly trenchant criticism from a somewhat unexpected quarter. Alasdair MacIntyre, Fellow of University College, Oxford, wrote an article in *Encounter* beginning: 'What is striking about Dr Robinson's book is that first and foremost he is an atheist,'[60] and his concluding sentence became one of the most famous *bons mots* to be produced by the whole controversy: 'The creed of the English is that there is no God and that it is wise to pray to him from time to time.'[61] The pages in between argued that modern Protestant theology, notably exemplified by Robinson's three main sources Bultmann, Bonhoeffer and Tillich, is inherently atheistic in tendency, as is the practice of most people in modern society. There is, argues MacIntyre, a fundamental inconsistency between Robinson's desire to retain the word 'God', along with other religious or theological terms, while accepting what is fundamentally an atheistic premise that the basic issue is 'how to describe our nature and not anything else'. In other words, on this view the ambiguity had collapsed as 'God' simply dissolved into an aspect of human nature, or another name for a part of it. But the chief thrust in MacIntyre's thesis lay in a socio-historical analysis of the decline in religious belief in modern Britain (and in retrospect one is struck by how few such analyses there were in 1963 – perhaps that simply reflects how the sociological approach to religious belief has blossomed since then).

Right down to the start of the industrial revolution, says MacIntyre, Christianity provided a common frame of reference, a sense of meaning and purpose, for all groups in society from the most conservative to the revolutionary. But industrial society proved inimical to a religious interpretation of its activities. And not even secular humanism has been able to maintain a Utopian vision for all. All classes in society are caught in the pursuit of immediate goals.

> What we do have is a religious language, which survives even though we do not know what to say in it. Since it is the only language we have for certain purposes it is not surprising that it cannot be finally discarded. But since we have no answers to give to the questions we ask in it, it remains continually in need of re-interpretation, re-interpretation that is always bound to fail. We should therefore expect to find continual attempts to use religious language to mask an atheistic vacuum, and sooner or later someone was bound to preserve the religious language and the atheistic

> content together by suggesting, although not of course explicitly, that the latter simply *is* the meaning of the former.[62]

Hence, implies MacIntyre, *Honest to God* is a symptom of our condition, 'a desperate attempt that cannot succeed'. The only cure lies in transforming our social structures.

From a Christian theological point of view one of the most serious criticisms of *Honest to God* was that Robinson, in criticizing 'traditional' Christian thought, seemed to display a paucity of awareness of the 'tradition'. This impoverished understanding applied in fact to many of Robinson's critics no less than to himself. Only rarely in the discussion was it ever brought to mind that the 'classical' Christian doctrine of God is not a monarchy, such as was implied by both the defenders and critics of the 'God up there' or 'God out there', but a Trinity. Robinson himself gave trinitarianism a dismissive nod as simply exemplifying the notion of God as self-sufficient, self-existent 'being' apart from the world, and ignoring the fact that, at least in terms of the 'economic' (or externally active) Trinity, Christian theism is not primarily concerned with a God 'apart from' or distanced from the world; rather, one who, though certainly different from the world, is as much united with it (in the Son) and within his creation (as the Spirit) as he is beyond it (as the Father). And even his freedom *from* the world is manifested in the freedom of his love *for* the world. These elemental categories were largely ignored. One theologian did intervene notably on behalf of orthodoxy, and his contribution has an especial significance in view of the reputation he was later to suffer when he himself became embroiled in controversy in another context. David Jenkins, at that time Chaplain at Queen's College, Oxford, maintained in answer to Robinson that the traditional theistic talk about a 'personal God' was no more and no less difficult than the language about 'ultimate reality' and 'ultimate concern'.[63] Robinson had asserted that one could not argue whether ultimate reality existed or not, only about what it was like. But, replied Jenkins, one could refuse or be unable to believe that ultimate reality has the character asserted. Robinson, suggests Jenkins, however hard he fights against the old 'imagery', cannot really keep out the substance of the classical belief:

> . . . *if* ultimate reality does have the character asserted of 'it', then it looks very much as if it remains true that there exists a personal God who is other than and more than the stuff and phenomena of our life, however true it must be that he is to be encountered only in and through this stuff.[64]

In which case, Jenkins continued, the need is for a symbolism which expresses the fullest possible giving of self on behalf of other selves. Before opting for such language as 'depth', one might have to reflect that such language might be redolent not so much of self-giving, of going out of oneself to others, but quite the opposite – of going into oneself, even the escapist journey back to the womb:

> It might perhaps be true that the problem of transcendence is the problem of the fulfilment of human personality in a fullness of personality that embraces all personal possibilities in a Transcendent which (who) is fully personal. To this end the best symbolism might be the challenge of height symbolism. Perhaps it may turn out that the doctrine of the Trinity (the transcendent 'personalness' of God which is more than 'persons' and yet the perfection of unified personality) is not all that irrelevant psychologically, metaphysically or theologically.[65]

In the view of many, therefore, *Honest to God* had clearly forced into the centre of public attention certain serious questions which had been fomenting in the spiritual consciousness of a generation both among academic theologians and many 'ordinary' believers. Not all interpreted the crisis in the same way. MacIntyre, for instance, saw it as the inevitable outcome of a two centuries' search by religious terminology to find a new home, and finally knocking in desperation on the door of secular humanism itself and claiming ownership to the title deeds. More generally, among the theologians who were prepared to give Robinson a hearing, there was a consensus that there did seem to be a dichotomy, or a gulf of meaninglessness, between traditional religious talk, and the expectations, aspirations and experiences of the contemporary world. That the question was a real one, and was neither invented by Robinson himself nor simply by fashion-seekers in theology, may be gauged from the fact that not-so-radical people had been putting it in their own terms. For instance, such a mainstream commonsensical philosopher of religion as H. D. Lewis had written in 1959: 'God is not a constituent of the world, one among many; he is somehow altogether beyond it. But many people, not finding God as they would find other things, despair, not unnaturally, of finding him at all. How can we get altogether outside our experience?'[66] Robinson's Tillichian answer was to replace the 'altogether beyond' of God by the 'depth' of human being, or 'ultimate concern'; and to reach this depth or ultimacy or ground one converted 'love' to 'Love'. Many who saw the problem refused to buy this answer because there are as many difficulties in relating to an immanent abstraction as there are in being committed to an 'altogether beyond' God, who in some sense is personal. To quote Dillistone again:

> I am not convinced that the image of depth and the method of existential reduction are alone sufficient to meet the crisis of our time. We need also an image, or images, of personal coherence and the method of conceptual integration if we are to build up a new structure worthy to symbolize that reality which is so obviously the object of Dr Robinson's ultimate concern.[67]

The consensus of sympathetic critics appeared, therefore, to be that there was indeed a problem in relating the Christian traditional language about God to the modern world – but that the answer was likely to be found in a re-examination of the resources of that tradition, not in its abandonment.

The distant view

After nearly a quarter of a century *Honest to God* can still make for arresting reading, even in disagreement, on account of the very features for which it was criticized initially – its compressed hurry, its bold questions and risky answers – and which raised, as no other approach could have done, the sharp theological questions of the age. The present writer is probably not alone in dating the beginning of his interest in theology from the discussions which swirled out from the controversy during student days. With hindsight a measure of detachment is possible and distance lends necessary perspective to the view. Three main features stand out.

First, while one of the great contributions of *Honest to God* was to popularize Bonhoeffer, Bultmann and Tillich beyond the academic domain, it has to be said that Robinson's use of these mentors was quite unexamined. Bonhoeffer and Bultmann were used, as we have seen, to demolish the old theism, and Tillich provided the new building. There was an assumption that what Tillich provided would fit neatly into the hole left by the other two. This procedure was highly questionable. At least it might have been asked why so little attention was paid to Bultmann's own reinterpretation of Christian faith which relied on a highly transcendental understanding of God, albeit a God who can only be understood in terms of his impact on human existence. Bultmann at least believed in a God who was in some sense active, to the extent at any rate of speaking his Word to (!) man. Robinson's 'Ground of Being' was static by comparison. From the Bonhoeffer standpoint an even more basic question emerges. Bonhoeffer's critique of religion began with a criticism of all approaches which relied on words alone. 'The time when people could be told everything by means of words, whether theological or pious, is over . . .'[68] From that standpoint, *Honest to God* might be considered an impatient attempt to find new words or even 'images' when what is needed is a time of 'prayer and righteous action' out of which a new language might emerge. Something rather more drastic than an enforced stay in bed is required for that project.

Second, there is the question of the social significance of the *Honest to God* debate. From the sociological perspective Robin Gill has presented the case that Robinson's views were indeed of perceived significance to a much wider circle than that of organized religion, as evidenced by the extraordinary media coverage.[69] At the same time we have noted that very little positive feedback came from outside the Churches. That *Honest to God* was of interest to many in society is indisputable. Whether the interest was directly in the theological argument as such is not quite so certain. Alasdair MacIntyre, we have seen, offered a theory (which Robinson himself did not accept) that religious language in the industrialized society has been looking for a home, and that it was understandably a sensation when it claimed for itself an atheist dwelling.

This is a realm where little more than speculation is possible, and ideological interpretation is all too possible. But what must not be overlooked in the public significance of *Honest to God* is the ethical aspect. Already, we have seen, there had been growing disquiet over what came to be called 'permissiveness' and the apparent acquiescence of many clergy in the 'new morality'. 1963 was also the year of the so-called Profumo scandal, when Mr John Profumo, Secretary for War in the Conservative Government, became embroiled in a call-girl racket and, partly because a security risk was involved, was forced to resign. The scandal fully and finally broke in the early summer (that is, after the publication of *Honest to God*), and some wasted no time in drawing what they saw as the connection between such libertinism and the kind of thinking represented in the chapter 'The New Morality' in *Honest to God*. Other Christian writers were also apparently eroding the foundations of absolute moral standards. *Towards a Quaker View of Sex* also appeared in 1963[70] and *No New Morality: Christian Personal Values and Sexual Morality* by Douglas Rhymes in 1964.[71] The fact that Rhymes was a Canon of Southwark Cathedral was merely added evidence, for those who wished to see it, for a South Bank-Cambridge conspiracy against true religion and morality.

'Morality' has the popular connotation of restraint and control, and it is likely that for many people, whether believers or not, 'God' functions as a seat of such control and restraint. To question the received notion of God, as John Robinson did, was therefore for many people more than just a metaphysical quibble. It was to make a statement about human nature as such, and about the ultimate authority and sanctions in human behaviour; and to say it, moreover, at the same time as social and cultural mores were undergoing a sea-change. The 'God out there' was, if nothing else, a notion that there is something absolute in itself to which human beings must relate in obedience. By questioning this, *Honest to God* was saying – and not just in the chapter on morality – that to be human does not entail servility, either to a supreme Being or to other human beings. It was calling people to a freedom and responsibility for themselves and each other, which was both exhilarating and daunting. That is what happens when the old gods are cast out. And it does not matter if the old gods were only half-believed in by many people anyway, for they still operate in psychologically powerful ways as symbols of how things ought to be and what values ought to hold sway. *Honest to God* was a powerful statement on behalf of human autonomy, not least at the level of challenging and encouraging spiritual autonomy within the Churches themselves, since it did imply that laypeople were, or ought to be, mature enough to think through tough theological issues without being talked down to by the clergy. When this is said on such a scale in the Church, it is bound to be felt outside as well. In a real sense, *Honest to God*, whatever its theological imperfections, marked and legitimated a coming of age, both religiously and socially.

The third feature of *Honest to God*, which is still more conspicuous from a distance, is its virtual lack of any philosophical framework. Even the I–Thou personalism of Buber receives only passing mention. To this lack must be attributed much of the ambiguity. Once a theologian moves outside biblical discourse, some parameters must be set to indicate how reality is being talked about. *Honest to God* was awash with such terms as 'distance', 'ultimate', 'freedom', 'depth', 'being', 'personal' and so on, with little definition as to their meaning and hence there was an open invitation to read into them as much or as little as one wished. Astonishingly, for a work so concerned with 'images', there was scant treatment of the time-honoured role of analogy in Christian thought. As often happens, where there is a philosophical vacuum the space becomes occupied by a sort of psychology: '. . . most of us still retain deep down the mental image . . .'; ' "depth" seems to speak to us of concern while "height" so often signifies unconcern'.

Secular Theology: The wider debate

Nothing was more illustrative of Robinson's theological innocence than his initial enthusiasm for Paul van Buren's *The Secular Meaning of the Gospel*, which appeared in the autumn of 1963.[72] Van Buren, an American Episcopalian who had studied under Karl Barth, did appear to share Robinson's concern to restate a doctrine of God meaningful to modern man. Robinson greeted it excitedly: 'A brilliantly original thesis and something of a theological *tour de force*, it seeks to do justice to an orthodox Christology based on Barth and Bonhoeffer at the same time as taking the philosophical critique of Wittgenstein and the linguistic analysts with equal seriousness.'[73] What van Buren showed brilliantly, however, was that if positivist linguistic analysis is taken so seriously on its own terms, insisting on passing all truth-claims through the grid of 'empirical verification', scarcely anything of orthodox belief, christological or anything else, can survive. For van Buren 'God' has become a meaningless term in the modern West. The most that can be extracted from the Christian corpus is the empirically observable influence of Jesus himself – his 'contagious freedom' which sets people free to live in a similar way. On such a view, looking for God in the depths was as much a waste of time as looking for him 'up there' or 'out there'.

Robinson was right, of course, in calling attention to van Buren's work as evidence that a new theology was stirring not just in Woolwich or Cambridge or even in Britain as a whole. 'Secular' and 'radical' theology would have arrived regardless of *Honest to God*, though the interest in it would not have been generated in the same way. Indeed the appearance of *Honest to God* nearly coincided with *God Is No More* by Werner and Lotte Pelz,[74] an Anglican priest and his wife, former refugees from Nazi Germany and now working in Lancashire. It is a highly original and imaginative book, far more positive than its title implies, and is an appeal to follow the words of Jesus as they stand, and to realize thereby the untold creative possibilities of life. But the most provocative forms of radical theology came from America: in addition to Van Buren, Harvey Cox's synthesis of urban sociology and theology in *The Secular City* (1965) and, most exotic of all, the famous 'death of God' theologies of William Hamilton and Thomas Altizer.[75] The nearest British equivalent to the 'death of God' theology was probably to be found in Alistair Kee's *The Way of Transcendence* (1971).

Moreover, as we have seen, the radical movement even in Britain had begun well before *Honest to God*, certainly with Ronald Gregor

Smith's *The New Man* in 1956.[76] Lecturing at Gregor Smith's university in Glasgow in 1964, Alec Vidler said:

> I apprehend that *The New Man* is a more intrinsically valuable instance of radical Christian thought than others that have received more publicity. If Professor Smith had been a bishop (which, I grant, is hard to imagine) and if the gist of his theme had appeared on the front page of the *Observer* with a suitably sensational title, it might well have had the same effect as *Honest to God*.[77]

(Vidler's detached view of *Honest to God* – shared by others at Cambridge despite the Woolwich–Cambridge conspiracy theory – was aptly, if inadvertently, illustrated by his letter to *The Times* on 6 April 1963, that is, at the height of the initial furore over *Honest to God*. He wrote, not on this or any other theological issue, but on a matter of correct English usage. The Church of England report on the Matrimonial Clauses Bill had used the phrase 'as to whether' instead of the plain 'whether', much to his annoyance.)

The British scene was entertained by, rather than fully participant in, the 'secular theology' debates where the main protagonists were American and continental. Gregor Smith's *Secular Christianity* (1966) was as much a critique of the Americans as an advocacy of radicalism, employing as it did Gabriel Vahanian's fine distinction between secularization, considered as a historical process in which human life is freed from false dependence on superhuman powers and religious authorities, and secularism, considered as a particular ideology or belief-system about human powers which in the end shuts off human freedom. On the conservative side, E. L. Mascall hewed mightily and with relish against both van Buren and Robinson in *The Secularization of Christianity* (1965).

There was both gain and loss in the *Honest to God* controversy and its associated debates. The gain was in the fructifying input of new theological ideas that had been confined to the academic realm thus far. There were many instances where controversy was shown to have an immense educational potential for both clergy and laypeople, once it was admitted that people had the right to ask fundamental and searching questions about belief, and that if such questions were not aired, there was little likelihood of anything worthwhile being learnt. The loss was in fact that, as often happens when people take sides and labels are worn, much important and creative theology suffered a lack of attention, either because it was assumed to belong to one side or another, or simply seemed to be less exciting than the sensational products being marketed elsewhere. Vidler's comment on Gregor Smith could be extended similarly to a writer like Daniel Jenkins, whose *Beyond Religion*[78] would have added a good deal of mature reflection on the actual forms of 'religion', in relation to Bonhoeffer's views on 'religionless Christianity'. It goes without saying also, that the impression was given to many students of that particular generation that this was the first time that a 'worldly' interpretation of faith had been sought by British theology, as though John Oman and H. H. Farmer, to name but two, had never lived.[79]

The real long-term product of the controversy of 1963 and after, cannot be precisely defined. It is not a matter of particular ideas that have carried the day – if anything theology is now in a much more fragmented state – but rather an underlying style which has come to inform so much theology and spirituality. It is a style which seeks the encounter with God in and through the concrete, human, this-worldly experience. At a popular level it found expression in the 1960s vogue for the prayers of Abbé Michel Quoist.[80] At a more theological level it is characterized by the work of one such as John Macquarrie, whose stated theological method is to 'begin at the human end'.[81] In fact, Macquarrie's work could well be described as the plant which flourished in the soil ploughed up by the *Honest to God* debate. It is a theology which, while still distinguishing itself from anthropology, is nevertheless very human and glad to be so.

The return of the native

Robinson did not stay still after *Honest to God*. Just as Campbell after 1907 was to learn that the theology which he had rejected was not the only one within the Christian tradition, so Robinson after *Honest to God* educated himself both theologically and philosophically. Even by late 1963 he was picking up what was already a fast-running current in theology on 'secularism' and 'secularization'. In March 1965 came *The New Reformation?*, consisting mainly of lectures given in the United States. There was the same ambivalence of the reluctant revolutionary: 'I do not in the least want to see the classical disciplines of theology discredited – that would be disastrous for lay theology as much as for any other. But if we are not to retire into the ark or die of inanition, we must find new sources of nourishment.'[82] Then there are passages which read as good and true though hardly original:

> Doctrine is the definition of the experience; the revelation discloses itself as the depth and meaning of the relationship. To ask men to believe in the doctrine or to accept the revelation before they see it for themselves as the definition of their experience and the depth of their relationship, is to ask

> what to this generation, with its schooling in an empirical approach, seems increasingly hollow.[83]

By the time of *Exploration into God* (1967) we find a theology much more mature than *Honest to God*, much more multi-faceted, employing more careful distinctions and drawing upon a much wider range of theologians, not to mention philosophers, social scientists, artists and the great mystical tradition of Christianity. We hear less of the God 'out there' or 'in depth', and much more of 'non-duality' (though carefully avoiding 'monism'), of a transcendence found always in and with the immanent. Robinson, in fact, was joining the general stream of theology again, and his later books were useful contributions in the area of 'process theology' which emerged in the later 1960s and 1970s – and, it need hardly be said, were nowhere near as controversial as *Honest to God* had been.

Robinson returned to Cambridge in 1969 as Fellow and Dean of Chapel at Trinity College. Increasingly, also, he returned to New Testament studies, surprising the public again in yet new ways by arguing for a much earlier dating of the New Testament documents than most modern scholars had assumed,[84] and accepting the authenticity of the Turin Shroud. His last major work in the doctrinal field was his christological study *The Human Face of God* (1973). The shift back to Cambridge could only unfairly be described as a retreat. As always, his pastoral work was one of his strongest gifts, and this he continued not only at Trinity, but also during vacations in the diocese of Bradford. He died, after a long illness, in December 1983. The *Church Times*, which twenty years before had effectively called for his removal from episcopal office, now commented that it was a mark of the breadth of the Church of England that it could count among its sons two such contrasting characters who had died at almost the same time – John Robinson and the evangelist David Watson. Whether that is a sign that Robinson had succeeded or had at least been vindicated as a 'radical', or merely that the institution of the Church had shown its ability to absorb and contain dissent while remaining essentially unchanged in itself, must remain an open question. As Kierkegaard said, the system is hospitable.

Notes

1 J. A. T. Robinson, quoted in Ved Mehta, *The New Theologian*, Harmondsworth: Pelican Books 1968, p. 102.
2 B. Cooper, *Baptist Times*, 4 July 1963.
3 From *Listener*, 21 February 1963, quoted in J. A. T. Robinson and D. L.

Edwards, *The Honest to God Debate*, London: SCM Press 1963, pp. 27–29. *The Honest to God Debate*, published in the autumn of 1963, provides a convenient compilation of contemporary reactions to *Honest to God*.
4 ibid., p. 7.
5 J. A. T. Robinson, *Honest to God*, London: SCM Press 1963, pp. 26, 44, 136–9.
6 A. R. Vidler, *Scenes From a Clerical Life*, London: Collins 1977, p. 179.
7 *On Being the Church in the World*, London: SCM Press 1960, p. 71.
8 *The Times*, 7 November 1960 (my italics).
9 ibid., and 14 November 1960.
10 Karl Barth, *Letters 1961–1968*, Edinburgh: T. & T. Clark 1981, p. 109.
11 Robinson, *Honest to God*, p. 13.
12 See above, chapter 2.
13 Robinson, *Honest to God*, p. 14.
14 ibid., p. 29.
15 ibid., p. 48f.
16 ibid., p. 59.
17 ibid., p. 66.
18 ibid., p. 66f.
19 ibid., p. 87.
20 ibid., p. 115.
21 ibid., p. 131f.
22 ibid.
23 Robinson and Edwards, op. cit., p. 126f. (Article originally in *Prism*, May 1963.)
24 ibid., p. 49.
25 ibid., p. 51.
26 ibid., p. 49f.
27 *Sunday Times*, 24 March 1986.
28 Robinson and Edwards, op. cit., p. 55.
29 ibid., p. 64.
30 ibid., p. 77.
31 *Sunday Times*, 24 March 1963.
32 *Observer*, 24 March 1963.
33 Robinson and Edwards, op. cit., p. 49.
34 Quoted, ibid., p. 95.
35 *The Times*, 25 March 1963.
36 *Church Times*, 22 March 1963.
37 ibid. Also reprinted in Robinson and Edwards, op. cit., pp. 85–7.
38 *Observer*, 1 April 1963.
39 *Church Times*, 5 April 1963.
40 *Image Old and New*, London: SPCK 1973, p. 3.
41 ibid., p. 10.
42 ibid., p. 14.
43 *Church Times*, 26 April 1963.
44 ibid., 10 May 1963.
45 *British Weekly*, 21 March 1963. Reprinted in Robinson and Edwards, op. cit., p. 82–4.

46 *Baptist Times*, 28 March 1963.
47 Letter from K. Robbins, *Baptist Times*, 18 April 1963.
48 *Baptist Times*, 16 May 1963.
49 The Religious Education Press 1963.
50 London: Church Book Room Press 1963.
51 London: Inter-Varsity Fellowship 1964.
52 *Theology* LXVI (June 1963), p. 254f.
53 *Observer*, 24 March 1963. Reprinted in Robinson and Edwards, op. cit., p. 91f.
54 *Baptist Times*, 23 May 1963.
55 See Buber's *The Eclipse of God*, London: Gollancz 1953.
56 Review in *Blackfriars* July/August 1963. Reprinted in Robinson and Edwards, op. cit., pp. 165–80.
57 ibid., p. 171f.
58 F. W. Dillistone, review in *Sunday Times*, 24 March 1963.
59 Robinson and Edwards, op. cit., p. 129.
60 'God and the Theologians', *Encounter*, September 1963. Reprinted (with abbreviations) in Robinson and Edwards, op. cit., pp. 215–28, with a reply by Robinson.
61 Robinson and Edwards, op. cit., p. 228.
62 ibid., p. 226f.
63 'Concerning Theism', ibid., pp. 194–206.
64 ibid., p. 202.
65 ibid., p. 203.
66 H. D. Lewis, *Our Experience of God*, London: George Allen and Unwin 1959, p. 15.
67 Dillistone, op. cit.
68 D. Bonhoeffer, *Letters and Papers from Prison*, London: SCM Press 1971, p. 279.
69 R. Gill, chapter 5, 'The Social Significance of the *Honest to God* Debate', in *Theology and Social Structure*, London: Mowbrays 1977.
70 London: Society of Friends 1963.
71 London: Constable 1964.
72 London: SCM Press 1963.
73 Robinson and Edwards, op. cit., p. 250.
74 London: Gollancz 1963.
75 W. Hamilton, *The New Essence of Christianity*, London: Darton, Longman and Todd 1966; T. J. J. Altizer, *The Gospel of Christian Atheism*, London: Collins 1967.
76 London: SCM Press 1956. See above p. 146.
77 A. R. Vidler, *Twentieth Century Defenders of the Faith*, London: SCM Press 1965, p. 109.
78 London: SCM Press 1962. See also Jenkins' essay, 'Religion and Coming of Age', in Robinson and Edwards, op. cit., pp. 207–14.
79 Cf. J. Oman, *Grace and Personality*, Cambridge: Cambridge University Press 1919; H. H. Farmer, *The World and God*, London: Nisbet 1935.
80 Cf. M. Quoist, *Prayers of Life*, Dublin: Gill 1963.
81 Cf. especially his *In Search of Humanity*, London: SCM Press 1982.

82 *The New Reformation?* London: SCM Press 1965, p. 73.
83 ibid., p. 40.
84 Cf. *Redating the New Testament*, London: SCM Press 1976, and *The Priority of John*, London: SCM Press 1985. The fullest account now available of Robinson's life and work is Eric James, *A Life of Bishop John A. T. Robinson*, London: Collins 1987.

8 'The Tension must be Endured'

> May I express through your paper my dismay and indignation that our recently-appointed fourth-highest bishop, from his remarks made before a very large television audience . . . apparently does not subscribe to the biblical doctrine of the Virgin Birth and the miraculous element in the life of our Lord; and further casts doubts on the actuality of the Resurrection of Christ.
>
> Of what value is it if our congregations are duly and faithfully taught the great credal statements of our faith, and the doctrine enshrined in them, if the Church of England appoints to its oversight persons who question, or even deny, those very truths?
>
> Is it not time to raise with all those involved in the appointment of our leaders the importance of taking most seriously their solemn responsibility before God and his Church in this matter?[1]

We seem to have come very little distance, or perhaps simply to have travelled full circle, from the Hensley Henson furore of 1917–18, to the David Jenkins trauma of 1984. A tour of the major theological controversies in England this century is likely to deposit us in the contemporary scene with the sense of *déjà vu*. The degree of reiterated discord in the theological and doctrinal camp over so long a period may have occasioned surprise. The phenomenon will certainly be interpreted variously. To some, it will supply evidence of a lengthy, sinister conspiracy to debase the doctrine of the Church in accommodation to modernity, in face of which the time has come to wrest the wheel firmly back on the course of traditional, dogmatic orthodoxy. To others, more world-weary, it may simply confirm them in their suspicion that theology is a futile, intellectual in-fight within the Churches, entertaining for the participants but of no interest or use to the mass of faithful Christians who plod on with such measure of credal and devotional equipment as happens to be theirs, not examining it too carefully and concerned only that it should provide some kind of framework of meaning, purpose and assurance to otherwise dull and confusing lives. There is another possibility, however. This is, that theological controversy of the kind that we have been considering is symptomatic of profound dilemmas and ambiguities in the modern Western consciousness, affecting us intellectually, socially and spiritually, and which we cannot expect to be resolved quickly or easily. The first chapter of this study has already indicated the roots of some of these dilemmas, which are the legacy of the breakdown of the medieval outlook, and the continuing impact of the Enlightenment. Added to this, there is a further possibility which will be argued later in this chapter, namely, that controversy and conflict, far from being accidental to the 'peaceable' nature of Christ's religion, has been, is, and always will be, inherent in it.

Before we examine such larger issues, however, we need to survey briefly some of the controversies which are part of the more immediate story. *Honest to God*, a quarter of a century ago, has slipped over the rim of history. Whole classes of present-day students were not even born in 1963. Not Robinson, but Nineham, Hick, Wiles and – especially – Cupitt and Jenkins are this generation's discomforters. Controversies have continued since *Honest to God* and the radically swinging 1960s. None have been so ecclesiastically bitter as those of 1912–22, none so convulsively exciting as *Honest to God* itself in the breadth of interest it aroused. There is both continuity and change in the relation between the past and more recent debates, but it is unwise to try to pretend that we can view the current scene with quite as much detachment as we have attempted in the case of the earlier ones. In addition, several issues have been running at once in a somewhat untidy race, and arguments about 'religious pluralism' have themselves been conducted in a highly pluralistic fashion. At least, by now we should be somewhat inured to the hyperbole of horror which has been the standard accompaniment of controversy.

Christology again: The Myth of God Incarnate

If the questions of the 1960s was the doctrine of God, that of the 1970s was the person of Christ. True, the collection of essays *The Myth of God Incarnate*[2] did not appear until 1977, but there had been plenty of critical analysis of traditional incarnational doctrine before then. For example, John Robinson's *The Human Face of God* appeared in 1973, with its suggestion that the traditional formula 'one person, two natures' could be restated as 'one person, two stories'. Moreover, the issues which surfaced publicly and dramatically in 1977 had, to a considerable extent, already been anticipated in a doctrinal controversy within the Baptist Union at the start of the decade. At the Baptist Assembly of 1971 in London, Michael H. Taylor, Principal of the Northern Baptist College, gave an address on 'How Much of a Man was Jesus Christ?' His thesis, that Jesus was as utterly human as everyone else, that no formula of divinity could be allowed which altered in any way his full humanity, that the New Testament itself never explicitly states that Jesus is God, and that it was preferable to speak of God *doing* something unique in Jesus, rather than Jesus himself *being* unique in his nature, was expressed with exceptional clarity and cogency. Equally, it proved unacceptable to many on the conservative wing of the denomination, particularly in view of Taylor's position of responsibility for preparing candidates for the ministry. For a tense year the theological and related issues were debated at every level in the denomination, from local churches to the Baptist Union Council, with a number of pamphlets emerging in defence of evangelical orthodoxy. The controversy, as often happens, brought out both the worst and the best in people. Taylor was subjected not simply to theological criticism but to quite unscrupulous abuse, often by persons who had only second-hand knowledge of what he had said. At the same time many Baptists rallied in support of him, not always agreeing with his theology but admiring his personal integrity and aware that in the Free Church tradition liberty of interpretation, for all its risks, was the essential prerequisite of authentic belief. The Assembly of 1972 quietened the issue with a somewhat ambiguous resolution upholding the biblical faith, and not mentioning Taylor by name. A few churches left the Union.

1977 saw the publication of Geoffrey Lampe's last major contribution to British theology, his 1976 Bampton Lectures, *God As Spirit*.[3] This too was a critique of classical incarnational and trinitarian theology, proposing instead a view of the immanent creativity of the divine Spirit in the whole processes of creation and salvation, uniquely focused in Christ. The cross was the 'climactic disclosure' both of the tragedy of human resistance and of the invincibility of the divine love – 'the focal moment in the continuous outreach of God to man'. It was, in some respects, an elegant restatement of the idealist Christology of the first two decades of the century. It was also an imaginative exposition of the totality of the Spirit's work in history and the cosmos, with a strong eschatological orientation. Much of what Lampe wrote was at least as radical as anything in *The Myth of God Incarnate*, but it did not hit the headlines as effectively as that book did.

The Myth of God Incarnate could not exactly be described as 'Birmingham theology', although three of the contributors, John Hick (who edited the volume), Michael Goulder, and Frances Young, were on the staff of Birmingham University, and they certainly supplied the impetus for the symposium. Of the other four, Don Cupitt was from Cambridge, while Dennis Nineham, Leslie Houlden and Maurice Wiles were from Oxford. The title was itself provocative, of course, and could not fail to strike an iconoclastic note, especially to a wider public who had not been educated into the technical nuances of the word 'myth' in modern religious and theological studies. Moreover the Preface declared baldly that the authors' aim was to open up the topic in England, 'where the traditional doctrine of the incarnation has long been something of a shibboleth, exempt from reasoned scrutiny and treated with unquestioning literalness'. It was launched amid a blaze of publicity with a press conference, and had no difficulty stirring controversy. It sold 30,000 copies in eight months, wiseacres saying that oil-rich Arab propagandists were buying it up as the best statement to date of the Islamic view of Christ. The Church of England Evangelical Council called for the Anglican authors (that is, all bar the Presbyterian Hick and the Methodist Young) to resign their orders.

It was, as Maurice Wiles later admitted, 'an untidy book'. It embraced a variety of approaches and an unevenness in the quality of both writing and argument. There was a critical consensus that much of the most thorough work came from Frances Young, who in 'A Cloud of Witnesses' used her expertise in New Testament and patristics to illustrate how the New Testament titles, in the first place, derived from their own cultural setting, and how later, Nicene, Christology has tended to be read back into them. Michael Goulder portrayed 'Jesus, the Man of Universal Destiny', as one who turned a moment of historical crisis into the creation of a new community through his teaching and exemplification, to the point of martydom, of the 'primacy of love'. 'It is impossible to justify any stronger claims than these – to Jesus' sinlessness, or his *complete* devotion to God's will, or his *invariable* attitude of love.'[4] In a subsequent chapter, 'The Two Roots of the Christian Myth', Goulder proceeded to a novel theory as to how the 'incarnational' myth ('The Word became flesh', John 1.14) derived from a marriage of Galilean messianic eschatology and a Samaritan gnostic cult – a theory to be queried, in turn, by Frances Young in her next essay, 'Two Roots or a Tangled Mass?' In 'The Creed of Experience', Leslie Houlden began from the recognition that 'There is not one christology in the New Testament, there are many,'[5] to argue that the titles and concepts applied to Jesus in the New Testament were indicators of religious *experience* evoked by Jesus, and, rather than detached, objective statements directly about Jesus himself, they were 'oblique statements about God', signs of how the relationship with him had been illuminated and brought to a new level. Houlden was led to reformulate the christological question thus:

> what must I say about Jesus when as a result of him, by innumerable routes, I have been brought to that experience of God which has been my lot and privilege? The resulting answer may be far from traditional words, but it will avoid the obstruction of technicality, it will have a refreshing realism, it will reach out towards spirituality, and it will be, strictly, theological. It may also turn out to bypass some of the traditional questions and draw the sting of anxiety which they so often retain: in what sense was Jesus unique? how was he both divine and human? how was he God incarnate? To use the bypass may strike as being an evasion of the city; to others it is a way of reaching the destination more quickly.[6]

Houlden does not seem inclined to announce a hymn at this point, but it is all somewhat reminiscent of T. R. Glover's 'Christ without theory'. Don Cupitt then proceeded to demolish the 'Christ of Christendom' as a departure from the Jesus of the Gospels, who is a prophet of the all-holy, all-gracious God, utterly submissive to this transcendent and hidden one. The doctrine of incarnation was an innovation, indeed a superimposition on what Jesus himself did and taught, whereby he himself, instead of God, became an object of worship, a legitimation of earthly imperial power and splendour.

Oddly, bearing in mind the book's title, it was not until now that the term 'myth' itself was examined, in Maurice Wiles' essay, 'Myth in Theology'. As well as a highly useful survey of the development of the term in its technical usage from the nineteenth century onwards, the essay showed a marked sensitivity to the need to maintain 'some ontological reality corresponding to the central character of the structure of the myth'.[7] The ontological truth behind 'incarnation', suggested Wiles, is the experience of grace, the union of divine and human at the heart of the human personality. But equally, acknowledged Wiles, incarnation has always been linked with the *particular* historical figure of Jesus. 'Would it be reasonable to continue to link the incarnation so specially with the historical figure of Jesus while interpreting it as a mythological account of a potential union of the divine and the human in the life of every man?'[8] This was perhaps the most mature statement in the whole volume. In fact earlier, in the first of the essays, 'Christianity without Incarnation?', Wiles had experimented with the possibility that 'the stories about Jesus and the figure of Jesus himself could remain a personal focus of the transforming power of God in the world. They could still properly fulfil that role, even without the concept of "incarnation", though they would not impinge upon us in precisely the same way.'[9]

The essays proper concluded with John Hick's 'Jesus and the World Religions'. To those who had previously thought of Hick as the moderating, centrist theologian and philosopher of religion, it came as something of a shock to find him asserting that

> the Nicene definition of God-the-Son-incarnate is only one way of conceptualizing the lordship of Jesus, the way taken by the Graeco-Roman world of which we are the heirs, and that in the new age of world ecumenism which we are entering it is proper for Christians to become conscious of both the optional and the mythological character of this traditional language.[10]

The 'deification' of Jesus – effectively seen already in the fourth Gospel's depiction of Jesus as proclaiming himself as incarnate Son – arose out of the Christian experience of reconciliation with God.

> The new life into which Jesus had brought his disciples, and into which they had drawn others, was pervaded by a glorious sense of the divine forgiveness and love. The early Christian community lived and rejoiced in the knowledge of God's accepting grace. And it was axiomatic to them, as Jews influenced by a long tradition of priestly sacrifice, that 'without the shedding of blood there is no forgiveness of sins' (Heb. 9.22). There was thus a natural transition in their minds from the experience of reconciliation with God as Jesus' disciples, to the thought of his death as an atoning sacrifice, and from this to the conclusion that in order for Jesus' death to have been a sufficient atonement for sin he must himself have been divine.[11]

So it was 'natural and intelligible' that this 'poetic' hailing of Jesus as Son of God should have 'hardened into prose and escalated from a metaphorical son of God to a metaphysical God the Son', and hence to the Nicene and Chalcedonian formulae. Such formulae have served their purpose well, but today such language has no non-metaphorical meaning. Moreover, it makes absolutist and exclusivist claims for a relation to God through Jesus which makes impossible any serious encounter with other world religions. Jesus must be released to be the 'man of universal destiny' to whom people of all cultures can respond in their own ways, regardless of the classical, orthodox formulae.

The essays, therefore, beyond sharing a general dissatisfaction with a continued, unexamined use of the classical incarnational doctrine, hardly displayed a uniformity of approach or level of insight. It was a variegated firework display on a somewhat foggy evening. There was, however, one concluding firecracker to be thrown into the box which, while no less radical in sympathy than the authors themselves, severely queried much of the basis of their conclusions. Dennis Nineham had, since the early 1960s, been known as a New Testament scholar of distinction. In a remarkable way, however, instead of following the normal path of critical scholarship, which consists in producing paper after paper, or book after book, on first this, and then that, problem of criticism or exegesis, he had single-mindedly advanced two major questions: How much do we actually *know* for certain of the history of Jesus and the early Church? and, linked with this, How do we cope with the vast cultural divide between the first century and today? There can be no quarrying of the Bible for theological or ethical guide-lines which ignores this problem, least of all by reading into the New Testament the later credal orthodoxy. This was the underlying theme of his *The Use and Abuse of the Bible* (1976),[12] and it was, of course, an irritant to a complacent orthodoxy. But Nineham, who was invited to contribute an epilogue to *The Myth of God Incarnate*, levelled the question to the de-incarnators also. It was, after all, remarkable that Goulder and Hick, having been so dismissive of the classical formulae as being incompatible with modernity, should be so confidently simplistic in their reconstruction of who or what Jesus of Nazareth and the early Christian movement 'actually' were. Thus, while rejecting the *metaphysical* uniqueness of Jesus, most of the de-incarnators still held to a *moral* perfection or uniqueness in Jesus, variously described in terms of 'the new humanity', 'the man wholly for others' and so forth. But what, asked Nineham, was the *historical* basis for such weighty assertions about Jesus? And, in view of the cultural divide between first-century Palestine and twentieth-century Europe, would such descriptions have meant the same then as now?

The critical reaction to *The Myth of God Incarnate* was on the whole negative, not simply from instinctive conservatives but also from many of those already well versed in the hermeneutical and philosophical problems associated with incarnational theology. John Macquarrie, for instance, in his review in *Theology* pointed out that the writers had not sufficiently distinguished between the myth, and the *metaphysics*, of incarnation.[13] There did indeed seem to be an underlying assumption that if one could demonstrate that a particular doctrine had a *history* (describable as the story of the origins and development of a myth), involving identifiable cultural and even political influences as well as religious ones, it was *ipso facto* suspect as far as its truth was concerned.

Within weeks of the book's publication there appeared *The Truth of God Incarnate*,[14] edited by Michael Green, Rector of St Aldate's, Oxford, and a leading Anglican Evangelical. He was joined by Stephen Neill, doyen of Anglican biblical and missionary studies, the Roman Catholic Bishop Butler, Brian Hebblethwaite of Cambridge, and even John Macquarrie. Green marched right up to the seven essayists with the stark banner of Biblical Testament Evidence:

> If . . . we are to make up our minds whether the incarnation of God in Jesus of Nazareth is a fact or a myth, we must begin with the New Testament, not with any speculative theories spun out by theologians in the fourth century – or the twentieth. What evidence does the New Testament afford on so momentous a matter? It offers a great deal.[15]

No Ninehamite questions here about what *kind* of documentation or 'evidence' is supplied by the New Testament, but instead an extraordinary faith in the power of C. F. D. Moule and his recent *Origin of Christology* – 'It is probable that if his book had been available a year ago *The Myth of God Incarnate* would not have seen the light of day.' Most polemicists are on surer ground when probing their opponents' presuppositions than when facing up to their own, and Green landed some well-weighted blows against the evident consequences of some of the essayists' line of thought, especially in his accusation that the authors were in danger of removing history altogether from the Christian faith, rather than taking history seriously, as they claimed.

Perhaps the most persuasive reply in the book was Brian Hebblethwaite's essay 'Jesus, God Incarnate', which at least had the merit of exposing the implications of incarnation for the doctrine of God. 'If Jesus is God *in person*, then our knowledge of God has an intelligible personal human focus . . . At the same time God does not overwhelm us by his self-revelation. Instead he invites and wins our personal response.'[16] In short, the replies were that we need not be nearly so sceptical of the New Testament evidence as the seven authors had maintained, and that to posit a unique relationship of Jesus to God, or rather a unique presence of God in Jesus, was both defensible theologically, and necessary spiritually and ethically. Stephen Neill, towards the end of his essay 'Jesus and History', remarked somewhat wearily that the ideas in *The Myth of God Incarnate* had been before the Churches for long enough and 'I am only one of many who have had before them for many years all the problems dealt with in this book, and have reached independently conclusions different from those here set forth.'[17]

In 1978, an impressive symposium was organized to carry forward the debate between the seven and their critics, the papers for which were subsequently published as *Incarnation and Myth: The Debate Continued*.[18] Brian Hebblethwaite, Nicholas Lash, John Rodwell (a scientist), Charles Moule, Stephen Sykes, Graham Stanton and Lesslie Newbigin were the interlocutors. By now it was becoming a little too contrived, a somewhat in-theological academic affair. But the symposium did at least get beyond the hands-off-the-New-Testament-and-creeds stances taken in the earliest popular reaction. Summarizing the exchanges would be a tedious task, and unnecessary for our immediate purposes. But an overdue element was introduced into the discussion, reflecting other current theological explorations, when some of the interlocutors queried the implicit assumption of a 'myth' versus 'fact' dichotomy. Dennis Nineham, in fact, in the original book had suggested that it was a shortage of *imagination* which weakened contemporary Christianity.

> Men find it hard to believe in God because they do not have available to them any lively imaginative picture of the way a God and the world as they know it are related. What they need most is a story, a picture, a myth, that will capture their imagination, while meshing in with the rest of their sensibility in the way that messianic terms linked with the sensibility of first-century Jews, or Nicene symbolism with the sensibility of philosophically-minded fourth-century Greeks.[19]

A prophet would be needed for this. Nicholas Lash considered that more than prophecy would be needed – 'profound transformations of language, relationship, behaviour and social institution', to our 'stuctures of feeling'. In other words, *how* religious truth is expressed and communicated is a far more subtle affair than the debate about myth and incarnation, dealing purely with verbalized concepts, had so far reckoned.

Stephen Sykes, in his essay 'The Incarnation as the Foundation of the Church', took up a closely related point from the more strictly theological end, namely, the fact that the 'doctrine of the incarnation' is essentially a *story*, and its narrative form is not incidental to what it is seeking to convey:

> Both the rendering of who God is in story form, and the telling of this particular story are indispensable to speaking of God. The form of a story is indispensable not simply because it is a vivid and pedagogically effective means of communication . . . [but] because it is in the end by means of stories that human identity is patterned . . .
>
> Accordingly, the story-form in which incarnation is told is not an illustrative device for saying something about God which could be told more clearly in another form. It is, in essence and intention, a story of primary existential import, whose rehearsal contains the meaning of the individual's life. It is an inclusive story in the sense that in the entry of the Son of God into the world, the nature of my own origins as a fleshly reality is given its significance; in his death, my own death is included; in his resurrection, God's power to raise me from death is told.
>
> Moreover, it is the telling of *this* story which is vital, not any story which might illustrate love or costly forgiveness or triumph over adversity. The

incarnation means the coming into flesh of one who stands in a unique relation to God.[20]

In the Christian tradition, this story has become 'the paradigm for construing who God is in the other scriptural stories in which God figures'. Perhaps here, in Sykes' assertion that God himself is known only in story form, not as a static essence, nor as a universal principle, we might see the beginning of the end of that tendency which, for the best part of a century, has beset British theology, namely, seeing the incarnation as ultimately no more than the supreme exemplar of a general truth of immanence, and hence, in the final analysis, as dispensable. The fact is that, whatever the particular matters of historicity under debate may be, it is the fear that the finality of Christ as God incarnate is being denied, which motivates the 'conservative' reaction to the approach of *The Myth of God Incarnate*. And there was something naive, to say the least, in John Hick's reconstruction of the 'natural and intelligible' development towards credal formulae, originating from the 'poetic' acclamation of Jesus borne out of the 'experience' of forgiveness and new life. Might not the sense of finality have been there from the beginning? How do we know just what the pure, pristine 'experience', if such there was, of the first Christians was? Might it not in turn have depended upon a certain early conceptualization? Might not the 'natural and intelligible' development of christological formulae from St Paul to Nicaea be equally well described as 'consistent and logical' in terms of the reality it was dealing with, quite apart from pseudo-pyschological considerations? In the opinion of many, therefore, the case set out by the original seven, particular historical points of value and interest notwithstanding, had to rest non-proven. There was plenty of life in the old tradition yet, without having recourse to either biblical or credal fundamentalism.

The essayists' paths tended to diverge after 1978. Frances Young developed a more sympathetic approach to the New Testament and the classical doctrinal tradition. Michael Goulder eventually felt compelled to espouse atheism. Don Cupitt went his own, highly original, way.

The Cupitt Odyssey

Dennis Nineham's Epilogue to *The Myth of God Incarnate* was not quite the last word in that volume. Don Cupitt, Dean of Emmanuel College, Cambridge, had *the* final word with the briefest of codas. In reply to Nineham, he admitted the limitations of historical knowledge about Jesus, but 'the core of a religion does not lie in the biography or personality of the founder, but in the specifically religious values to which, according to tradition, he bore witness'.[21] The values, or 'principles of Spirit' to which Jesus bore witness were embodied in the call to repent in face of God's Kingdom. 'As principles of transcendence they are the only non-relativistic criterion of the subsequent development of the tradition.' A brief comment it was, but, in retrospect, a significant landmark on a journey being undertaken, and still being pursued, by one of the most forthright of modern controversialists in theology. Not least, his reputation has been made by his being one of the few academics, in any discipline, to operate really effectively on television, and it was in that medium, in 1978, that he first came to prominence (and, for some, notoriety) in his BBC series *Who Was Jesus?*

Cupitt's writings prior to *The Myth of God Incarnate* had focused particularly on Jesus and his proclamation of the Kingdom of God – a hidden, utterly transcendent God who could not be visualized or embodied or codified, to whom only surrender could be made in a life transcending the possibilities of the old life. Subsequent to the *Myth* essays, it is with the 'principles of Spirit' rather than directly with Jesus himself, that he has engaged, above all in his provocative trilogy *Taking Leave of God* (1980), *The World to Come* (1982), and *Only Human* (1985). These books are, or can be, too well known and accessible to require any detailed exposition here, and again, his documentary television series *The Sea of Faith* aroused widespread interest and comment. In one sense, Cupitt represents an entirely novel approach to the question of religious truth, as compared with the entire range of controversialists we have surveyed in this study, for his case rests on the premise that a shift of Copernican proportions is taking place in our awareness of the actual reference of religious language and commitments:

> Our perception of religious meaning is undergoing profound change. The place where it is to be found is shifting from tradition and external authority to individual subjectivity, and as a result it is leaving the metaphysical domain and becoming concentrated in the domain of ethics and spirituality. Religious meaning is becoming less a matter of metaphysical facts and more a matter of insights and ideals that are discovered to be illuminating, life-guiding and life-transforming. This process has been going on irregularly for centuries and is now reaching completion. Its upshot is that Christianity has now to be seen not as a body of supernatural facts certified to us by various authorities and evidences, but as a body of ideals and practices that have the power to give ultimate worth to human life.[22]

'God' as a 'real', 'objective' other, or Person, external to us, is no longer defensible. Instead, 'God' is the ultimate, unifying symbol of our moral and spiritual ideals. All the attributes of utter holiness, omniscience and power belong therefore not to a supernatural 'object', but to the religious ideal itself, the command to become spirit, and to live uncompromisingly at the behest of the religious demand. Kant and Kierkegaard are the chief prophets bidding this turn towards inwardness and subjectivity, in place of the 'external', authoritative God.

At one level Cupitt is not as novel, and would not claim to be, as might appear at first sight. There have been a number of attempts to describe Christianity as primarily a 'way of life' for which 'God' acts as some kind of idealizing symbol, rather than a belief in an 'objective God'. On the other hand, no one has claimed as strongly as Cupitt the value and indeed the need for this shift in perspective, on religious grounds. In contrast to the pseudo-Bonhoefferian 1960s slogans about the need to preserve Christianity by stripping 'religion' away from it, Cupitt believes passionately that it is precisely the 'religious' element – that is, utter transparency to the transcendent claim of the demand to be spirit – that needs preserving. In face of that demand, 'objective' or 'realist' doctrines of God can be allowed to slide, or at least their inner, subjectivist function should now be exposed.

Cupitt's attack on 'objective theism', and his readiness to describe himself as a 'Christian Buddhist' has, predictably, led to calls for him to forsake the Church of England, though he has, apparently, been left alone by authority. He is, after all, not a bishop. The measure of his actual 'following' would be hard to determine, but there are certainly those, and possibly an increasing number, in both pulpit and pew, who would say that he articulates the reason why they still attend Church, or find some meaningful contact with Christian tradition. The stories, the sacraments, the prayers, keep them in touch with a sense of what is continually worth striving for, morally and spiritually. What there is beyond this sense, they are not prepared to say, and perhaps would not be inclined to probe. But they would rather, Sunday by Sunday, be brought into the presence, by word and sign, of a human life making and calling for a sacrifice costing not less than everything, than attempt to survive unaided the bruising of human dignity and compassion of which their world largely consists.

At the same time, Cupitt's non-theistic religion has to bear within itself some mighty paradoxes, if not contradictions, approaching in gravity those which he sees in the 'objective theism' he rejects. The religious ideal is all-consuming in its demand for spiritual transparency and integrity. H. H. Farmer's 'Absolute Demand' could not be put more strongly. But Farmer used to describe the religious experience of encounter with God as also the sense of 'Final Succour'. Where is the grace, the succour in the 'religious ideal'? It seems a somewhat moralistic substitute for the old theism that we are left with. But if the 'religious ideal' is then said to be *also* gracious, accepting of us and forgiving, then it seems we are back on the way to having some kind of 'personal Other' to us, for the synthesis of both demand and acceptance is the hallmark of the personal. Otherwise we have sheer contradiction, or two principles (which would be religiously inadequate). Cupitt's great merit is his logical hardness. But he drives dichotomies hard, to the point where any coherence of experience and comprehension becomes impossible: *either* fact *or* value, *either* God as an 'object' *or* God as a subjective idea. In the final analysis, oddly, it is his initial starting-point of an utterly transcendent God which lies at the root of his self-imposed dilemmas. His God is utterly hidden, other. He cannot be conceived – yet he is known to be inexorably demanding in his call to become spirit. Since, apparently, this is all that can be known of him, it is but the shortest of steps to saying that this is all there is, in reality, of him: the religious demand. An insistence on God's 'otherness' in so stark a manner, has therefore the paradoxical result of denuding God of his reality in himself, and transforming him into our own subjectively held ideal. God is then, in the end, 'only human'. Cupitt, by a kind of paradox, here reflects Karl Barth. The early Barth, author of the pivotal *Commentary on Romans* which led to the downfall of liberal theology and the emergence of 'neo-orthodoxy' at the end of the First World War, likewise stressed the 'wholly otherness' of God. For Barth, this led to such a stress on the sheer reality of God as to leave problematical any genuine independent place for human existence and activity, even in faith. Cupitt, by contrast, leaves little room for an independent God. Barth was able, in due course, to make some resolution of the problem by his theology of the God who is 'other' not, finally, in his hiddenness but in his *freedom*, a freedom which is sovereign precisely in its graciousness, in the love which creates, posits and welcomes man as his partner. Whether Cupitt's 'only human' God remains as free, and hence able to liberate man, will be an interesting question.

David Jenkins, Bishop of Durham

Martin Luther would not have been at all surprised that, one night in the early summer of 1984, York Minster caught fire, most probably having been struck by lightning. Luther, however, would probably not have associated it with the recent consecration there of David Jenkins as a bishop of the Church of England, for in his view such was often the fate of the church as the highest building in any locality. It was merely a parable of the fact that judgement always begins with the household of God.

The Jenkins facts are well known and scarcely need sketching here.[23] Jenkins was last seen in this study as the Chaplain of Queen's College, Oxford, who in the *Honest to God* debate was about the only English theologian to provide a critique of John Robinson's efforts from a classical trinitarian standpoint. His *Guide to the Debate about God* (1968) was widely welcomed as one of the most balanced and mature introductions to the theological issues behind the controversy, and his 1966 Bampton Lectures on Christology, published in 1967 as *The Glory of Man*, were a thoughtful defence of the classical formulae of the person of Christ, expressive of a profound affirmation of the potentialities of human personality as a medium for revelation of, and communion with, the divine. After working on the World Council of Churches' *Humanum* study project in Geneva he became Director of the William Temple Foundation, with its particular concerns of theological reflection upon human issues arising out of contemporary industrial, educational, social and political life. From 1979 he was Professor of Theology at Leeds University.

In March 1984 his appointment as Bishop of Durham was announced. On 29 April, he took part in the ITV programme *Credo*, and his interviewer asked him, among other things, about belief in the miraculous items in the creeds. The resurrection, said Jenkins, was not a single event, but a series of experiences. Jesus was raised up, that is, 'the very life and purpose and personality which was in him was continuing'. As for the virgin birth, 'I wouldn't put it past God to arrange a virgin birth if he wanted, but I very much doubt if he would because it seems contrary to the way in which he deals with people and brings his wonders out of natural personal relationships.' Next day the *Daily Mail* headlined the story: 'The fake miracles of Jesus, by a Bishop'. The storm soon came, led by Bath Deanery with a protest resolution and a reaffirmation of its belief in the virgin birth and the resurrection. To some extent the atmosphere had already been charged by a controversial London Weekend TV series, *Jesus – the Evidence*, which many, and not just conservatives in theology, considered tendentious and biased. Not only was there a spate of letters in the religious press, but one William Ledwich, chaplain of Hereford Cathedral School, launched a nationwide petition inviting the Archbishop of York to affirm publicly the Creeds. Ledwich himself was in due course to leave the Church of England for the Orthodox Church, and published his own account of the Durham Affair in his book of that title.[24] The events of the summer and autumn are well known: the provocative but mostly misquoted remark about God performing a conjuring trick with bones (which Jenkins said the resurrection was *not*), the consecration service in York Minster, at which Dennis Nineham preached, the bizarre controversy surrounding the subsequent Minster fire, and finally the enthronement sermon in Durham Cathedral itself, at which the new Bishop struck even more fame with his remarks upon the then running coal dispute, and in particular upon Mr Ian MacGregor, Chairman of the National Coal Board.

To those who had known Jenkins and his work on theological reflection upon human issues, very little of what he had said, either about the resurrection or about human relations in industry and in the increasingly deprived north-east of England, came as any surprise. As Henson before him, he was warmly received in his own diocese, and a year later a special report in the *Church Times* on his first months in office emphasized how much whatever opposition there had been, had waned. As usual in such controversies, his opponents vastly exaggerated the effect of his pronouncements. One correspondent in the *Church Times* referred darkly to the trail of devastation which Jenkins had left in inummerable parishes across the country. There was little evidence of such damage, however, and it was even less apparent what might constitute such evidence. The incident revived, however, the whole issue of the relation between the miraculous and the divine, to a degree unknown since the first two decades of the century. And for many Anglicans, especially on the Evangelical wing, it provoked a repudiation not only of Jenkins, but of the whole 'liberal' tendency of the past eighty years. Whereas those of liberal tendency had felt able to appeal to the length and breadth of liberalism embedded in the modern Anglican tradition, a significant body of conservative opinion now wished to repudiate this stream rather than embrace it within the comprehensiveness or *via media* of *ecclesia anglicana*. Three Anglican members of the Department of Theology at Durham University appeared to think that Jenkins was somehow a modern-day gnostic intent on denying the bodiliness of human existence. In an open letter to John Habgood, Archbishop of York, they said:

St Irenaeus has been held in the highest regard throughout Christian

> tradition . . . By contrast the 1939 Report on Doctrine, a belated product of the erosion of Christian belief under the onslaught of the Enlightenment, tried to paper over the cracks caused by the reassertion in the Church of England of heterodox doctrine by cautiously affirming a liberty of interpretation.
>
> In effect the Church of England in 1938 seemed prepared to declare null and void the outcome of the debates of the Early Church which led to the formulation of the historic creeds. However, although the 1938 Report on Doctrine was 'received' by the Church, moves to use it as the basis for a modern restatement of doctrine were wisely rejected and it remains *entirely unofficial.*[25]

Even Hensley Henson, argued the authors, was prepared to declare his assent to the Creed, whereas Jenkins. . . ? The Durham affair had evidently uncovered not merely a theological issue, but a struggle for power within the Church of England. The Durham open letter, in referring to the 1938 Report as attempting to 'paper over the cracks' was tendentiously making that Report into something it was never intended to be. The 1938 Report (on which all theological viewpoints, including evangelical and high church were represented) was simply an attempt to set out what *was* held as essential belief by Anglicans at that time, and to indicate those variations in doctrinal interpretation which, attended by a significant following in the Church, had grounds for toleration if not acceptance. The fact that by 1984 the whole spirit, let alone the contents, of that Report could be repudiated is symptomatic of the change that had come over Anglicanism.

Several Christianities, one Christ?

From the mid-1970s onwards there has been no lack of effort by official Anglican bodies to reconcile conflicting doctrinal interpretations, or at least to define where the crucial differences lie. In 1976, only a year before *The Myth of God Incarnate* appeared, the Doctrine Commission of the Church of England produced its report *Christian Believing: The Nature of the Christian Faith and its Expression in Holy Scripture and Creeds*. The Commission, as in 1938, was certainly representative of the spread of Anglican opinion. It was chaired by Maurice Wiles, and included Evangelicals such as J. I. Packer and Michael Green, liberals like J. L. Houlden and Geoffrey Lampe, and, more in the catholic tradition, J. R. Lucas and John Macquarrie. The report, however, could do little more to promote 'reconciliation' than to insist on the need for continued dialogue between views which could not simply coexist in 'benevolent tolerance' of each other as if their intrinsically polemical tendencies could be ignored:

> It is tempting in the weariness and distress of conflict between followers of a common Lord to opt for a radical and simplistic solution by which a decision is taken to rule out one or more of these competing attitudes. But we are convinced that any such tension would be disastrous to the health of the Church. The tension must be endured. What is important is that everything should be done (and suffered) to make it a creative tension – that is, not a state of non-communication between mutually embattled groups but one of constant cross-fertilization of ideas and insights.[26]

Since then a succession of commissions and reports has appeared, including that produced by the bishops in 1986, which cautiously reaffirmed the reality of the resurrection and the miraculous, and which David Jenkins reputedly found 'dull', down to the report *We Believe in God* in 1987. Some, like Don Cupitt, see the process as one of ecclesiastical manoeuvring in the interests of safety-first, an attempt to ensure that the theological men in grey have the final word.[27]

Surveying the story of twentieth-century theological controversies in England as a human story, certain human elements form patterns which are almost too obvious to need stating. The role of the secular media in publicizing issues, sometimes in distorted, selective and sensational ways, but sometimes usefully (perhaps providentially) short-circuiting the usual channels of communication and discussion within the ecclesiastical communities themselves, is one such obvious feature. The *Daily Mail* thus treated R. J. Campbell, the *Daily Express* likewise Hastings Rashdall, and the *Observer* got the *Honest to God* debate moving. Television is now on the scene with potent force, as the stories of Alec Vidler and David Jenkins certify. It has often been said that sensational reportage and quick-fire discussion under the lights are not the media in which religious and theological language can do itself justice, and that the nuances of theology cannot therefore be appreciated. Over-simplification and crudity are therefore almost inevitable. Dietrich Bonhoeffer's plea that the modern Church, where it cannot for the present adequately interpret the great traditional doctrines for contemporary people, should preserve them from profanation by maintaining a silence, is immensely attractive. Bonhoeffer in 1944, however, after more than a decade of totalitarian suppression of public debate and freedom of information, could not have reckoned with an information-hungry mass media homing in on the Church, cameras and jotting-pads at the ready.

The second obvious observation is that, in retrospect, in the heat of controversy both 'radical' and conservative protagonists tend to exaggerate the significance of the debate in terms of its overall effect on the Church. Controversy certainly seems to have very little 'weakening' effect on the Churches. If anything, it has a useful side effect in some quarters, namely an educative one, and it raises the profile of the Churches in society. Conservatives tend to project their own anxieties on to the scene with dire warning about how 'disturbed' the mass of faithful believers are, as Lord Halifax and Watts-Ditchfield did with the Henson episode, as Archbishop Garbett did with Barnes, and as hefty evangelicals have been doing with David Jenkins. This is not to say that important issues of truth are not at stake. It is simply to recognize that whenever issues of truth are debated, human motivations for power and dominance over others, or feelings of threat at apparent dominance and rejection by others, come into play. The question of truth is also a question about the nature and identity of the *Church*, and that is never an abstract question. It is a question as to who rightfully owns the Church, who is really at home within it.

Concerning the actual theological issues, it is dangerously easy to over-simplify and attempt to identify one underlying 'issue' which all the controversies have 'really' been about. History does not actually repeat itself, though, as we have seen, there were important similarities between what R. J. Campbell and John Robinson were attempting, and between the idealistic approaches to Christology of the Anglican modernists around 1920 on the one hand, and *The Myth of God Incarnate* on the other – not to mention the 'experimental' Jesus of T. R. Glover and the similar emphasis of a number of authors in that volume. However, one major and continuing preoccupation can be highlighted. It is what may be called the tension between unity and otherness.

The human mind requires a sense of wholeness, of coherence, in its vision and understanding. W. B. Sanday had spoken of the 'unification of thought' as summarizing the liberal outlook. There is, after all, only one world and for the Bible God is known only in his actions within this one world which he shares with man. But religious belief apprehends a sense of 'otherness'. Things as they are, are not the whole story. There is that which does not simply fit in with the world as it is, which transcends it, is 'beyond it' and not conditioned by it. How, then, can the desire for unified wholeness, and the itch for transcendence, be wedded, if at all? R. J. Campbell sought a direct apprehension of the divine by a monistic route, which proved theologically untenable and religiously useless. John Robinson sought a kind of transcendence which would not involve a disruption from secular human experience, by speaking of God as the 'depth' or 'ground' of what we already experience in human relationships. Idealistically based Christology, from Rashdall to Wiles, essentially views God as a continually active principle or agent within the world, of which the Christ-event is the supreme disclosure. Don Cupitt sees the only possibility for post-Kantian religion as lying within an intra-human unity, in which 'God' is not a detached 'other' but expresses the 'otherness' of the religious life as a wholly human possibility. All such approaches have, in one way or another, sought to maintain the rationality and coherence of human experience of the world as a unified whole. Behind them all, regardless of their end-results, lies the valid and important perception that faith and the totality of human experience cannot be dichotomized. There must be integration (which by no means necessarily implies assimilation). The 'otherness' is glimpsed through the worldly, and expressed in a new direction of worldly living. God as ultimate reality cannot be sundered from creation, nor superimposed upon the finite realm in a sheerly arbitrary and irrational manner. Faith is neither magic nor madness. Further, such approaches tend to lay great store by the *inwardness* of faith. It is the 'experience' of Jesus, rather than doctrines about him or unusual events associated with his birth and posthumous existence, which are the basics of such faith.

Conservatism, broadly speaking, still finds it necessary to insist upon the 'objective' occurrence of certain events such as the virgin birth and physical resurrection, as the basis of experiencing God, not simply as *expressions* of that experience. Only so, it is asserted, can it still be maintained that 'God acts' in his world. They would not deny much that liberals would wish to assert about the universality of the divine dimension and activity in the world, but would insist that faith, if it is not to lapse into sheer subjectivism, needs anchorage in such events. On this view, only an 'interventionist' God can guarantee the 'otherness' apprehended by true religion. The natural and historical continuum has to be visibly ruptured at some point or other – else what 'otherness' is there?

Can these two versions of Christian faith – or even as some would say, two Christianities – be reconciled? Our historical survey gives little ground for any such hopes. The issues are far too deeply embedded within the fabric of the post-Enlightenment Christian West, either to countenance any quick resolution, or for one side to hope for outright victory over the other. Controversy seems endemic, and, for the foreseeable future, a permanent feature of the modern Christian landscape. The reason lies not simply within the perversity of human nature, from which, as we have seen, theologians are by no means immune, nor even in the sheer intellectual difficulty besetting the questions of transcendence, historical knowledge and the meaning of religious language. The main reason lies in the way in which *both* sides can cite valid and profoundly *religious* reasons for their respective stances. It just is not the case, for example, that the liberal view is a 'doubting' stance in contrast to the 'firm convictions' of the conservatives. However shocking it may appear to their opponents, those who reject a literal virgin birth or a physical resurrection often do so out of a deep conviction that to take these as literal events within space and time is derogatory to the manner of the divine working. Paradoxically, to insist on a 'physical' return to life of Jesus can lead to a trivializing of the whole message of resurrection, which is nothing less than the new creation, and hence no less mysterious than the original creation. There are, at root, positive and firmly held convictions as to what God is actually about in the universe, and how.

Do, however, such convictions justify one group de-churching, or even de-Christianizing the other party? What constitutes heresy today? We would do well to pay heed to Professor Stephen Sykes' warning against allowing theology, as such, to be wholly determinative of the question of Christian identity, and hence unity.[28] Sykes points out the lesson of modern New Testament scholarship that conflict seems to have been an essential feature of the Christian movement from the first. Even Jesus and his own mission carried an ambiguity for the earliest Church. Was the Jesus movement a reform of Judaism, or a movement designed for the wider world? Contrasting and often conflicting interpretation was inevitable. Conflict cannot be eliminated, only contained within bounds. And, according to Sykes, the profoundest reason for theological conflict lies in the *inward* dimension of belief, which can never find adequate expression in purely verbal and conceptual terms. He writes:

> A verbal resolution of the tension between external rite and internal intention . . . necessarily belongs to one of the external dimensions of Christianity; it is theology. No matter how precise theological formulations may strive to be, or indeed actually are, they are never immune from the charge that they have failed to capture the ultimately mysterious meaning and truth of the heart. On this account of the matter Christians had better reconcile themselves to the perpetuation of internal conflict; and indeed they would do well to go beyond mere resignation, and seek the positive advantages to be gained from such disputes.[29]

The inwardness of faith, its peculiarly personal character as a communion with the ultimately mysterious God, means a continual dialectic with theological formulation. 'The assertion of a single authoritative version of Christianity is a profoundly non-historical response, a mere assertion in the face of an overwhelming quantity of contrary evidence.'[30] The external expression, in story, myth and doctrine, has to be continuously interrelated with the inseparable 'internal experience of new life'. Conflict arises because of the problem of the precise delineation of boundaries, and the inherent ambiguities of the problems Christianity inherits and has to undertake. The 'proper conduct' of controversy requires 'an inwardly appropriated sense of what has to be achieved in the world'. Therefore, the basis of a unity within which Christians find their identity is not, Sykes argues, exact theological agreement, but worship. It is in worship that Christians are united in what *is* crucial and central in Christianity, namely, committed attention to Jesus as the decisive revelation of God in history, an existential relation in which, for the moment, theological formulae are relativized *vis à vis* eath other.

I find considerable attraction in Sykes' argument, provided it is no excuse for evasion of continued hard wrestling with genuine theological difficulties, or a pretext for escape into the hymnbook in T. R. Glover fashion. We do, however, need to face the question of where legitimate conflict within Christianity becomes a conflict of Christianity versus something else – to repeat, what constitutes heresy today. It is in fact extremely difficult to give an abstract description of what heresy is, just as it is hard to define sin beyond saying that it is faithlessness and disobedience to God. We can, however, say that Christianity places the person and work of Jesus Christ at the centre of everything to be believed about God and his purpose for mankind. The crucial heresy is to say that for Christians, Jesus is not definitive of God, and that trust for life and salvation can be placed elsewhere than in Jesus. Precisely in what *way* Jesus is decisive for our knowledge of God and our salvation is another matter. That is an affair for theological reflection – perhaps disagreement and maybe even conflict. Here a glance at another context in modern history may be helpfully illustrative.

No one was clearer on the need for the full-bodied affirmation of the revealed Word of God in Jesus Christ, than Karl Barth. The high-point of his stance was the formulation, in which he had a major part, of the Barmen Confession of 1934, which provided the charter for the Protestant resistance to the nazification of the Church in Germany. Its opening affirmation has justly become famous:

> Jesus Christ, as he is testified to us in the Holy Scripture, is the one Word of God, whom we are to hear, whom we are to trust and obey in life and in death.
>
> We repudiate the false teaching that the church can and must recognize yet other happenings and powers, personalities and truths as divine revelation alongside this one Word of God, as a source of her preaching.

In the context of the early days of the Third Reich, the pressure was mounting for the Church to conform to the nationalistic and racist spirit of the times – a spirit which took some highly subtle and attractive theological forms – and to admit some racial criterion for membership of the German Church. In that context, this would have been the supreme heresy – to allow some definition of the Church, some qualification for membership, other than faith in Christ. Barmen represented a concerted attempt to state the identity of Christianity, to recover where its *centre* was and to state again what the *source* of Christian truth was, namely, the person of Jesus Christ himself. This was a mighty and fundamental assertion and recovery of the integrity of the Church. It stated where, or more precisely *who*, was the *source* of Christian truth, namely Christ known through the Scriptures. It left open, however, a good deal of room for theological debate, simultaneously with allegiance to that recognized centre of belief. During the Second World War, Rudolf Bultmann – whom it should be remembered was himself a member of the Confessing Church – of Marburg caused a stir within the Confessing Church by his celebrated paper on 'The New Testament and Mythology', setting off the whole 'demythologizing' debate which after the war spread throughout the European and North American religious and theological scene. From the beginning there were those in Germany who wished to arraign Bultmann for heresy. From over the Swiss border, Barth decisively rejected Bultmann's attempt to rid the *kerygma* of myth as an ill-conceived, reductionist assault on the New Testament, and moreover, saw the whole existentialist movement in theology as a recrudescence of the nineteenth-century liberal emphasis upon the religious *man*, instead of the self-revealing *God*. Barth poured scorn on Bultmann's 'hermeneutical' project of 'understanding' the New Testament in terms of modern existentialist self-understanding, not least when he delivered his comment on Bultmann in an essay ironically entitled 'Rudolf Bultmann – An Attempt to Understand Him'. But Barth preserved a sense of detachment, and, moreover, a sense of humour over the whole business. He refused to shoulder a gun when, in the 1960s, some well-meaning conservatives in Germany were drawing up the lines of battle. Barth's reply to one such individual, of somewhat unstable tendency, is a gem of pastoral wisdom and worth quoting to all who gird up their loins for (their version of) the truth of God:

> It is not thanking God, nor is it good therapy . . . to proclaim the *status confessionis hodie*, to imitate Luther at Worms or Luther against Erasmus, to compose thoughtlessly generalizing articles and paltry battle-songs, to write me (and assuredly not only me) such fiery letters, to pour suspicion on all who do not rant with you, indeed, to punish them in advance with your scorn, etc. Instead you should be watching and praying and working at the place where you have been called and set, you should be reading holy scripture and the hymn-book, you should be studying carefully with a pencil in your hand the theological growth springing up around you to see whether there might not be some good grain among the tares. Lighting your pipe and not letting it go out, but refilling and rekindling it, you should not constantly orient yourself only to the enemy – e.g., to senilely simplistic statements such as those recently made by the great man of Marburg in the *Spiegel* – but to the matter in relation to which there seem to be friends and enemies. Then in the modesty in which is true power . . . you should preach good sermons in X, give good confirmation lessons, do good pastoral work – as good as God wills in giving you the Holy Spirit and as well as you yourself can achieve with heart and mind and mouth. Do you not see that this little stone is the one thing you are charged with, but it is a solid stone in the wall against which the waves or bubbles of the modern mode will break just as surely as in other forms in the history of theology and the church they have always broken sooner or later? Dear pastor, if you will not accept and practise this, then you yourself will become the preacher of another Gospel for which I can take no responsibility. You will accomplish nothing with it except to make martyrs of your anger those people who do not deserve to be taken seriously in this bloodthirsty fashion and whom you cannot help with your 'Here I stand, I can do no other.' With the modesty indicated, be there *for* these people instead of *against* them in this most unprofitable style and effort.[31]

We may take Barth's remarks as an important ingredient in the 'proper conduct' of controversy. We might also venture the opinion that, if the story of English controversies this century reveals anything at all, it is the relative weakness of the place of systematic theology on the English scene. Historical and biblical studies, with philosophy of religion, predominate as might be expected in a context where theology is taught as a university discipline rather than a seminary subject, and where any subject suggestive of confessional rather than historical or philosophical interest seems out of place. But, for example, the notion that belief in God uniquely incarnate in one person is logically impossible – as Rashdall and a number of authors of *The Myth of God Incarnate* assumed – cries out for a doctrine of God which takes seriously his own 'becoming' in time as a fulfilment, not a contradiction, of his being. There has been nothing here so far, to compare with an Eberhard Jüngel.

Further, while agreeing strongly with Professor Sykes about the role of worship as the locus of Christian identity, it should be asked whether the theologians, *qua* theologians, can be allowed to escape their own responsibilities in promoting that interrelation between the inward and external elements in Christianity. Crucial here is the aim and method of theological education itself. Time out of mind in the story of modern controversies, laments have been heard that if laypeople were shocked and bewildered by what they heard the avant-garde theologians were saying, it was because their own priests and ministers had not been doing their job of educating their people with the findings of modern scholarship and theological exploration. That may well be so. The pulpit and study-group have too often played for safety, providing immediate and simple reassurance rather than the challenge of illumination. I have just attended a service on Trinity Sunday. At the beginning of his sermon, the visiting preacher cheerfully announced that he was glad and relieved to leave the doctrine of the Trinity to the minister who would be occupying the pulpit at the evening service. A coy titter ran round the pews. But this church was in a university city. Lecturers, teachers, doctors, local government and business administrators were in the congregation – yet a minister evades the proclamation of, let alone the wrestling with, the great and glorious mystery of the Christian doctrine of God. It is, in pious mock modesty, thought to be beyond both pulpit and pew. Every time this sort of thing happens, real questions are evaded, laypeople are shielded from the challenge of exploration, their spiritual and intellectual maturation is deferred and the long fuse of yet another public theological explosion is lit.

But if this is happening, questions must be asked about the theological education of the clergy themselves. They may have learnt about a number of doctrines as concepts, but not necessarily how to think doctrinally about the practical issues which confront themselves and the people they serve. They may have learnt a smattering of modern theology, of Barth's, Bonhoeffer's or Rahner's God, but scarcely apprehended their own. The interrelation between inwardness and theological formulation must begin within the classroom itself, so that creation or atonement or Kingdom of God are apprehended in terms of what these mean in experience, decision and discipleship. Only a theology that is personally owned can really be communicated to others. That is what Harry Williams discovered.

Finally, it should be recognized that if worship is the locus of unified Christian identity, that is partly because of the eschatological orientation of communal worship. The congregation gathers to celebrate God's past coming in Christ, recaptured and presented in the Spirit here and now, and anticipating the fullness of the Kingdom to come. The proper conduct of controversy requires therefore an eager longing for the appearance of that further light and truth which, as the seventeenth-century Puritan John Robinson said, the Lord hath yet to break forth from his word. The fact that even as I quote that Pilgrim Father I can almost hear the groans from those who dismiss his words as 'hackneyed' indicates the present mood in both Church and society today. There is a looking back to the past for authoritative reassurance, rather than an anticipation of some new thing, a continual desire to return and check that the tomb is empty before taking the road out of Jerusalem to wherever Christ is to be met anew. Theology is always in danger of succumbing to whatever is the current fashion prescribed by contemporary social, cultural and political trends, and the danger is no less real when those fashions are reactionary, as they are today, than when they were buoyantly progressive twenty years ago. (For that reason, if invited to hazard a prophecy, the next really intense and wide-ranging controversy in Britain may well involve an attempt at a thoroughgoing political theology, with which previous flirtations with the Latin American liberation theologians will pale by comparison.) Reaction and novelty both provide temptations to simplistic and illusory resolutions of problems. We may believe in an ultimate unity of truth, though not apprehended as yet, and only seen in a glass darkly. The resolution of theological conflict is a *hope* and it will be fulfilled only when there is no more to be taught us by the Spirit of truth.

Notes

1 Letter, *Church Times*, 11 May 1984.
2 J. Hick (ed.), *The Myth of God Incarnate*, London: SCM Press 1977.
3 Oxford: Oxford University Press 1977.
4 Hick (ed.), op. cit., p. 53.
5 ibid., p. 125.
6 ibid., p. 131.
7 ibid., p. 161.
8 ibid., p. 162.
9 ibid., p. 9.
10 ibid., p. 168.
11 ibid., p. 176.
12 London: Macmillan.

13 *Theology* LXXX (September 1977) pp. 370–2. Reprinted in *The Truth of God Incarnate* (see note 14).
14 M. Green (ed.), *The Truth of God Incarnate*, London: Hodder and Stoughton 1977.
15 ibid., p. 17.
16 ibid., p. 103.
17 ibid., p. 86.
18 M. Goulder (ed.), *Incarnation and Myth: The Debate Continued*, London: SCM Press 1979.
19 Hick (ed.), op. cit., p. 201f.
20 Goulder (ed.), op. cit., p. 123.
21 Hick (ed.), op. cit., p. 205.
22 *The World to Come*, London: SCM Press 1982, p. 139f.
23 For a reasonably fair journalistic account, see T. Harrison, *The Durham Phenomenon*, London: Darton, Longman and Todd 1985. For an account by one of Jenkins' fiercest opponents, see W. Ledwich, *The Durham Affair*, Welshpool: Stylite Publishing Ltd 1985. For David Jenkins' most recent statement of his position, see his *God, Miracle and the Church of England*, London: SCM Press 1987.
24 See note 23.
25 Quoted in Ledwich, op. cit.
26 *Christian Believing*, London: SPCK 1976, p. 38.
27 *The World to Come*, p. 141f.
28 S. Sykes, *The Identity of Christianity: Theologians and the Essence of Christianity from Schleiermacher to Barth*, London: SPCK 1984.
29 ibid., p. 46.
30 ibid., p. 250.
31 K. Barth, *Letters 1961–1968*, trans. and ed. by G. W. Bromiley, Edinburgh: T. and T. Clark 1981, p. 230.

Bibliography

Aubrey, M. E. 'T. R. Glover. Review and Reminiscence', *Baptist Quarterly* XV (October 1953), pp. 175–82.

Barnes, E. W. *Should Such a Faith Offend?*, Hodder and Stoughton 1927. *Scientific Theory and Religion: The World Described by Science and its Spiritual Interpretation*, Cambridge University Press 1933. *The Rise of Christianity*, Longmans 1947.

Barnes, J. *Ahead of His Age. Bishop Barnes of Birmingham*, Collins 1979.

Barth, K. *The Epistle to the Romans*, Oxford University Press 1933. *Letters 1961–1968*, T. and T. Clark 1981.

Bateman, C. T. *R. J. Campbell: Pastor of the City Temple*, S. W. Partridge 1903.

Bell, G. K. A. *Randall Davidson, Archbishop of Canterbury*, Oxford University Press 1935.

Bogdanor, V., and R. Skidelsky, (eds) *The Age of Affluence 1951–1964*, Macmillan 1970.

Bonhoeffer, D. *Letters and Papers from Prison*, SCM Press 1971.

Booker, C. *The Neophiliacs*, Collins 1970.

Buber, M. *The Eclipse of God*, Gollancz 1953.

Campbell, R. J. *City Temple Sermons*, Hodder and Stoughton 1903. *Christianity and the Social Order*, Chapman and Hall 1907. *The New Theology*, Chapman and Hall 1907. *A Spiritual Pilgrimage*, Williams and Norgate 1916.

Chadwick, O. *Hensley Henson. A Study in Friction between Church and State*, Clarendon Press 1983.

Chase, F. H. *Belief and Creed*, Macmillan 1919.

Clements, K. W. 'God at Work in the World: Old Liberal and New Secular Theology', *Baptist Quarterly* XXIV (July 1972) pp. 345–60. *The Theology of Ronald Gregor Smith*, E. J. Brill 1986. *A Patriotism for Today: Love of Country in Dialogue with the Witness of Dietrich Bonhoeffer*, Collins Liturgical 1986.

Cockshut, A. O. J. *Religious Controversies of the Nineteenth Century: . Selected Documents*, Methuen 1966.

Cupitt, D. *Taking Leave of God*, SCM Press 1980. *The World to Come*, SCM Press 1982. *Only Human*, SCM Press 1985.

Davies, R. Horton *Worship and Theology in England: The Ecumenical*

Century 1900–1965, Oxford University Press 1965.

Edwards, D. L. *Leaders of the Church of England 1828–1944*, Oxford University Press 1971. *Religion and Change*, Hodder and Stoughton 1974.

Farmer, H. H. *The World and God*, Nisbet 1935.

Gill, R. *Theology and Social Structure*, Mowbrays 1977.

Glazebrook, M. G. *The Faith of a Modern Churchman*, John Murray 1918.

Glover, T. R. *The Conflict of Religions in the Early Roman Empire*, Methuen 1909. *The Jesus of History*, SCM Press 1917. *The Free Churches and Reunion*, Heffers 1921. *Democracy in the Ancient World*, Cambridge University Press 1927. *Fundamentals*, Baptist Union Publication Department 1931. *The Ancient World*, Cambridge University Press 1935.

Gore, C. *The New Theology and the Old Religion*, John Murray 1907. *The Basis of Anglican Fellowship in Faith and Organization: An Open Letter to the Clergy of the Diocese of Oxford*, A. R. Mowbray 1914.

Goulder, M., (ed.) *Incarnation and Myth: The Debate Continued*, SCM Press 1979.

Grant, J. W. *Free Churchmanship in England 1870–1940*, Independent Press 1955.

Green, M., (ed.) *The Truth of God Incarnate*, Hodder and Stoughton 1977.

Hamilton, W. *The New Essence of Christianity*, Darton, Longman and Todd 1966.

Harrison, T. *The Durham Phenomenon*, Darton, Longman and Todd 1985.

Hastings, A. *A History of English Christianity 1920–1985*, Collins 1986.

Henson, H. (ed.), *Church Problems: A View of Modern Anglicanism*, John Murray 1900. *Christian Liberty and Other Sermons*, Macmillan 1918. *Retrospect of an Unimportant Life* (2 vols), Oxford University Press 1941–43.

Heron, A. C. *A Century of Protestant Theology*, Lutterworth 1980.

Hick, J., (ed.) *The Myth of God Incarnate*, SCM Press 1977.

Holloway, D. *The Church of England: Where is it going?*, Kingsway 1985.

Iremonger, F. W. *William Temple: Archbishop of Canterbury*, Oxford University Press 1948.

Jenkins, Daniel *Beyond Religion*, SCM Press 1962.

Jenkins, David *The Glory of Man*, SCM Press 1967. *Guide to the*

Debate About God, Lutterworth 1968. *Living With Questions*, SCM Press 1969.
Jones, R. Tudur *Congregationalism in England 1662–1962*, Independent Press 1962.
Knox, R. A. *Some Loose Stones*, Longmans, Green and Co. 1913.
Lampe, G. *God as Spirit*, Oxford University Press 1977.
Lash, N. *Theology on Dover Beach*, Darton, Longman and Todd 1979.
Ledwich, W. *The Durham Affair*, Stylite Publishing Ltd 1985.
Levin, B. *The Pendulum Years: Britain and the Sixties*, Jonathan Cape 1970.
Lewis, H. D. *Our Experience of God*, Allen and Unwin 1959.
Lloyd, R. *The Church of England in the Twentieth Century*, Longman, Green and Co. 1946.
Macleod, G. M. *Only One Way Left: Church Prospect*, Iona Community 1956.
Macquarrie, J. *Twentieth Century Religious Thought: The Frontiers of Philosophy and Theology 1900–1960*, SCM Press 1963. *Principles of Christian Theology*, SCM Press 1966. *In Search of Humanity*, SCM Press 1982.
Mascall, E. L. *Up and Down in Adria*, Faith Press 1963. *The Secularization of Christianity: An Analysis and a Critique*, Darton, Longman and Todd 1965.
Matthews, W. R. *Memories and Meanings*, Hodder and Stoughton 1970.
Mehta, V. *The New Theologian*, Pelican 1968.
Montefiore, H. *Truth to Tell: A Radical Restatement of Christian Faith*, Collins Fontana 1966.
Morris, L. *The Abolition of Religion*, Inter-Varsity Fellowship 1964.
Mozley, J. K. *Some Tendencies in British Theology: from the Publication of* Lux Mundi *to Present Day*, SPCK 1951.
Newbigin, L. *The Other Side of 1984: Questions to the Churches*, World Council of Churches 1984.
Nineham, D. E. *The Use and Abuse of the Bible*, Macmillan 1976.
Nowell-Smith, S., (ed.) *Edwardian England 1901–1914*, Oxford University Press 1964.
Oman, J. *Grace and Personality*, Cambridge University Press 1919.
Pelz, W. and L. *God Is No More*, Gollancz 1963.
Pullan, L. *Missionary Principles and the Primate on Kikuyu*, Oxford 1915.
Purcell, W. *Fisher of Lambeth*, Hodder and Stoughton 1969.
Quoist, M. *Prayers of Life*, Gill 1963.

Ramsey, A. R. *From Gore to Temple: The Development of Anglican Theology between* Lux Mundi *and the Second World War 1889–1939*, Longmans 1960. *Image Old and New*, SPCK 1973.

Rashdall, H. *Jesus, Human and Divine*, Andrew Melrose 1922.

Reardon, B. M. G. *Religious Thought in the Nineteenth Century*, Cambridge University Press 1966.

Reports: *Doctrine in the Church of England: The Report of the Doctrinal Commission on Christian Doctrine Appointed by the Archbishops of Canterbury and York in 1923*, SPCK 1938. *Christian Believing: The Nature of the Christian Faith and its Expression in Holy Scripture and the Creeds*, SPCK 1976. *The Nature of Christian Belief: A Statement and Exposition by the House of Bishops of the General Synod of the Church of England*, Church House Publishing 1986. *We Believe in God*, Church House Publishing 1987.

Rhymes, D. *No New Morality: Christian Personal Values and Sexual Morality*, Constable 1964.

Robinson, J. A. T. *On Being the Church in the World*, SCM Press 1960. *Honest to God*, SCM Press 1963. *The New Reformation?* SCM Press 1965. *Exploration into God* SCM Press, 1967. *The Human Face of God*, SCM Press 1973. *Redating the New Testament*, SCM Press 1976. *The Priority of John*, SCM Press 1985. (with D. L. Edwards), *The Honest to God Debate*, SCM Press 1963.

Robinson, T. H. *Terrot Reaveley Glover, Scholar and Christian*, Carey Press 1943.

Sanday, W. B. *The Position of Liberal Theology: A Friendly Examination of the Bishop of Zanzibar's Open Letter*, Faith Press 1920.

Schweitzer, A. *The Quest of the Historical Jesus*, Adam and Charles Black 1910.

Sell, A. P. F. *Theology in Turmoil: The Roots, Course and Significance of the Conservative–Liberal Debate in Modern Theology*, Baker Book House 1986.

Smith, H. M. *Frank, Bishop of Zanzibar: Life of Frank Weston 1871–1924*, SPCK 1926.

Smith, R. Gregor *The New Man: Christianity and Man's Coming of Age*, SCM Press 1956. *Secular Christianity*, Collins 1966.

Spinks, G. S. *et al. Religion in Britain Since 1900*, Andrew Dakers 1952.

Stephenson, A, M. G. *The Rise and Decline of English Modernism*, SPCK 1984.

Streeter, B. H. (ed.), *Foundations: A Statement of Christian Belief in Terms of Modern Thought. By Seven Oxford Men*, Macmillan 1912. *The Four Gospels: A Study of Origins*, Macmillan 1924.

Sykes, S. *The Identity of Christianity: Theologians and the Essence of Christianity from Schleiermacher to Barth*, SPCK 1984.

Vidler, A. R. *Windsor Sermons*, SCM Press 1958. (ed.) *Soundings: Essays Concerning Christian Understanding*, Cambridge University Press 1962. (ed.) *Objections to Christian Belief*, Constable 1963. *Twentieth Century Defenders of the Faith*, SCM Press 1965. *The Church in an Age of Revolution*, Penguin Books 1971. 'Bishop Barnes: A Centenary Retrospect', *Modern Churchman* XVIII (Spring 1975) pp. 87–98. *Scenes From a Clerical Life*, Collins 1977.

Vine, C. H., (ed.) *The Old Faith and The New Theology*, Sampson Law, Marston and Co. 1907.

Warschauer, J. *The New Evangel: Studies in the 'New Theology'*, James Clarke 1907.

Welsby, P. A. *A History of the Church of England 1945–1980*, Oxford University Press 1984.

Weston, F. *Ecclesia Anglicana – For What Does She Stand? An Open Letter to Edgar, Lord Bishop of St Albans*, Longmans 1913.

Wiles, M. *The Remaking of Christian Doctrine*, SCM Press 1974. *Working Papers in Doctrine*, SCM Press 1976. *Faith and the Mystery of God*, SCM Press 1982.

Williams, H. A. *Some Day I'll Find You: An Autobiography*, Collins Fount 1984.

Williams, T. Rhondda *The Evangel of the New Theology*, W. Daniel 1903.

Wood, H. G. *Terrot Reaveley Glover. A Biography*, Cambridge University Press 1953.

Newspapers, journals and periodicals from which material has been drawn:

Baptist Times
British Weekly
Church Times
Daily Mail
Expository Times
Modern Churchman
Observer
Sunday Times
Sword and The Trowel
Theology
The Times

Index